Fascist Virilities

Fascist Virilities

*Rhetoric, Ideology, and
Social Fantasy in Italy*

Barbara Spackman

 University of Minnesota Press
Minneapolis
London

Published by the University of Minnesota Press
111 Third Avenue South, Suite 290, Minneapolis, MN 55401-2520
Printed in the United States of America on acid-free paper

Library of Congress Cataloging-in-Publication Data

Spackman, Barbara, 1952–
    Fascist virilities : rhetoric, ideology, and social fantasy in
Italy / Barbara Spackman.
        p.   cm.
    Includes bibliographical references and index.
    ISBN 0-8166-2786-X (hc). — ISBN 0-8166-2787-8 (pbk.)
    1. Masculinity (Psychology)—Italy.   2. Rhetoric—Political
aspects—Italy.   3. Fascism and sex—Italy.   4. Fascism and women—
Italy.   5. Fascism—Italy—Psychological aspects.   6. Italy—
Politics and government—1922-1945.   I. Title.
HQ1090.7.I8S67   1996
305.3–dc20   95–53733

The University of Minnesota is an
equal-opportunity educator and employer.

Contents

Acknowledgments

A University of California President's Research Fellowship in the Humanities and an Irvine Faculty Research Grant gave me the time and support I needed to complete the research and writing of this book. I am grateful as well to the American Academy in Rome for making my stay in Rome in the fall of 1992 a pleasant one.

A number of colleagues and friends deserve special thanks for their comments, criticisms, suggestions, and support, in particular Thomas Albrecht, Albert Ascoli, Margaret Brose, Ellen Burt, Liz Constable, Carla Freccero, John Freccero, Keala Jewell, Marilyn Migiel, J. Hillis Miller, Margaret Morton, Graziella Parati, Robin Pickering-Iazzi, Karen Pinkus, Juliana Schiesari, Nancy Harrowitz, Jeffrey Schnapp, Rebecca West, and Hayden White. Irina Costache came to the rescue at a critical moment and provided me with precious materials. The students in my graduate classes at Northwestern, the University of California, Irvine, and New York University have helped me untangle knots and made me think harder and better. I am grateful to Biodun Iginla for his interest in the project and to Elizabeth Knoll Stomberg and Hank Schlau for their valuable help in the production process. Andrzej Warminski has been both critical reader of my work and loving partner in my life. To him, and to Chico, I dedicate this book: for being home.

•

A preliminary version of chapter 1 was published in *Stanford Italian Review* 8:1–2 (1990) 81–101, and is reprinted here with permission; a version of chapter 2 was published in Robin Pickering-Iazzi, ed., *Mothers of Invention:*

Women, Italian Fascism, and Culture (Minneapolis: University of Minnesota Press, 1995), 100–120, and is reprinted with permission; parts of chapter 3 were published in *Modernism/Modernity* 1:3 (1994) 89–107, and are reprinted here with permission of Johns Hopkins University Press.

Preface

This book treats Italian fascism as a discursive formation whose principal node of articulation is "virility." It argues that a knowledge of fascist ideology may be gained not through cataloguing the often ideologically incompatible elements or ideas that circulated in it, but rather through an analysis of the way in which those heterogeneous elements are articulated or bound together. As a means of articulation, rhetoric thus comes to be crucial to an understanding of ideology; it also provides a shuttle between political and literary texts and allows the book to explore the question of fascism in the text.

The coupling of the terms "fascism" and "fantasy" is by now (at least after the publication of Klaus Theweleit's *Male Fantasies*)[1] no surprise; the terms "fascism," "rhetoric," and "ideology," however, have a history of conflictual relations. The question of the relation between Italian fascism and ideology has been answered in two contradictory ways: on the one hand, fascism is said to have no ideology, and, on the other, fascism is said to be synonymous with ideology. The discrepancy in part derives from differing notions of ideology but is, this book argues, merely apparent: both say the same thing, and for the same reason. The denial of the existence of a fascist ideology is deeply rooted in the political condemnation of fascism and relies upon a conception of ideology as a coherent worldview. To recognize an ideology or philosophy in fascism would thus be to dignify it with an intellectual stature that it does not merit. The political usefulness (and, at a certain historical moment, necessity) of this position is clear: if fascism has no ideology, then it becomes easier to close that particular "parenthesis in history" (as Benedetto Croce called it) and to consider fascism a historical aberration. The equation of fascism and ideology, while more often relying upon a conception of ideology as unconscious and contradictory, serves much the same purpose: if fascist ideology is irrational, the "institutionalized unconscious" (as Julia Kristeva puts it) or the postmodern equivalent of evil, then we may still consider ourselves to be rational, good, and outside of that thing called fascism. In other words, for both arguments, fascism is a black box whose contents are unspecified but whose moral significance is given in advance.[2]

The question of the relation between rhetoric and fascism has been answered in a similar, indeed circular, way: fascism has no ideology, the argument goes, but is instead sheer "rhetoric" — by which is meant empty, insincere speech that can be opposed to some nonrhetorical use of language.[3] This too is a strategic account: there were no ideas and hence no appeal to rational faculties; there was only rhetoric and, behind that rhetoric, state violence. Supporters of fascism and, ultimately, reason itself (as well as "nonrhetorical" language) are thus saved from the taint of complicity, for reason and rational belief had, according to this account, no part in fascism. This view opens the way to the various theories of bedazzlement according to which the supporters of fascism were hypnotized and spellbound by the charismatic leader's "rhetoric" and hence oblivious to the violence done to them, and to reason.

If this book offers rather different answers to these questions, it is because the historical distance that now separates us from the *ventennio nero*, the "black twenty years," has perhaps paradoxically made it possible to come closer to being able to analyze the inner workings of fascist discourse than was possible for postwar scholars, involved, as many were, in the reconstruction of their countries. To take fascism seriously as "verbal revolution" or "reign of the word" is no longer considered an endorsement, but rather a recognition that rhetorical and semiotic transformations were among fascism's principal modes of self-definition. And to speak of ideology in relation to fascism no longer carries with it the taint of complicity. As the theoretical work of Louis Althusser and Ernesto Laclau has argued, ideologies need not be entirely "coherent," on the one hand, nor entirely "irrational," on the other, in order to be recognized as such and to interpellate subjects and create consent. On the contrary, "The ideological unity of a discourse is perfectly compatible with a wide margin of logical inconsistency."[4] The notion of ideology that I work with here is indebted to Laclau's essay entitled "Fascism and Ideology" in particular, for there he brings Althusser's theorization to bear on fascism and suggests that one can come to know its ideological unity by examining the way in which the different and specific interpellations are related to one another, are "articulated," in Laclau's terms. How, that is, are different interpellations — religious, political, familial, racial, and gender — bound together to form a unified fascist discourse? In focusing on virility, I have concentrated here on one interpellation that I argue fulfills "a role of condensation with respect to the others"; that is, it manages to evoke all the others and stand as their representative.[5]

Rhetoric articulates and binds together; "fantasy," as I understand it here, also binds and articulates. This book works with two notions of fantasy, one based loosely on the work of Jean Laplanche and J.-B. Pontalis and the other derived from Slavoj Žižek's theorization of what he calls ideological fantasy. I take from Laplanche and Pontalis the notion that the position of the subject in a fantasy, and hence the anchor of its meaning, is located not in this or that element, this or that character, but rather in relations among elements, in the "syntax" of the fantasy.[6] This focus on the syntax of fantasy allows me to map the syntax of a "literary" fantasy onto the syntax of a social and cultural fantasy and to suggest structural analogies. From Žižek I borrow the notion of fantasy as modeled on fetishistic disavowal. Just as the fetishist's "Je sais bien, mais quand même . . . " (I know very well, but all the same . . .) binds together a knowledge and a nonknowledge, so ideological fantasy names a reality structured by a disavowal, in which the fantasy acts as structuring illusion. Translating these terms from the realm of the subject to the realm of the text, I suggest that one might speak of a "splitting of the text" analogous to Freud's "splitting of the ego" in which a textual nonknowledge is caused by a textual knowledge (or, to put it in the closely related terms of Marxian fetishism, a textual doing is unaffected by a textual knowing). This model lends itself particularly well to the study of fascist ideology that, as Alice Y. Kaplan has argued, functions precisely by binding and splitting.[7]

This book follows rhetorics of virility as they move through literary texts, political manifestos, and political speeches. My choice of texts may seem somewhat idiosyncratic at first glance: F. T. Marinetti's manifestos from the so-called second futurism and his early 1909 novel *Mafarka le futuriste* (Mafarka the futurist); Valentine de Saint Point's futurist manifestos and Teresa Labriola's fascist feminist writings; a selection of Gabriele D'Annunzio's speeches during the occupation of Fiume and his 1895 novel *Le vergini delle rocce* (The virgins of the rocks); and finally Mussolini's rhetorical practice in general and in two of his most important and widely cited speeches. The reasons for grouping these texts and figures together are several, some motivated by the assumptions and claims of existing scholarship and some produced, as my own work on the book progressed, by the metonymical reading that is part of every research project. I began the project with the D'Annunzio-Marinetti-Mussolini trio, for it constitutes an established linkage in discussions of the sources of fascist rhetoric and ideology. My aim was not to produce a comprehensive study of all aspects of their rhetorical practice but rather to explore their differing conceptions of "virility" and the reproductive fantasies that issued from them. This particular cluster brought into play another question that has been debated in studies of fascism, namely, the degree to which one may point to precursors of fascist rhetoric and ideology in the fin de siècle and among the futurists; hence the inclusion of the earlier novels by Marinetti and D'Annunzio, both of which stage reproductive fantasies and thematize the very notion of a precursor. The futurist Valentine de Saint Point and the fascist feminist Teresa Labriola appeared serendipitously as I followed the trails of virility in fascist discourse. And all roads led to Mussolini. Seen through the double focus of virility and reproductive fantasies, Mussolini's "Discorso del 3 gennaio" (Speech of January third) (1925) and his "Discorso dell'ascensione" (Ascension Day speech) (1927) offered the most fertile ground.

Chapter 1, "Rhetorics of Virility: D'Annunzio, Marinetti, Mussolini, Benjamin," gives an overview of the rhetoric of virility in fascist discourse and in several critical discourses that claim to analyze fascism (Carlo Emilio Gadda, Maria-Antonietta Macciocchi, Walter Benjamin). The chapter argues that virility is not simply one of many fascist qualities, but rather that the cults of youth, of duty, of sacrifice and heroic virtues, of strength and stamina, of obedience and authority, and of physical strength and sexual potency that characterize fascism are all inflections of that master term, virility. It shows how both Mussolini's self-presentation and the analyses of the critics collude in the creation of a scenario in which the virile leader "rapes" the feminized masses. The chapter then focuses on the models of virility found in the political writings of F. T. Marinetti and Gabriele D'Annunzio, writers often cited as the sources of fascist rhetoric. The Marinettian model is characterized by what Eve Kosofsky Sedgwick has called "homosexual panic": in an effort to stabilize the boundaries between homosociality and homosexuality, Marinetti's texts superimpose national borders onto sexual ones. Lined with nationalism, virility defines and defends itself against femininity, homosexuality, and Bolshevik internationalism. The D'Annunzian model is, on the other hand, one in which virility is defined and molded through the feminine; its opposite is the "adiposity" of "plutocratic" nations, and its model is the paradoxically female virility of a Caterina Sforza, the Renaissance virago. Such mixing and matching, I argue, is inimical to the way in which the discourse of fascism-as-regime collapses gender and sex and biologizes both.

In fascist rhetoric, the adjectives "masculine" and "virile" as applied to women were terms of abuse meant to deride the intellectual, "feminist," and hence supposedly sterile woman not properly devoted to her reproductive mission. Chapter 2, "Fascist Women and the Rhetoric of Virility," probes the ideological ramifications of the adoption of the fascist rhetoric of virility by women themselves: Does the rhetoric, when wielded by women, produce what Michel Foucault has called a "reverse discourse," or does it instead merely recirculate the same strategy, leaving intact its logic of exclusions and prohibitions? The chapter examines the writings of two women who flaunt the prohibition on virilization, the futurist Valentine de Saint Point and the fascist Teresa Labriola, and shows how fascist discourse comes to turn upon itself.

Chapters 3 and 4 return to Marinetti and D'Annunzio in order to ask the question of "fascism in the text": How, and to what extent, can literary texts be said to be "fascist" or "sources of fascist ideology"? I have chosen two novels that treat the theme of the production of a superhuman son, Marinetti's *Mafarka le futuriste* (1909) and D'Annunzio's *Le vergini delle rocce* (1895).

Mafarka le futuriste brings together a number of elements that might be called fascist: a rhetoric of virility, imperial fantasies tied to the colonization of Africa, misogyny, a reproductive project, and an obsession with self-sufficiency. In an analysis of what I call Marinetti's "homophobic economics," I propose that Marinetti's fantasy of sexual autarky — the son is to be generated through male parthenogenesis — shares an ideological structure with the fascist regime's fantasy of economic autarky. Marinetti's fantasy of male autarky is built upon misogyny, threatened with bankruptcy by same-sex relations, and therefore requires the reintroduction of the other in the form of the woman (to be raped). The fantasy of national autarky, I argue, is similarly structured: built upon nationalist xenophobia, it is threatened by the erasure of difference within and therefore requires the reintroduction of the other in the form of the

colony (to be raped). The analysis is supplemented with contemporaneous texts that describe the problems of "national virility and the Italian
colonies."

Like *Mafarka*, D'Annunzio's antidemocratic, antiparliamentarian novel, *Le
vergini delle rocce*, takes as its theme the generation of a superman: the novel's
protagonist sets out to choose from among three sisters a genitrix who will
bear him an exceptional son. Surrounding this fairy tale are politically explicit declamations that have prompted critics to point to this text — a text
about the making of a precursor, by the author who will come to be known
as the "John the Baptist of fascism" — as a precursor of fascist ideology. The
chapter explores the precursorial relation through an analysis of the novel
as what Žižek has called "ideological fantasy." The concept of ideological
fantasy allows the chapter to address the splittings and bindings of the text
and in particular to bind together what I call the "political narrative" and
the "virgins' narrative." I propose that the novel binds together a protest
against commodity fetishism and a longing for a refetishization of social relations. It imagines not a totalitarian leader (as is the cliché), whose rule is
legitimized through underlining the defetishization of social relations, but
rather a king whose rule is possible only without subjects. The chapter then
juxtaposes Freud's "Theme of the Three Caskets," which also treats of a
choice among three women, to the novel. Freud's is a democratic fantasy, I
argue, whose fetish is choice; he knows very well that there is no choosing
of death, and yet all the same he puts this nonexistent choice in the place
of necessity. D'Annunzio's fantasy, on the other hand, is an antidemocratic
one that puts necessity — and Necessitas, mother of the fates — in the place
of suffrage (and the protagonist's choice among women); it knows very well
that there is choice (and suffrage), and yet all the same puts necessity, in the
form of monarchy in the political narrative, and the mother, in the fairy-
tale narrative, in its place. This antidemocratic fantasy blocks the choice
of the protagonist, who thereby cannot fulfill his destiny as precursor; this
blockage affects the ideological structure of the novel as a whole and puts
into question its precursorial status.

The final chapter, "Fascism as Discursive Regime," begins with a survey
of linguistic and rhetorical studies of Mussolini's rhetoric. Imposed through
the schools and the media as correct, "fascist" Italian, Mussolini's style, his
grammatical, syntactic, and rhetorical practice, was generalized and codified. The section "The Elements of Fascist Style" questions the attribution
of stable ideological content to such elements and examines the "resemanticization" that is part of the popular-democratic interpellation in fascist

discourse. The bulk of the chapter is devoted to rhetorical analyses of two representative Mussolinian speeches, the "Discorso del 3 gennaio" (1925) and the "Discorso dell'ascensione" (1927).

In the section titled "Fascist Violence, Fascist Rhetoric," I argue that the "Discorso del 3 gennaio," in which Mussolini took responsibility for the illegal violence of the fascist squads that had brought him to power, illustrates the interdependence of rhetoric and violence in fascist discourse. Theorizations of the performative and positional functions of language allow us to think of fascism as a discursive regime in which the relation between language and event is not one in which language functions to mystify a reality of pure force, but rather one in which language itself functions as one of the realities of force and violence. The "Discorso del 3 gennaio" is, I argue, a collection of speech acts that rhetoricize the violence "out there" and recycle it as performative language — as promise and threat. The positing of nonverbal violence gives meaning to the rhetoric, while the rhetoric gives new meaning, as performative threat, to violence already committed. The tide-turning importance of the speech is explained through its rhetorical mode, for I argue that the speech brings into existence, through its speech acts, the juridico-political conditions that grant the performative its felicity; it consequently validates itself and establishes itself as event. The rhetoricization of violence also accounts for the turn to rape at the end of the speech; the elements of violence, nationalism, and sexuality are bound together to produce what Teresa de Lauretis has called a "violence of rhetoric," the violence resulting from the implication of all representations of violence in a particular model of sexual difference. The speech introduces a feminized "Italia" whose function is to redirect the violence that threatened to erupt among men (the threat to which the speech responds) toward a "woman" to be raped.

The final section, "Demographic Delirium in the Prophylactic State," examines the "Discorso dell'ascensione," which established as policy some of the elements of the fascist reproductive fantasy and gave official form to the demographic delirium that led Mussolini, in 1934, to blame the First World War on the "unborn French." I show how the fantasy of the social body, as organic whole unriven by antagonism, underlies the fascist reconfiguration of public and private and produces a national reproductive fantasy in which national prophylaxis, as Mussolini calls it, is required to guard against the social reproduction of antifascists and personal prophylaxis is prohibited in order to promote the biological reproduction of fascists. The fantasy is not only that more and more bodies would be produced but that the offspring would physically embody a political doctrine; this, I argue, is fascist racism. And one body, more than all the others, embodies such doctrine: the Duce's. Public and private, political and personal, the Duce's body is produced through a condensation of fantasies of the integrity of the male body and the unity of the social body.

1 / Rhetorics of Virility: D'Annunzio, Marinetti, Mussolini, Benjamin

Virilities

Dacchè tutto era, allora, maschio e Mavorte: e insino le femine e le balie e le poppe della tu' balia, e l'ovario e le trombe di Falloppio e la vagina e la vulva. La virile vulva della donna italiana.[1]

[For everything then was male and Martial: even broads and wet nurses, and the tits of your wet nurse and the ovary and the fallopian tubes and the vagina and the vulva. The virile vulva of the Italian woman.]

Thus Carlo Emilio Gadda maliciously summarizes the fascist era in his novel *Eros e Priapo* (Eros and Priapo), by carrying the obsession with virility in fascist discourse to its limit: the virilization of woman herself. Gadda's aim is to ridicule fascist discourse by pointing to what he takes to be the absurdity of mixing and matching gender and sex: so outlandish is the fascist rhetoric of virility, his logic goes, that it even extended virility to women's genitalia! But such a gendering is ridiculous only if one assumes a naturalized relation between gender and sex, in which masculinity is the natural property of the male and femininity the natural property of the female, and only if one assumes that virility can be detached neither from masculinity nor from the male. I would like to begin by putting into question such assumptions and suggesting that we cannot assume that we know what interpretants to assign to such a highly charged term as "virility," even before we move on

---

Unless noted otherwise, all translations throughout the book are my own.

to its more properly rhetorical use in fascist discourse. If some of the discourses we are about to examine will often subscribe to those assumptions, indeed will sometimes vehemently enforce them, others may line up instead on the side of the possibility of mixing and matching. We cannot therefore assume that "virile" is equivalent to "phallic" or to "masculine," that its contrary is "effeminate," nor that the term occupies the same area in English as in Italian. In English, according to the *OED*, "virility" may refer to "the period of life during which a person of the male sex is in full vigour, mature or fully developed manhood or masculine force"; it may refer specifically to the "generative organs" or to capacity for sexual intercourse; it may refer to "manly strength and vigour of action or thought, energy or force or a virile character." As an adjective, "virile" may refer simply to a stage in life in contrast to youth and old age; in Renaissance usage, it may be applied to a woman to mean "nubile"; it may be defined, broadly, as "of, belonging to, or characteristic of man; manly, masculine, marked by strength or force." Zingarelli's Italian dictionary is even more loquacious on the topic, offering as examples of "that which is proper to man, as male," a list of nouns that might be described by the word "virile": "sex, appearance, beauty, nature, member." And as qualities that are "proper to the physically and mature adult male," the following examples appear: "force, voice, age, energy, wisdom, courage." In Italian the notion of virility appears to have undergone further cultural elaboration and may refer to "that which is proper or suitable to the strong, well-balanced, and self-confident person, aware of his role, duties, responsibilities, etc." Because the gender of possessive adjectives in Italian refers not to the possessor but to the thing possessed, this last definition appears unmarked by gender in much the same way as "man" in English functions as the universalized, "unmarked" term. These definitions are simply the raw material, the semantic field, that fascism will mine in both senses of the word: all possibilities will be excavated and explosive devices planted where one least expects them.

Yet even this elementary reading of dictionaries is illuminating. Zeev Sternhell, for example, lists virility as one of many qualities and cults that characterize the "new civilization" desired by fascism, yet those cults in fact read like dictionary entries for a single master term.[2] As mentioned in the preface, these cults — of youth, duty, sacrifice, strength, obedience, sexuality, war, and so on — all are inflections of the term "virility." Indeed, Mussolini's public image appears to be similarly dictated by a series of dictionary entries. In Philip Cannistraro's account of the orders given the press regarding the image of the Duce to be created, "virility" once again appears as a subcategory of a series of which it in fact stands as rubric.[3] No news of the Duce's illnesses or birthdays, nor of the fact that he had become a grandfather, was to be published. Mussolini himself shaved his head so that no grey hair might mar the appearance of a man in his prime. He was simply not to grow old. The lights left burning late into the night in his Piazza Venezia office similarly signaled not only devotion to his "duties" but vigor and stamina. He was not to be shown participating in "nonvirile" activities (and here the term *non virili* is used) like dancing but was instead to be shown participating in vigorous sports such as riding, flying, motorcycling, and so on. No references were to be made to his family life, to his role as husband and father. The image of the family man would presumably soften his virility. Interestingly, none of the directives cited by Cannistraro excludes information about the lovers and amorous exploits Mussolini was "known" to have.

It is, of course, a commonplace that an obsession with virility is one of the distinctive traits of fascist discourse, a commonplace that is sometimes psychologized, sometimes simply taken for granted as a sort of linguistic tic.[4] References to virility do indeed pepper the writings of fascist intellectuals as though the word itself were proof of the writer's fascist credentials, a kind of verbal campaign button. But the latter approach often accepts masculine adjectivation as self-evident, rather than symptomatic. The linguist Giovanni Lazzari's study of the most exploited semantic fields in fascist discourse, *Le parole del fascismo,* is typical in this regard.[5] "Virility" appears in his study alongside such categories as "Rome," "war," and "the Duce," yet no attempt is made to analyze the interrelations among these fields. In Lazzari's case we might attribute this lack of analysis to the restricted scope dictated by the discipline of linguistics itself; what he presents is raw data awaiting analysis of a different type. But these raw data reappear, still unrefined, in Furio Jesi's suggestive *Cultura di destra* when Jesi takes it for granted that virilization is one of the distinctive rhetorical strategies of fascist discourse. Jesi analyzes the variations in what is presumably the "same" speech given in commemoration of Giosuè Carducci on two different occasions in 1907: one in public and one in a Masonic lodge. What is interesting for the present study is that Jesi's index for protofascism in the former version is not a philosophical or political position but a rhetoric of virility: "Locutions and stylemes that will later be those of fascist rhetoric are the signs of [the speaker's conviction that he is] entering into a relation with that value: 'un maschio viso' [a masculine face], 'viril fierezza' [virile pride], 'momenti storici fatidici' [fatal historical moments]."[6] The "value" in question is that of the past as undifferentiated value, yet Jesi does not pursue the question of the relation between virilization and the attitude toward the past that it presumably signals.

While linguistic and literary studies accept virilization as unremarkable, psychological studies read the fascist obsession with virility as pathological. These studies tend either to indulge in the social fantasy that links homosexuality and fascism or to oppose pathological fascist virility to a model of "healthy virility" usually to be found in Marxism. Representative of the latter tendency is John Hoberman's rather dramatic claim, in *Sport and Political Ideology*, that a cult of virility not only is present in all fascist cultures but is indeed constitutive of them and never appears in Marxist cultures.[7] Wilhelm Reich, in *The Mass Psychology of Fascism*, is perhaps the most notable and notorious author of psychologizing theories of the former tendency followed by Jean-Paul Sartre, who attributes homosexual tendencies to the collaborator in "Qu'est-ce qu'un collaborateur?"[8] In what will become one of the more pernicious topoi of representations of fascism, Sartre bypasses the homosocial to arrive at the notion of the homosexual as politically aberrant: men *desaxés*, as Sartre puts it, by the Axis.[9] More recently Klaus Theweleit, in *Male Fantasies*, has analyzed the misogyny and psychosexual development of the "soldier male" whose murderous fantasies are taken as synecdochic for those of Nazism (and sometimes those of Western civilization as a whole).[10] What is interesting and important about these psychological studies is that they take the obsession with virility seriously and examine it as a symptom. What is, instead, dangerous is that such analyses risk associating what they consider to be sexual aberration with what they hope to present as historical "aberration," thereby coming perilously close to the famous Crocean interpretation of fascism as a "parenthesis" in history — the term "parenthesis" implying that its roots could not be traced in all that had come before it and that it did not leave seeds for future fascisms. The association of sexual "aberration" with historical aberration has been perpetuated in various narrative forms, among them cinema. One might think, for example, of Roberto Rossellini's film *Open City*, where the Italian collaborator with Nazism is not only wanton but a lesbian to boot, or of the more recent Bertolucci film *1900*, in which the fascist is not only sadistic but portrayed as sexually perverted.[11] These two approaches — that of the linguistic tic and that of pathological aberration — represent the Scylla and Charybdis of approaches to fascism: trivialization and demonization. Demonization, though historically associated with political opposition to fascism, turns analysis into exorcism, while trivialization precludes analysis altogether.

I would like to chart a third course, suggested by a possible objection to the project itself: one might object that political rhetoric always includes a rhetoric of virility and that the problem is therefore not a specifically "fascist" one at all. To be sure, the introduction of gender into political discourse is hardly a fascist innovation. Just as Klaus Theweleit analyzes the way in which Bolshevism is figured as a sexual threat by the Freikorps of-ficers, so Neil Hertz has analyzed the way in which, in the context of the 1848 revolution and the Commune, a political threat may be represented as a sexual threat.[12] And several of the texts we will be examining explic-itly or implicitly invoke a Machiavellian genealogy for their virile virtues. An investigation of the rhetoric of virility would thus seem doubly banal: not only do we "know" that fascist rhetoric is a rhetoric of virility; we also "know" that all political rhetoric is a rhetoric of virility.[13] But such "knowl-edge" is based upon an ideological sedimentation so thick that it seems as natural as the ground we walk upon, and easily leads to an acceptance of those gender politics as equally natural. Though layer upon layer of culture have made it appear "natural," that common ground is a commonplace — rhetorical and ideological — that is neither trivial (simply to be expected) nor demonic (completely unprecedented). Without a rhetorical and ideo-logical analysis of this commonplace, our understanding of the culture that produced fascism and of the culture that fascism produced remains not only partial but ideological as well, for we risk accepting the gender politics of that culture. One such layer of culture can be found in the literary roots of fascist rhetoric.

This literary treatment of fascism is rendered necessary by Italian fas-cism's refusal (or incapacity) to define itself philosophically, a refusal (or incapacity) that has plagued historians and political scientists who find themselves hard pressed to define their object of study. Their solution is often a chronological, rather than philosophical or ideological, one: "The word Fascism with a capital 'F' refers specifically to the political system of Italy from the early 1920s through the early 1940s and should not be a problem; the problem concerns the word fascism with a small 'f,' " writes the historian Edward Tannenbaum.[14] Such a chronological solution is a heuristic device that merely displaces the problem onto "fascisms." Indeed, "fascist philosophy" and "fascist ideology" come to be viewed as almost oxymoronic combinations, as contradictions in terms.[15] Yet fascism seems to compensate for this refusal (or incapacity) by overdefining itself rhetorically and semiotically: hence the need to change calendar and holidays, to eradicate all traces of foreign words and dialect from the "official" language, to identify the fascist by the clothes he wears and the slogans he repeats, and, in general, to attempt a realignment of signifiers and signifieds. Thus, in oxymoronic fashion, war comes to be aligned with life and peace with death; socialism comes to be national; the revolution is conservative; and neologisms (in particular, invective) abound. If this "verbal revolutionism," as it has been called, stands in the place of an "authentic" revolution, it is also one of fascism's primary modes of self-definition. Hence the fascination that fascism seems to hold for literary scholars: fascism is a movement in semiotic overdrive.

Here we will deal with a small part of that semiotic movement by focusing on the rhetoric of virility of two of Mussolini's most notorious "precursors": F. T. Marinetti and Gabriele D'Annunzio. Though it is well known that Mussolini adopted slogans from both writers and that the Duce's political style owed much to D'Annunzio's style during his occupation of Fiume, the writings from which both slogans and style were culled remain to a large extent unread. Marinetti's neglected political writings (*Democrazia futurista* [Futurist democracy] [1919], *Al di là del comunismo* [Beyond communism] [1920], *Futurismo e fascismo* [Futurism and fascism] [1924]) and D'Annunzio's speeches and writings from the Fiume period (collected in *Il sudore di sangue* [Blood sweat], *L'urna inesausta* [The inexhaustible urn], *Il libro ascetico della giovane Italia* [The ascetic book of young Italy]) belong to the same cultural context in which protofascism, fascism as a movement, had not yet solidified into fascism as regime. The revolutionary aspects of protofascism still coexist, in their works, with the reactionary trend that will out in the end. This combination is often played out as a split between the good revolutionary, Marinetti, and the bad reactionary, D'Annunzio, a split that can be maintained as long as one does not actually read the texts in question.[16] Maria-Antonietta Macciocchi, for example, attempts to salvage Marinetti and lay all blame on D'Annunzio:

> D'Annunzio relegates woman to her boudoir with her feathers, her sequins, her veils, her simpering, and her fainting, in the style of Sarah Bernhardt and Belle Otero. Woman was "a thousand times woman." Like a true D'Annunzian (his same whore-mongering tastes will lead him to defend bordellos during the fascist period), Mussolini will choose the sexual and cultural poverty of women as a system of power. Anti-Dannuzianism — represented by Marinetti and clearly marked by the Bolshevik revolution — was in the meantime headed in the opposite ideological direction (a letter from Gramsci

to Trotsky — September 1927 — reveals the extent to which futurist discourse was widespread in the centers of workers' culture in Turin). Marinetti's futurism, before being put in step and distorted by fascism, upset the traditional bourgeois ethic and its familialism that were always accompanied in D'Annunzio by a morality of debauchery for the privileged elite. He extolled divorce, free love, the abolition of women's servitude, women's suffrage. The futurist documents of the twenties addressed to women had as titles: "Manifeste de la femme futuriste" (Manifesto of futurist women), "Contro il lusso femminile" (Against feminine extravagance), "Contro il matrimonio" (Against marriage).[17]

This passage is typical in a number of ways: it confuses D'Annunzio's biography with D'Annunzio's literary texts; it accepts Marinetti's own characterization of his relationship to "D'Annunzianesimo" at face value; it adheres to a split between a first, revolutionary futurism, and a second, "distorted" (read: fascist) futurism. Such splitting makes it impossible to read anything other than titles, for when the texts that follow those titles are read, one discovers that the two "moments" of futurism are ideologically simultaneous rather than sequential: "tutte le belle libertà" [all the beautiful freedoms] (as Marinetti himself puts it in *Come si seducono le donne* [How to seduce women]) that futurism has to offer women are designed not only to liberate women from slavery to men and to the bourgeois family but also to safeguard virility and ensure the future of the nation and of the race. Marinetti's writings on "women's issues" are the breeding ground for his rhetoric of virility, and so it is to those texts that we now turn.

Marinetti's Border Patrol

"Contro il matrimonio," a manifesto that appears in *Democrazia futurista,* is divided almost exactly in half between the "left" and the "right," the "first" moment of futurism and the "second." In the first half, the bourgeois family is lambasted as an absurd, prehistoric prison in which all participants are victims; marriage is denounced as a hypocritical mask for legal prostitution; the abolition of property, both of land and of women, is declared: "Noi vogliamo distruggere non soltanto la proprietà della terra, ma anche la proprietà della donna" [We want to destroy not only the ownership of land, but also the ownership of woman]. As Macciocchi notes, Engels would have approved. But just as one is about to applaud (and Macciocchi, who quotes only the first half, does applaud), the argument takes a nationalistic turn: "La donna non appartiene a un uomo, ma bensì all'avvenire e allo sviluppo della razza" [Woman does not belong to a man but rather to the future and to the race's development]. This appearance of nationalism coincides — not coincidentally — with the introduction of a rhetoric of virility, confirming George Mosse's suggestion that the ideal of manliness is a fellow-traveler of nationalism.[18] Indeed, the second half of the manifesto gives a series of quite different reasons for the abolition of family and marriage:

> Sarà finalmente abolita la mescolanza di maschi e femmine che — nella prima età — produce una dannosa effemminazione dei maschi.
> I bambini maschi devono — secondo noi — svilupparsi lontano dalle bambine perchè i loro primi giuochi sieno nettamente maschili, cioè privi d'ogni morbosità affettiva, d'ogni delicatezza donnesca, vivaci, battaglieri, muscolari, e violentemente dinamici. La convivenza di bambini e di bambine produce sempre un ritardo nella formazione del carattere dei bambini che immancabilmente subiscono il fascino e la seduzione imperativa della piccola femmina come piccoli cicisbei o piccoli schiavi stupidi.[19]

> [We will finally do away with the mixture of males and females that during the earliest years always produces a harmful effeminizing of the male.
> Little boys must — according to us — develop far away from little girls in order that their first games be clearly masculine, that is, free of emotional morbidity or womanly delicacy, lively, feisty, muscular and violently dynamic. When little boys and girls live together, the formation of the male character is always retarded. They always succumb to the charm and the willful seductiveness of the little female, like little ladies' men or stupid little slaves.][20]

The logic of this passage runs counter to the commonplace that "boys will be boys": given half a chance, boys will be girls. That dreaded opportunity might be forestalled by segregation, separate but not quite equal, at an early age. But even then the boy's masculinity is not assured, for the manifesto continues and ends with yet another example of harmful mixture. History itself may still intervene at a later age, and men will jump at the chance:

> La vasta partecipazione delle donne al lavoro nazionale prodotto dalla guerra, ha creato un tipico grotesco matrimoniale: Il marito possedeva del denaro o ne guadagnava, ora l'ha perduto e stenta a riguadagnarne. Sua moglie lavora e trova il modo di guadagnare un denaro abbondante in un momento in cui la vita è essenzialmente costosa.
> La moglie ha per il suo lavoro stesso la necessità di una vita poco casalinga, il marito invece non lavorando concentra tutta la sua attività in una assurda preoccupazione di ordine casalingo.
> Rovesciamento completo di una famiglia dove il marito è diventato una donna inutile con prepotenze maschili e la moglie ha raddoppiato il suo valore umano e sociale.
> Urto inevitabile fra i due soci, conflitto e sconfitta dell'uomo.[21]

[The wide participation of women in the national work produced by the war has created a typical matrimonial grotesque: the husband had money or was earning it, now he has lost it and has difficulty earning it back. His wife works and finds a way to earn a handsome income at a time when cost of living is high.

On account of her job, the wife needs a nonhousewifely life, while the husband who does not work concentrates all his activity in an absurd housewifely preoccupation.

Complete overturning of a family in which the husband has become a useless woman with masculine pretensions and the wife has doubled her human and social value.

Inevitable clash between the two spouses, conflict and defeat of the man.][22]

The virile soldier returned from the segregated barracks and trenches to find the familial, patriarchal hierarchy inverted. The first, eminently quotable half of the manifesto calls for the liberation of woman from family and patriarchy; the second recasts that argument in terms of the liberation of man from evirating woman: marriage and the family are threats to virility. This refrain is taken up again in the manifesto "Orgoglio italiano rivoluzionario e libero amore" (Revolutionary Italian pride and free love):

Il matrimonio deprime e avvilisce la donna abbreviandone la gioventù e troncandone le forze spirituali e fisiche. Il matrimonio scoraggia e soffoca lo sviluppo del figlio, tronca la gioventù e la forza virile del padre, effemmina l'adolescente, monotonizza e affloscia in un ambiente di mediocrità tre o più individui che avrebbero dato il loro massimo rendimento slegati in libertà e in piena avventura. Il matrimonio è un nemico di ogni audacia e di ogni eroismo.[23]

[Marriage depresses and disheartens woman by cutting short youth and stunting her spiritual and physical forces. Marriage discourages and suffocates the development of the son, cuts short the youth and virile strength of the father, effeminates the adolescent, monotonizes and withers, in an atmosphere of mediocrity, three or more individuals who would have fulfilled their potential unfettered in freedom and in high adventure. Marriage is an enemy of all boldness and all heroism.]

One might, of course, point out that there is a good deal of "cutting off" ("troncandone ... tronca") going on in this passage and that this "cutting off" has a withering and feminizing effect. But while such castratory language comes as no surprise in this context, it is not really the point—as in the case of the *bambine* cited above, the mere proximity of woman seems enough to wither and feminize.

This latter point is brought home with remarkable clarity in the manifesto "Contro il lusso femminile," which appears in *Futurismo e fascismo*. Here the inversion of the familial hierarchy, noted in "Contro il matrimonio," is translated into an "inversion" of another sort, as Marinetti associates feminization with homosexuality, or, as he puts it, "pederasty":

> I gioelli e le stoffe dolci al tatto distruggono nel maschio l'assaporamento tattile della carne femminile. I profumi sono ugualmente contrari al vero desiderio, poiché raramente collaborano cogli odori della pelle, spesso si combinano con essi spiacevolmente, sempre distraggono e astraggono l'olfatto-immaginazione del maschio.
>
> Il maschio perde a poco a poco il senso potente della carne femminile e lo rimpiazza con una sensibilità indecisa e tutta artificiale, che risponde soltanto alle sete, ai velluti, ai gioielli, alle pellicce.
>
> Diventano sempre più rari i maschi capaci di prendere e gustare una bella donna senza preoccuparsi del contorno e del contatto di stoffe scintillii e colori. La donna nuda non piace più. I maschi si trasformano in gioiellieri, profumieri, sarti, modiste, stiratrici, ricamatori e pederasti. La *toilettite* favorisce singolarmente lo sviluppo della pederastìa e si dovrà giungere presto a quel provvedimento igienico di un doge di Venezia, che obbligò le belle veneziane ad esporsi colle poppe nude alla finestra, fra due candele, per ricondurre i maschi sulla retta via.[24]

[Jewels and fabrics sweet to the touch destroy in the male the tactile tasting of female flesh. Perfumes are equally contrary to true desire, for rarely do they collaborate with the skin's odors; often they combine with them in an unpleasant way; and they always distract and abstact the male's olfactory imagination.

Little by little, the male loses the potent sense of female flesh and replaces it with an indecisive and completely artificial sensitivity that responds only to silks, velvets, jewels, and furs.

Males capable of taking and enjoying a beautiful woman without worrying about the trimmings and contact with fabrics, glitters, and colors are ever more rare. The naked woman no longer pleases. Males are transformed into jewelers, perfumers, tailors, stylists, ironesses, embroiderers, and pederasts. Toilettitis particularly favors the development of pederasty, and soon we will have recourse to that hygienic measure taken by a Venetian doge who required the beautiful Venetian women to expose their naked breasts at the window, between two candles, in order to lead males back to the straight and narrow.]

Marinetti needs to create two different kinds of women (even if those two kinds are only differentiated by the presence or absence of clothes), two different kinds of proximity, since dispensing with women entirely would leave the male without means to prove his masculinity.[25] It is difficult to imagine a more direct countertext to what might be called the "Decadent Manifesto," Baudelaire's "Éloge du maquillage" (and equally difficult to imagine that Marinetti, reader of Baudelaire and Mallarmé, did not have Baudelaire in mind). Baudelaire, of course, had praised cosmetics and the *mundus muliebris* as the model for the artist whose poetics were those of cosmesis rather than mimesis. And in "Un mangeur d'opium," proximity to the *mundus muliebris* is quite explicitly the incubator of genius:

> L'homme qui, dès le commencement, a été longtemps baigné dans la molle atmosphère de la femme, dans l'odeur de ses mains, de son sein, de ses genoux, de sa chevelure, de ses vêtements souples et flottants,
>
> > Dulce balneum suavibus
> > Unguentatum odoribus
>
> y a contracté une délicatesse d'épiderme et une distinction d'accent, une espèce d'androgynéité, sans lesquelles le génie le plus âpre et le plus viril reste, relativement à la perfection dans l'art, un être incomplet. Enfin, je veux dire que le goût précoce du *monde* féminin, *mundi muliebris,* de tout cet appareil ondoyant, scintillant et parfumé, fait les génies supérieurs.[26]

> [The man who, from the beginning, has long been bathed in the soft atmosphere of woman, in the odor of her hands, her breast, her knees, her hair, her supple and flowing clothes,
>
> > Dulce balneum suavibus
> > Unguentatum odoribus
>
> has contracted an epidermal delicacy and a distinction of accent, a sort of androgyny without which the most severe and virile genius remains, in relation to perfection in art, an incomplete being. In short, I mean that the precocious taste for the feminine world/cosmetics, for the whole flowing, scintillating, perfumed display, makes superior geniuses.]

For Baudelaire, androgyny can be contracted and virile genius completed through physical proximity to women and their *toilette,* "scintillant et parfumé." For Marinetti, instead, what is contracted from the *manìa morbosa* (morbid mania) of the *toilette* ("I profumi...stoffe scintilli colori") is not androgyny but pederasty. *Toilettite* (toilettitis), as Marinetti calls it, "perverts" masculine desire, and only a naked woman can lead the man back to the *diritta via* of heterosexuality. And once again, the rhetoric of virility is coupled with nationalistic sentiment:

> Noi futuristi, barbari raffinatissimi, ma virilissimi, viviamo in tutti gli ambienti; siamo, se non sempre amati, mai trascurati. Abbiamo interrogati i

maschi più fortunati. Sono del nostro parere. Siamo dunque competenti e ottimisti non delusi. Parliamo in nome della razza, che esige maschi accesi e donne fecondate. La fecondità, per una razza come la nostra, è in caso di guerra, la sua difesa imdispensabile, e in tempo di pace la sua ricchezza di braccia lavoratrici e di teste geniali.

In nome del grande avvenire virile fecondo e geniale dell'Italia, noi futuristi condanniamo la dilagante cretinerìa femminile e la devota imbecillità dei maschi che insieme collaborano a sviluppare il lusso femminile, la prostituzione, la pederastìa, e la sterilità della razza.[27]

[We futurists, extremely refined barbarians, but extremely virile, live in all environments. If not always loved, we are never ignored. We have interrogated the most fortunate males. They agree with us. We are therefore competent and undeluded optimists. We speak in the name of the race, which demands ardent males and inseminated females. Fecundity, for a race like ours, is its indispensable defense in times of war, and in times of peace, its wealth of working arms and genial heads.

In the name of the great, virile, fecund, and genial future of Italy, we futurists condemn the spreading feminine idiocy and the devoted imbecility of males that together collaborate to develop feminine extravagance, prostitution, pederasty, and the sterility of the race.][1]

These concluding demographic preoccupations are "pure" Mussolini and appear in a manifesto that Macciocchi implies *preceded* the distortion of futurism by fascism. The point is not that futurism in 1920 was already distorted (in which case only prewar futurism would be "pure") but rather that it was always already "distorted."[28] One must not forget that the 1909 founding manifesto of futurism included, as article number nine, the glorification of war, militarism, patriotism, and "il disprezzo della donna" (scorn for woman), and that article number ten called for the destruction not only of museums but also of feminism. Nor should one forget that Marinetti's argument for women's suffrage, in "Contro l'amore e il parlamentarismo," is based upon the premise that since women are absolutely inferior in both character and intelligence, they will be mediocre legislative instruments and will therefore involuntarily aid in the cause of destroying the parliamentary system. But it is not, after all, the texts themselves that are distorted; rather, we, as readers, distort them by sorting out the "left" from the "right" and privileging either the one or the other. They are bound together: the "progressive" cause, women's suffrage, is but a means to a "reactionary" end, the destruction of the parliamentary form of government.[29] This binding creates an ideological double bind with regard to the preservation of virility: the proximity of women turns boys into girls and heterosexuals into "pederasts," but only the proximity of women (naked breasts at the window . . .) can make the boy a man and the man a patriot.

This patriarchal double bind has been astutely analyzed by Eve Kosofsky Sedgwick as the result of a prescription of homosocial behavior (male bonding) and an equally strong proscription of homosexual behavior.[30] The boundaries between the homosocial and the homosexual are unstable and always shifting, creating what, as mentioned earlier, Sedgwick calls "male homosexual panic": When does camaraderie become pederasty (as Marinetti would say)? What is the correct proximity of man to man? This double bind manifests itself in Marinetti's texts not in terms of proximity of man to man but in terms of man to woman. Divorce, free love, and destruction of the bourgeois family are all tactics that will enforce intermittent proximity of men to women, as if to draw new boundaries that would protect virility from the "effemination" that results from cohabitation, and at the same time refuel virility through sporadic contact with women. What distinguishes Marinetti's texts from the texts discussed by Sedgwick, however, is that here the patriarchal double bind is lined with nationalism; the rhetoric of virility is the site where boundaries between the homosocial and the homosexual, and borders between nations (which can be more clearly drawn and more openly defended than those between the homosocial and the homosexual), cross. Internationalism thus becomes the greatest threat to both, for the elimination of or expansion of national borders may also expand or eliminate the boundaries that stake out virility. Indeed, Marinetti's anticommunist manifesto, "Al di là del comunismo," attacks Bolshevism because it would eliminate boundaries between individuals, between classes, but most importantly between nations:

> Non si può abolire l'idea di patria se non rifugiandosi in un egoismo assenteista. Dire per esempio: io non sono italiano, sono cittadino del mondo, equivale a dire: "m'infischio dell'Italia, dell'Europa, dell'Umanità: penso a me."
> Il concetto di patria è indistruttibile quanto il concetto di partito.
> La patria non è che un vasto partito. Negare la patria equivale a isolarsi, castrarsi, diminuirsi, denigrarsi, suicidarsi.[31]

[One can't abolish the idea of a fatherland without taking refuge in an absenteist egotism. To say, for example: "I am not Italian, I am a citizen of the world," is equal to saying: "I don't give a damn about Italy, Europe, or humanity; I'm thinking of myself."

The concept of a fatherland is as indestructible as the concept of a political party. The fatherland is nothing other than a vast political party.

To negate the fatherland is to isolate oneself, castrate oneself, diminish oneself, denigrate oneself, commit suicide.]

Any internationalist movement, be it socialist or communist, is castratory not because it kills the father (apart from the word *patria*, there is little justification for such a reading in these texts) but because it effaces differences between nations, classes, intellects, and sexes. The futurist commutation appears to be a simple, if not brutally simplistic, one: no nations equals no wars, and no wars equals no virility. Marinetti states:

L'umanità sogna di stabilire la pace mediante un tipo unico d'uomo mondiale, che dovrebbe essere subito castrato, perchè la sua virilità aggressiva non dichiarasse nuove guerre.[32]

[Humanity dreams of establishing peace by creating a single type of man the world over, who should be castrated immediately in order that his aggressive virility not declare new wars.]

Scornful of the prospect of a peaceful, and therefore (to his mind) undifferentiated world where there are no national borders to defend, no class struggles to be won, Marinetti fantasizes the final frontier:

La pace assoluta regnerà forse colla sparizione delle razze umane. Se fossi un comunista mi preoccuperei della prossima guerra tra pederasti e lesbiche, che is uniranno poi contro gli uomini normali.[33]

[Absolute peace will perhaps reign with the disappearance of the human races. If I were a communist, I would worry about the next war between pederasts and lesbians, who will then unite against normal men.]

New "nations" will form in the absence of the old, and virility can once again be defended at the border.

If the destruction of national borders leaves virility open to attack, their aggressive defense allows virility's border patrol to relax. It is in this context that we can make sense of *Come si seducono le donne*, the seemingly anomalous futurist self-help manual published in 1916. Why, indeed, should Marinetti set about writing such a "D'Annunzian" text (though D'Annunzio, of course, would never write such a manual) in the midst of a war? The answer, and the text, lie at the crossroads between national borders and boundaries of virility:

Più della metà dei maschi italiani hanno la forza che seduce e capisce il bel sesso. In Spagna ed in Francia essa è molto meno sviluppata che da noi. In Russia e in Inghilterra quasi non esiste.[34]

[More than half of Italian males have the strength that seduces and understands the beautiful sex. In Spain and in France it is much less developed than in Italy. In Russia and in England it barely exists.]

Once again, cohabitation produces a harmful mixture

La convivenza è sempre nociva poichè distrugge quel bisogno di pericolo, di agguato, di lotta o d'incertezza che è favorevole al maschio specialmente e anche alla femmina.³⁵

[Cohabitation is always harmful because it destroys that need for danger, ambush, struggle, or uncertainty that is always favorable to the male in particular and also to the female].

Uncertainty and ambush can be created instead in rapid-fire seductions and the *conflagrazione generale* that is the war:

Eroismo: ecco l'afrodisiaco supremo della donna!... Ecco perchè ora soltanto, durante la conflagrazione generale si può godere e giudicare la donna. Ecco perchè durante la nostra grande guerra igienica, per il raggiungimento di tutte le nostre aspirazioni nazionali, i neutralisti italiani (professori e filosofi germanofili, sozzalisti ufficiali, giolittiani) sono tutti o quasi tutti cornuti. Per non inzaccherare questo libro elastico, aerato, balzante e futurista, non ho parlato più delle molte mogli neutralisti, alle quali ho inculcato rapidamente e con disinvoltura l'ineluttabile necessità dell'intervento!³⁶

[Heroism: that's the ultimate aphrodisiac for women!... That's why only now, during the general conflagration, can one enjoy and judge woman. That's why during our great hygienic war for the fulfillment of all our national aspirations, the Italian neutralists (Germanophilic professors and philosophers, official dirty socialists, followers of Giolitti) are all, or almost all, cuckolds. To keep from muddying this elastic, airy, bouncy, and futurist book, I have not spoken about the many neutralist wives into whom I have rapidly and casually inculcated the ineluctable necessity of intervention!]

Only during the war can proximity to women be celebrated, for fighting on the national front allows the male to ease up on another. Girded with nationalistic ardor, the futurist can even cross the border between homosociality and homosexuality: the sexual act itself is "nationalized," intercourse becomes intervention, and the double-entendre *inculcare-inculare* enacts the "pederasty" that usually lies on the other side of the enemy lines. If Italy's own intervention in the war was finally decided on the basis of a promise that its borders would be expanded, Marinetti's intervention in neutralists' wives similarly expands the boundaries of virility.³⁷ The futurist can *inculare* both literally and figuratively while heroically defending the nation and fighting for the expansion of its borders.

This same mechanism might explain the otherwise puzzling approval of homosexuality in "Discorso futurista agli inglesi" (Futurist speech to the English), included in *Guerra sola igiene del mondo* (War, only hygiene of the world) and republished in *Futurismo e fascismo*. Chock-full of national stereotypes, the speech condemns the English for their own hypocritical condemnation of homosexuality, citing both the "unforgivable" trial of Oscar Wilde and an "intensification of camaraderie" in youth:

> Quanto ai vostri giovanotti di vent'anni, sono quasi tutti, per qualche tempo, omosessuali. Questo loro gusto rispettabilissimo si sviluppa per una specie d'intensificazione della *camaraderie* e dell'amicizia, negli sports atletici, prima della trentina, età del lavoro e dell'ordine, in cui essi ritornano bruscamente da Sodoma per fidanzarsi a una signorina sfacciatamente scollacciata, affrettandosi a condannare severamente l'invertito-nato, il falso uomo, la mezza donna che non si corregge.[38]

> [As for your young men of twenty, they are almost all for some period of time homosexual. This highly respectable taste of theirs develops out of a sort of intensification of camaraderie and friendship in athletic sports before the age of thirty, the age of work and of order, when they suddenly return from Sodom to get engaged to a brazenly decolleté young lady and hasten to condemn severely the born invert, the false man, the half-woman who does not mend his ways.]

Crossing national borders one also crosses the unstable boundaries that separate homosexuality from homosociality; crossing national borders *allows* one to cross the boundaries of sexualities. We have in fact already encountered this "young lady" with the low neckline: she is one of the Venetians exposing her breasts at the window, the naked woman who converts the pederast and leads him away from Sodom. It is the same scenario, and only nationality and nationalism separate the English hypocrite from the virile Italian male.

D'Annunzio and the Virile Vulva

From the balconies of Fiume, D'Annnuzio, too, defended borders and contributed to what will become the fascist rhetoric of virility. The borders he championed, however, were those of the mother (Italy, "Madre-patria," and *mater dolorosa*), and the virility he praised was closer to Roman *virtù* than to that of Marinetti's Italian male. Nationalism and the rhetoric of virility are bound together by a rhetoric of maternity in D'Annunzio's speeches at Fiume. Indeed, the Fiuman writings are something of an anomaly in D'Annunzio's corpus; nowhere else is christological language employed so consistently, and nowhere else does D'Annunzio speak so piously of mothers and of motherhood.[39] This particular combination of piety and maternity would seem, in the abstract, to be a recipe for what will become the regime's rhetoric of maternity: "madri degli eroi della razza" [mothers of the heroes of the race], fecund mothers producing sons as martyrs to the "Madre-patria." And "in the abstract" — that is to say, by splitting off the rhetoric of virility from those of maternity and nationalism — it is easy enough to find examples that fit the bill: "madri degli eroi, le sorelle degli eroi, le donne degli eroi" [mothers of heroes, sisters of heroes, women of heroes] clamoring to be the first to decorate the graves of their fallen men.[40]

As we have seen, however, such splitting works to produce an ideological homogeneity that allows Macciocchi, for example, to distinguish the "good" Marinetti from the "bad" D'Annunzio. Thus in studies on Marinetti, there has been a tendency to discard the "right" in order to preserve the "left" (the "anarchic" Marinetti, the "anticlerical" Marinetti, the "revolutionary-form" Marinetti); in D'Annunzio's case, on the other hand, the tendency has been to carve out the "right," in all its flamboyance, and dismiss the "left."[41] Here I assume the existence of the "bad" D'Annunzio, the homogenized, "fascist" D'Annunzio, in order to show how the binding of left and right is at work in D'Annunzio's texts as well as Marinetti's. If I highlight the "left" in D'Annunzio, it is always against the background of the "right."

In the Fiuman texts themselves, then, the rhetoric of virility binds together those of nationalism and maternity and produces a mixture that will be inimical to the regime's attempts to enforce the stability of gender. In fascist discourse, gender and sex are not to be mixed and matched: virility is the property of man, and femininity the property of woman. Any attempt to redistribute those properties — and in particular, to allow women to enter the public, political arena, and hence "masculinize" them — was to be squelched. The adjectives "masculine" and "virile" as applied to women were exclusively terms of abuse meant to deride the intellectual, "feminist," and hence sterile woman not properly devoted to her reproductive mission.[42] It is here that D'Annunzio's own "decadent genealogy" interferes with (even as it contributes to) fascist rhetoric and ideology, for virility in the Fiuman speeches is not only, nor even above all, the province of males, just as, in his earlier novels, femininity is not only the province of women. The "feminine" was not a term of invective for D'Annunzio, and no disclaimers marked the inclusion of women's suffrage in the *Carta del Carnaro*, the constitution that he and Alceste de Ambris wrote for Fiume.[43] It is not against the feminine that virility is defined and defended, as in Marinetti, but rather against gluttony, greed, and "adiposity."[44] Thus among the romanizing, fascistizing topoi of Italy as the wounded mother, the bleeding, mutilated mother, and Fiume as a locus of fortitude, forbearance, self-discipline, and endurance, we also find a female source of "la Costanza virile":

> Ma il nome di tutte le donne fiumane è Ardenza; ma il nome di tutte le donne fiumane è Pazienza. Non mai il "pazientissimo ardore" dei Santi Padri fu testimoniato con una vigoria così maschia. Non mai, nella storia delle grandi lotte civiche, le ispiratrici e le sostenitrici rivelarono uno spirito così potente.[45]

> [But the name of all Fiuman women is Ardor; but the name of all Fiuman women is Patience. Never has the "most patient ardor" of the Holy Fathers been proven with such masculine vigor. Never, in the history of great civic struggles, have the female animators and supporters revealed such potent spirit.]

This patristic endorsement of patience and the underlying ideology of sacrifice are perfectly consonant with fascist discourse; what is not is the *vigoria maschia* attributed to women. Such crossing of the lines of gender and sex (and here those lines are grammatical as well as ideological, for the feminine ending in *a* of the adjective *maschio* represents a kind of grammatical equivalent of the mixing of sex and gender) would be "perversion" for Marinetti; D'Annunzio instead crossed them in Baudelairian fashion, extending the boundaries of virility to occupy (and speak through) the foreign land that was the woman's body. I have elsewhere analyzed the modalities and consequences of this occupation in D'Annunzio's early prose works. Here that body is specifically the body of a (nationalized) mother — of Rome, of Italy, and of Fiume "herself."[46] Indeed, in *Il Sudore di sangue,* the mother is the exemplary model of virility:

> Nell'atto di offrire il sacrifizio, sapendo qual sacrifizio ella (Roma) offrisse, non esclamava più, non parlava più. Severo spettacolo, maschio esempio. Rimaneva taciturna, come chi guarda il proprio fato e si sente a lui pari, anzi a lui sovrastante.
>
> Oggi noi vogliamo celebrare quel silenzio, Italiani, non altro che quel silenzio guerriero.
>
> L'Italia aveva partorito il suo futuro con uno spasimo atrocissimo; aveva ansiato prima di assalire; aveva sanguinato prima di combattere.[47]

> [In the act of offering the sacrifice, knowing what sacrifice she (Rome) offered, she exclaimed no longer, she spoke no longer. A severe spectacle, a

masculine example. She remained taciturn, like someone who looks upon her fate and feels equal to it, indeed superior to it.

Today we want to celebrate that silence, Italians, nothing other than that warrior's silence.

Italy had given birth to her future with a most atrocious spasm, she had gasped before attacking, she had bled before fighting.]

As if to underline the reversal in the "normal" order of things — "she" supplies the masculine example — D'Annunzio ends the passage with a double hysteron proteron, the figure in which the "normal or logical order" of things is reversed, the latter is put as the former: she had gasped before attacking (rather than after) and had bled before fighting (rather than after). The text insists upon the feminine gender of Rome even as "she" offers a masculine example, for Rome's virility in the face of sacrifice is metonymically compared to mother Italy's fortitude in the face of the pain of childbirth. One could imagine this analogy being turned back against women in a fascist version of the arguments against the *parto indolore* (painless childbirth) that the church will later formulate: that is, to be good fascist Christians, women should follow the example of the virile fascist and refuse painkillers in childbirth. Yet at the same time, the mixing and matching present here would make the analogy unpalatable. The analogy itself combines at least two traditional topoi: the figuration of Rome, or Italy, as a woman is, of course, at least as old as Italian literature itself — one thinks of Dante's Florence, the provincial lady become whore, or of his widowed Rome, crying out for her Caesar; and the comparison of war and parturition has roots in classical antiquity.[48] What is striking about the D'Annunzian version, however, is that here the subject of virility can be either masculine or feminine, and its source is what Gadda might have snidely called the "virile vulva of the Italian woman":

É bello che l'antica libertà comunale si ristampi, di generazione in generazione, nella matrice eroica. La risposta cruda di Caterina Sforza, dall'alto della torre romagnola, è appropriato a questo coraggio feroce: "Qui n'ho il conio."

I figli sono stampati a simiglianza delle madri, come abbiamo veduto. Hanno bevuto un latte così forte che possono resistere lungamente al digiuno e al disagio. Pare che la mammella materna li sostenga anche quando è inaridita: la sinistra sotto cui batte il cuore infaticabile.[49]

[It is beautiful that the ancient freedom of the communes is remolded, from generation to generation, in the heroic matrix/womb. The crude response of Caterina Sforza from the top of the Romagnolo tower befits this ferocious courage: "Here I have the 'mint.' "

The sons are molded in their mothers' likeness, as we have seen. They
have drunk a milk so strong that they can long endure fasting and discomfort.
It seems that the maternal breast sustains them even when it has dried up: the
left breast, under which beats an indefatigable heart.]

Gadda's "virile vulva" aims to ridicule fascism by implying that, after all,
not everything can be virile; as we have seen, his is a ridicule based on
the assumption, shared with fascist discourse itself, of a naturalized relation between gender and sex. Mixing and matching constitutes an absurd
impossibility only insofar as it is understood to violate such a "nature."
D'Annunzio's "virile vulva" is, I would like to argue, part of an opposing strategy, one with a history of its own. This particular image, in fact,
brings along with it a rich political history, for by citing the Caterina Sforza
story, D'Annunzio evokes a Machiavellian genealogy and an intertextual
depth that we need to sound in order to read its politics in the context
of D'Annunzio's speech at Fiume.

The anecdote to which D'Annunzio refers is recounted in the sixth chapter of book 3 of Machiavelli's *Discourses* and is a moment in the history
of a conspiracy against the Riario family in the town of Forlì in 1488.
The historical details are not a matter of obscure archival interest, however,
for this particular episode had long been popular myth, and Caterina's life
had, as recently as 1893, been the subject of a three-volume biography.[50]
D'Annunzio's audience, therefore, would have known the outlines of the
story, beginning with the murder of Caterina Sforza's husband, Girolamo
Riario, at the hands of conspirators. After his death, Caterina was, along
with her children, mother, and two half sisters, taken prisoner. In order to
consolidate their power, the conspirators needed to take possession of the
fortresses of the city, still loyal to the family. They met with nothing but
resistance until a shrewd castellan agreed to surrender on condition that he
be allowed to speak first with Caterina in the fortress. After several hours
of discussion — some of the conspirators smelled a rat — permission was
granted; "after all," writes Ernest Breisach, "they still held her children,
her mother, and two half sisters. What woman could ignore a threat to
such loved ones?"[51] Once inside the fortress, however, Caterina appeared
defiantly on the battlements and hurled insult upon her former captors.
When the conspirators threatened to kill her children, she responded, some
versions of the story say, by lifting her skirts to expose her genitals and
retorting that she had the means to make more.[52]

Of this account, historians dispute only the exposure of the genitals. Literary critics are, of course, interested in little else, and for good reason:

Caterina Sforza's gesture is not unique to her but rather is a variation of a topos that consistently forges a link between women and political action. As Neil Hertz has shown, the topos gripped those who found themselves on the wrong (that is to say, politically "right") side of the barricades in the French Revolution and was, Hertz argues, the product of "male hysteria under political pressure." In his "Reply" to responses to his essay, Hertz links the reactionary hysterization of history specifically to the Caterina Sforza story, citing it as yet another manifestation of the Medusan imagination in politics. Indeed, in an essay titled "Medusa and the Madonna of Forlì: Political Sexuality in Machiavelli," which focuses on Caterina, John Freccero has suggested that Medusa is the face worn by republicanism as seen by the aristocracy. But the specific meaning of the Caterina Sforza episode is, for Freccero, more political than psychoanalytical:

> To see the Medusa's face in the body of Caterina Sforza is to read historical significance into the reproductive force of nature. It is also to see in the body of a woman no longer the passive sign of political power, an object to be possessed, but rather an autonomous force.[53]

Freccero's reading is thus more like that of Catherine Gallagher, who, in response to Hertz, reads the gesture of exposure as a threat to patriarchal control of reproduction and hence to property relations in general.[54] Of course, this reading cannot simply be transposed to the D'Annunzian text, for it addresses both the specificities of Machiavelli's text and its historical context. But it gives us access to one layer of the intertext and draws upon another closer historically to D'Annunzio: Antonio Gramsci's reading of Caterina Sforza as an emblem of the irruption of the proletariat into history.[55] Once again, Gramsci is interpreting and appropriating the figure as it appears in Machiavelli's text; it is significant, however, that Gramsci, D'Annunzio, and Machiavelli all interpret Caterina's action as an emblem of positive political action, in contradistinction to Hertz's "male hysterics," who see her gesture as castratory. All three writers clearly see it as a threat not to themselves but to their enemies: an apotropaic shield bearing the head of Medusa. To put it in crude psychoanalytic terms, what for their foes may appear to be a threat of castration represents, to these three, a refusal to be castrated: the threat to kill Caterina's children is, after all, an attempt to castrate her politically, and her gesture can thus be read as a refusal to be castrated. The psychoanalytic translation into the Medusa, however, partially blinds us to the potential political meaning of the gesture by subsuming it under the fascination of the phallic mother, a fantasy that is more reassuring than not for the fetishizing male fantasy. While Caterina shares with Hertz's revolutionary women the gesture of exposure, it is her Medean rather than Medusan aspect that distinguishes her. An alternate, and still Machiavellian, interpretation would be to say that Caterina makes the private public, exposes what "should" remain private, and refuses to be shoved back into the private sphere. The point of the anecdote is that her enemies think they have conquered her because they hold her children hostage — that is, they can defeat her because she is a mother. The point of her gesture is that she is something *in addition to,* in excess of, a mother — a political being, who cannot be drawn back into the private sphere by the tug of the umbilical cord.

What happens when Caterina is transplanted to D'Annunzio's speech at Fiume? Is she still the emblem of republicanism, the face of the proletariat? Surely not, for no single image is of itself "left" or "right"; no individual "element" has a stable meaning; and no rhetorical strategy is inherently fascist or democratic — if they were, the binding machine of fascist rhetoric would have come grinding to a halt. Yet the Caterina Sforza story as ideologeme brings with it an intertextual and political history that must be factored into our analysis. The interpretation I have just outlined would allow us to read her as an antimother who exceeds and violates the parameters fascist discourse sets for women. As the model and mold of female virility, she violates the rigidly gendered, and ultimately Aristotelian, opposition between virile courage and maternal love, an opposition that Mussolini will elaborate in a famous equation: "La guerra sta all'uomo come la maternità alla donna" [War is to man as maternity is to woman].[56] The line D'Annunzio attributes to Caterina underlines its anti-Aristotelian twist: "Qui n'ho il conio" gives to Caterina ownership of the mold or form, precisely what the male is, for Aristotle, presumed to supply in reproduction. And D'Annunzio could not resist an interlingual pun: the *con* has become *conio.*

Unlike the mother of fascist propaganda, who exalts the son's virility, Caterina as antimother is the original model of virility: the sons are "printed" in the *mother's* likeness.[57] This *matrice eroica* is not meant to be the incubator for a demographic boom, but rather the matrix and model of political resistance. In the context of D'Annunzio's Fiuman writings, then, we might say that Caterina Sforza stands defiantly on her tower, not an example of "l'antiféminisme petit-bourgeois du fascisme"[58] but rather of a powerfully female political gesture, and of a paradoxically female virility.

For Marinetti and later for the discourse of the regime, virility is possible only if women are excluded from it; for D'Annunzio, virility is defined and molded through the "feminine." This contrast between Marinetti and D'Annunzio might be subsumed under what Christine Buci-Glucksmann has described as "two statutes of difference": one that is antiegalitarian and conservative and another that is transgressive of the boundaries between masculine and feminine. Buci-Glucksmann identifies the first of these with the "masculine order (der *Männerbund*)" and with what she calls a "virile homosexualization of values that relegates women to nature, originary chaos, and to the procreative mother."[59] The second, transgressive order engenders instead a space of new knowledge that makes possible the Freudian discovery of bisexuality. Buci-Glucksmann links the second of these to the Baudelaire-Nietzsche line, in other words, to the decadents whom she had examined in *La raison baroque,* the line to which D'Annunzio belongs.[60] The first of these is, with an important modification, the line to which Marinetti belongs, that is, a virile homosexualization of values that is a *homophobic* homosocialization of values (or, as Irigaray might put it, a "hom(m)o-sexualization").

It would be unfair, however, not to note the way in which Caterina Sforza is domesticated within D'Annunzio's speech. If I have dwelt at such length on the first of the two paragraphs cited, it was in order to highlight the potentially disturbing valence of D'Annunzio's invocation of the topos and therefore to swim upstream against a strong current of D'Annunzian criticism. But what happens in the second paragraph? I cite it again:

I figli sono stampati a simiglianza delle madri, come abbiamo veduto. Hanno bevuto un latte così forte che possono resistere lungamente al digiuno e al disagio. Pare che la mammella materna li sostenga anche quando è inaridita: la sinistra sotto cui batte il cuore infaticabile.[61]

[The sons are molded in their mothers' likeness, as we have seen. They have drunk a milk so strong that they can long endure fasting and discomfort. It seems that the maternal breast sustains them even when it has dried up: the left breast, under which beats an indefatigable heart.]

The paradoxical female virility that Caterina's gesture conjured up is upstaged by the nursing mother: as the *conio* is replaced by the maternal breast as focus of attention, the body of the mother reverts to being a passive matrix, vehicle for the milk of a national tradition. The virility of the sons takes the place of that of the mother, as it will in the propaganda of the regime.[62]

This D'Annunzian paradox will not outlive the occupation of Fiume; it is rather the Marinettian "panic" — stripped of its ambiguously progressive elements — that will become the currency of the regime. But it is not only "the feminine" (in the realm of discourse) and women (in the world of action) who will be affected. Other meanings will be added to "virility." If Marinetti and D'Annunzio set into motion the semiotic machinery that Mussolini will exploit, neither, finally, determines the direction it will take with Mussolini at the wheel. What Mussolini will absorb from his "precursors" must be weighed against what he will discard; the Duce will mint his own version of virility, welding new materials to old. By 1924, a little more than a month after the assassination of Giacomo Matteotti, Mussolini was already hard at work forging a new definition of the "virility" of fascism:

> Insomma, per certi signori, la normalizzazione dovrebbe consistere in una volontaria abdicazione del fascismo agli attributi della sua virilità e poscia nel ritorno a quei giochi e giochetti del tempo antico, che avevano suscitato lo sdegno generale. Del resto, Partito e Governo procedono sulla via dell'unica normalizzazione possibile, che è quella fascista.[63]

> [In sum, certain people suggest that normalization should consist of a voluntary abdication by fascism of the attributes of its virility and hence of a return to the little games of old that had caused the general disdain. In fact, both party and government are proceeding along the path of the only possible normalization, which is fascist.]

This virility is a barely disguised euphemism for the fascist militia and the violence it meted out against its political opposition. It is this virility that fascism will normalize and rhetoricize and that the fascist regime will not abdicate until its fall nearly twenty years later.

Raping the Masses

Critics often trope the texts they analyze, repeat the structures they claim to demystify, or participate unwittingly in the problems they aim to elucidate. Such is the case with an ideologeme that recurs with disturbing frequency in studies of fascism: the scenario of the rape of the masses. This scenario functions, I would argue, to perpetuate rather than criticize the fascist rhetoric of virility and makes an appearance even in Walter Benjamin's classic essay, "The Work of Art in the Age of Mechanical Reproduction." I want therefore to conclude this chapter with a glance at the afterlife of the rhetoric of virility in antifascist critiques.

The novelist with whom we began supplies us with a literary example of this scenario in *Eros e Priapo*. Gadda's parody is doubly malicious, for the novel is a critique of fascism not only through an idiosyncratic psycho-analysis but also through a figuration of the receptive masses as woman, and a subsequent attack upon those masses through a not-so-idiosyncratic misogynist discourse. The "feminine," a term of invective in fascist dis-course, is retained as a target of invective in Gadda's presumably antifascist parody:

> Kù-cè, Kù-cè, Kù-cè, Kù-cè. La moltitudine, che al dire di messer Nicolò amaro la è femmina, e femmina a certi momenti nottìvaga, simulava a quegli ululati l'amore e l'amoroso delirio, siccome lo suol mentire una qualunque di quelle, ad "accelerare i tempi": e a sbrigare il cliente: torcendosi in ne' sua furori e sudori di entusiasta, mammillona singultìva per denaro. Su issù poggiuolo il mascelluto, tronfio a stiantare, a quelle prime strida della ragazza-glia e' gli era già ebbro d'un suo pazzo smarrimento, simile ad alcoolòmane, cui basta annasare il bicchiere da sentirsi preso e dato alla mercè del destino. Indi il mimo d'una scenica evulvescenza, onde la losca razzumaglia si dava elicitare, prosperare, assistere, spegnere quella foja incontenuta. Il bombetta soltanto avea nerbo, nella convenzione del mimo, da colmare (a misura di chella frenesia finta) la tromba vaginale della bassàride. Una bugia sporca, su dalla tenebra delle anime. Dalle bocche, una bava incontenuta. Kù-cè, Kù-cè, Kù-cè, Kù-cè.[64]

> [Kù-cè, Kù-cè, Kù-cè, Kù-cè. The masses, who in the words of bitter old Nick are female, and a female at times "of the night," mimicked love and amorous delirium with those howls, just like any of that ilk fakes it, in order to "speed things up" and dispatch her client: writhing in the furors and sweat of an enthusiast, an old bag gasping for money. Up there on his little parapet, old Big Jaws, puffed up to the point of bursting, at those first cries of the rabble was already drunk in a mad rapture of his own, like an alcoholic for whom one sniff of the glass suffices to capture him and give him over to des-tiny. Whence the mimicking of a scenic evulvescence so that the disreputable rabble gave itself over to eliciting, increasing, assisting, and extinguishing that uncontained lust. Only Mr. Bowler Hat had the backbone, in keeping with the conventions of the mimicry, to fill (equal to that fake frenzy) the vaginal funnel of the riff-raff. A dirty lie, up from the darkness of their souls. From their mouths, an uncontained drool. Kù-cè, Kù-cè, Kù-cè, Kù-cè.]

Gadda invokes an illustrious genealogy for his introduction of gender into an analysis of political discourse: none other than "messer Nicolò," Machi-avelli himself. Sliding the attribution of femininity from *fortuna* to the masses, he recalls the famous conclusion to chapter 25 of *The Prince,* where the *vir* behind the *virtù* steps forth to rape a not unwilling *fortuna.* Here, however, a frenzied female crowd, chanting a barely disguised "Duce," oc-cupies the place of fortune and is not a willing victim but a whore who "fakes it" in order to speed up her client. Consent to fascism is thus simulated consent; the relation between the leader and his followers is neither love affair nor rape but a "dirty lie" shared by "consenting" adults. The antifascism of this move lies in its denial that the masses were ever truly fascist; in their whorish hearts, they remained pure. But in order to salvage their purity, those same masses must be turned into "woman." The antifascist critique thus participates in the rhetoric of virility that it set out to ridicule.

This unwitting participation is not limited to literary writing about fascism but seems to pervade even historical assessment. Three years before the publication of Gadda's novel, the historian Eugen Weber had written (apparently unaware of his Machiavellian genealogy): "The fascist leader conquers a crowd and subdues it as he would a woman or a horse."[65] In the equivalence that Weber establishes between women and horses, as in Gadda's misogyny, there is an equivocal collusion between what claims to be an antifascist critique and an implicit adherence both to the gender politics and to the image of the Duce promulgated by fascism itself. The analogy is patterned once again upon that of Virtue raping Fortune. That Machiavelli is evoked both indirectly by the historian and quite explicitly by the novelist is due to a chain of association in which Machiavelli seems to stand as the source of a political rhetoric that is also a rhetoric of virility. The hypervirilization of fascist discourse thus comes to be seen as an enactment of a Machiavellian metaphor.

Yet another enactment of the Gaddian-Machiavellian metaphor can be found in Macciocchi's historical analysis of the relation of Italian women to fascism and to Mussolini in particular. Macciocchi suggests that women — no longer a metaphorical "woman" but historical beings — were indeed enthralled by Mussolini's virile charm. In her scenario, Mussolini is procurer rather than client:

> Like a true pimp, Mussolini had grabbed the bludgeon and begun to wave it about in his speeches addressed to women with the arrogance of the male who reminds his woman that love will come after the blows.[66]

Macciocchi claims that, despite Mussolini's disdain for them, women were "fanatic" supporters of the regime, and she attributes women's fanaticism for Mussolini and for fascism to a masochistic pleasure derived from sacrifices requested of them. Those sacrifices ranged from acting as incubators for the demographic boom Mussolini desired, to donating their wedding rings to the state, to "refraining" from seeking employment that might (in Mussolini's words) "masculinize" them and rob their husbands of their virility. (In fact, women were excluded by decree from various types of jobs, their employment opportunities limited by hiring quotas and their salaries decreed, in 1927, half that of corresponding male salaries.)[67] Mussolini would have been pleased with this portrait of himself as the manly man who knows how to keep women in their place. What's more, by assuming the efficacy of the interpellation, Macciocchi replays and reinforces the gender politics of the scenario she criticizes, for she lays the blame for fascism at the feet of women's masochism. She thereby tropes a standard feature of the rape scenario by blaming the victim.[68] An alternative reading of Mussolini's virile display might suggest that his public speeches addressed to women were designed less to persuade women to do voluntarily what his less flamboyant decrees coerced them to do than to demonstrate one aspect of his virility to quite another addressee: other men. Macciocchi's controversial analysis (one of the first to deal with the question of women under fascism) only hints at the possibility that such triangulation may be at work in the "performance" she describes when she quotes Hitler as saying, "In politics, one must have the support of women, men will follow by themselves."[69] Yet the staging of Mussolini's sexual forcefulness may also, and perhaps above all, be construed as an interpellation of other men, for in what Irigaray has named the "hom(m)o-sexual economy," women serve as the alibi and mediation of relations, economic as well as sexual, among men.[70] Such an interpellation would therefore be a "hom(m)o-sexual," or homosocial, one whose success is facilitated and cemented through the mediating presence of "women."[71]

Even more disturbing is the role played by the rhetoric of virility in what has become the fetish of studies on fascism: Walter Benjamin's "The Work of Art in the Age of Mechanical Reproduction." The essay is framed by fascism and by what appears to be a contradiction between its opening claim and its conclusion. It begins by making a distinction between certain outmoded concepts (*überkommener Begriffe*) that lend themselves to fascism and the concepts introduced in the essay that will instead be "completely useless for the purposes of fascism"; it ends by showing how it is that fascism makes use not only of the "outmoded concepts" but also of some of those concepts the essay introduced as "useless."[72] What accounts for this reversal? The very term "reversal" suggests an answer — the apparent contradiction must be the result of the dialectical movement of thought in the essay. It opens, after all, with an example of dialectical thought in Marx (capitalism not only exploits the proletariat ever more intensely but through that very exploitation creates the conditions for its own destruction) and announces its intention to analyze the same sort of movement in the superstructure. It takes as object, then, a dialectic in the superstructure, and the story it has to tell about photography and film is structured as one of dialectical reversals: a phenomenon turns into its opposite; quantity is transformed into quality; and so forth. It would seem reasonable to suppose that the relation between the beginning and the end of the essay could be described as such a reversal, an example of the dialectic functioning smoothly. As we shall see, however, the rhetoric of virility that we have been tracking makes an appearance precisely at the moment of reversal and introduces a gendering that does violence to camera and dialectic alike.

Since this violence takes place as a blockage of the movement of the entire essay, we must briefly rehearse Benjamin's argument. A summary would go like this: techniques of reproduction — in particular photography and film — have had a number of consequences for art and for human perception. Reproduction eliminates the qualities that belonged to the work of art as unique object: its presence in space and time, its authenticity and authority, what, in a word, Benjamin calls the "aura." This notoriously hazy concept seems here to be defined provisionally as "that which withers in the age of mechanical reproduction," and that which withers is "the unique phenomenon of distance, however close it may be" (221). This withering has as much to do with relations of production as it does with techniques of reproduction; that is, aura as a phenomenon of distance is described as an individual phenomenon inseparable from social privilege, whereas film and photography are mass phenomena.[73] What Benjamin aims to describe here, he writes, is the way in which the masses adjust to reality, and reality adjusts to the masses. On the one hand, film and photography are forms of mass art that reveal the relations of production implicit in the auratic work of art. On the other, the decline of the aura can be attributed to the desire of the masses to bring things close to themselves and to their tendency to equate all things, to sense, as Benjamin puts it, the universal equality of things. This tendency is itself the effect of the mode of production, for what Benjamin seems to be describing is the effect of commodity fetishism on human perception. The abstraction that makes exchange possible and that underlies what Marx calls the "mystery of money" has led the masses to see things as equivalent. That commodity fetishism is at work — or has already done its work — on human perception is clear from Benjamin's comments on ritual in the fourth section of the essay: "The unique value of the 'authentic' work of art has its basis in ritual, the location of its original use value" (224). If in ritual we can locate use value, in mechanical reproduction and the universal equivalence of things we can locate exchange value. This wrenching of art from ritual — due to the market economy and commodity fetishism — has, as the result of a dialectical reversal, an emancipatory effect: "For the first time in world history, mechanical reproduction emancipates the work of art from its parasitical dependence on ritual" (224). As a result of this emancipation, the function of art is reversed; instead of being based on ritual, it begins to be based on another practice: politics. By the end of the fourth section of the essay, the ground has thus been prepared for the "aestheticization of politics" introduced only in the afterword.

In the intervening sections, an important notion is introduced, one that would seem to be one of those concepts "useless" for fascism:

> Mechanical reproduction of art changes the reaction of the masses toward art. The reactionary attitude toward a Picasso painting changes into the progressive reaction toward a Chaplin movie. The progressive reaction is characterized by the direct, intimate fusion of visual and emotional enjoyment with the orientation of the expert. (234)

Mechanical reproduction and film in particular transform the relation of the masses to art into a progressive, forward-stepping one. Benjamin is quite specific about the characteristics of film that foster this relation. The viewer necessarily adopts the "attitude of the expert," described a few pages before as "inherent in the technique of film" (231). This expertise is a consequence not only of the fact that anyone can be filmed but of the position taken by the viewing public: "The audience takes the position of the camera; its approach is that of testing" (228–29) ["*Es übernimmt also dessen Haltung: es testet*" (151; Benjamin's emphasis)]. The public, like the apparatus, tests and changes position with respect to the performance and thus adopts a critical attitude. The sentence that follows will be crucial to an understanding of the essay's afterword: "This is not the approach to which cult values may be exposed" (229). The statement is categorical: this is an aspect of film, of the technique itself, that cannot produce cult values. This critical stance is reinforced by Benjamin's description of the mass reaction to film:

> The greater the decrease in the social significance of an art form, the sharper the distinction between criticism and enjoyment by the public. The conventional is uncritically enjoyed, and the truly new is criticized with aversion. With regard to the screen (*im Kino*), the critical and the receptive attitudes of the public coincide. The decisive reason for this is that individual reactions are predetermined by the mass audience response they are about to produce, and this is nowhere more pronounced than in the film. (234)

[... Und zwar ist der entscheidende Umstand dabei: nirgends mehr als im Kino erweisen sich die Reaktionen der Einzelnen, deren Summe die massive Reaktion des Publikums ausmacht, von vornherein durch ihre unmittelbar bevorstehende Massierung bedingt.] (159)

The last sentence of this passage is puzzling and rendered even more obscure by the translation. How precisely are the critical and receptive attitudes made to coincide? A straightforward, but erroneous, answer would be to say that the whole is the sum of the parts; the mass reaction is the sum of the individual reactions, some of which are critical, some receptive. The final sentence, however, suggests a different temporality. The mass reaction is not just the sum of the individual reactions; rather, individual reactions are determined by the impending massing of those reactions, which is to say that the whole yet to be constituted determines the parts that will constitute it, and those parts in turn determine the nature of the whole. The fusion of critical and receptive attitudes appears to derive from this dialectical temporality associated with the collectivity as well as from the nature of the space in which viewing takes place. That this is so is supported by Benjamin's statement in this section that the viewing of paintings in galleries and salons was bound to provoke a reactionary response, because "there was no way for the masses to organize and control themselves in their reception" (235). This is not the case for the viewing of films; indeed, what is translated into English as "with regard to the screen" and "in film" appears in the German as *im Kino,* not "in regard to the screen," but in the cinema, in the movie house, in a space that organizes the masses in a certain way.

It is important to note that all of these are formal features, part of the "nature" of mechanical reproduction and film itself: the testing approach of the public that identifies with, takes the position of, the camera; the collective viewing of the film that makes critical and receptive attitudes coincide; the space of the movie house that allows the masses to organize themselves in a certain way. Benjamin makes it quite clear that even when the content of the film is reactionary, film retains its progressive, forward-stepping characteristics: "So long as the movie-makers' capital sets the fashion, as a rule no other revolutionary merit can be accredited to today's film than the promotion of a revolutionary criticism of traditional concepts of art" (231). In other words, even if the film does not criticize social conditions, the distribution of property, and so forth, it may still offer a revolutionary criticism of traditional (*überkommenen,* which recalls the *überkommener Begriffe* of the foreword of the essay) concepts such as the aura.

How is it, then, that film can be pressed into the service of "auratic" fascism? Standard accounts of the afterword elide this moment of reversal and go something like this: the categories of the traditional auratic work — authenticity, distance, presence, genius, ritual — are transferred from the aesthetic sphere, chased away by mechanical reproduction to the sphere of politics.[74] Politics thus becomes a spectacle to be contemplated from a distance, and war as spectacle is the culmination of this politics. The categories of genius, authority, and presence (the "outmoded concepts") are resurrected in the cult of the Führer. And this is the fascist aestheticization of politics.

But these outmoded concepts are not the only ones to appear in the afterword. What is elided in such an account, in fact, is an explanation of how it is that film and the apparatus — the concepts introduced in the essay as not useful for fascism — come nevertheless to serve its cause. If the progressive reaction to film is built into the medium itself, if the public and the apparatus take up a position that is not that to which cult values (*Kultwerte* [151]) can be exposed, how can film be "pressed into the production of ritual values" (241)? The translation itself smooths over the contradiction, rendering *Kultwerte*, elsewhere in the essay translated as "cult values," as "ritual values." How indeed can the camera that destroys cult values now be made to produce them? What dialectical turn can account for this reversal? It is here that the rhetoric of virility makes its appearance:

> The logical result of fascism is the introduction of aesthetics into political life. The violation of the masses [*Vergewaltigung der Massen*], whom fascism, with its Führer cult, forces to their knees, has its counterpart in the violation of an apparatus [*Vergewaltigung einer Apparatur*] which is pressed into the production of ritual values [*Kultwerten*]. (241; German, 168)

Once again, the translation smooths over the disturbance in the text; the German *Vergewaltigung*, which Harry Zohn translates as "violation," refers instead quite specifically to rape.[75] This is not a matter of a parking violation, of an infringement of a rule. What takes place is rather a double (and syntactically parallel) rape in which fascism rapes both camera and masses. The relationships between fascism and the masses, between fascism and the camera, are now gendered ones. In the first case, of course, the rape is grounded once again on the figuration of the masses as female and facilitated by grammatical gender (*die Masse*). In the second case, the camera is feminized syntactically, through the parallel construction or isocolon, grammatically (the feminine *Apparatur* appears here, rather than the masculine *Apparat*), and ideologically, for whoever, and in this case whatever, is raped is, socially speaking, raped as a woman.[76] Even the rape of a machine feminizes.[77] It is as a result of this rape that the camera is made to serve the production of cult values. But what does it mean to rape a camera? What happens to film's progressive, forward-stepping form? What happens if one now rereads the essay — following Benjamin and Adorno's own dictum that every sentence should be mediated through the totality of the essay — with this gendering in mind, with the possibility of rape before us?[78] What kind of narrative would that produce? More locally, what kind of model of history does this suggest? In what kind of model of history can "rape" be offered as historical explanation of political events? Certainly this is no dialectical turn; rather, it is the dialectic that turns upon itself. The progressive, forward-stepping movement of history, and of historical explanation, gets stopped in its tracks.

In the place of such dialectical explanation, the text produces first a citation from an unidentified Marinetti manifesto and then a series of "unnatural" figures:

> If the natural utilization of productive forces is impeded by the property system, the increase in technical devices, in speed, and in the sources of energy will press for an unnatural utilization, and this is found in war. (242)

War makes it possible to mobilize both technical resources and masses while maintaining the property system. The "natural" movement would have been the stepping forward together of masses and technology; war (here synonymous with fascism) blocks this "natural" movement, forces it into an "unnatural" direction. The metaphor of the human stream that appears at the end of the paragraph underlines this sense of "unnatural" deviation: "Society directs a human stream into a bed of trenches" (242). A natural order is violated; the "natural" course of history is deviated; and both masses and technology are channeled into war. It is, in other words, the nature of fascism and war to be unnatural. The rape of the apparatus is, in fact, merely the first of a series of figures that add up to the topos of the "world upside-down": not women are raped, but cameras; not rivers are drained, but human streams; "instead of dropping seeds from planes, it drops incendiary bombs." And finally: "Mankind, which in Homer's time was an object of contemplation for the Olympian gods, now is one for himself" (242). Though this last sentence does not say that mankind contemplates himself at the movies, the final footnote of the essay makes this explicit — the masses experience their own destruction at the movies, watching newsreels:

Mass reproduction is aided especially by the reproduction of masses. In big parades and monster rallies, in sports events, and in war, all of which nowadays are captured by camera and sound recording, the masses are brought face to face with themselves. This process, whose significance need not be stressed, is intimately connected with the development of the techniques of reproduction and photography. . . . This means that mass movements, including war, constitute a form of human behaviour which particularly favors mechanical equipment. (251)

On the contrary, the significance of this process *must* be stressed, since it is not at all clear what that significance *is*. Here the reaction of the masses, watching the spectacle of their own destruction at the movies, seems not to be a fusion of critical and receptive attitudes, but rather wholly receptive. As Benjamin writes in the final paragraph of the essay, humankind "can experience its own destruction as an aesthetic pleasure of the first order" (242). The critical attitude has fallen away, we know not how — except, of course, as a result of "rape." Rape is the figure for this otherwise inexplicable receptivity. The consequences of this are, I would argue, far-reaching, since it is this last, "unnatural" situation that grounds Benjamin's definition of fascism as the aestheticization of politics. The figure of rape functions not only as condemnation of fascism but also as an essential explanatory turn in the argument of the essay. This is no dialectical turn, no negation of a negation. The point is not, however, that Benjamin was a failed dialectician but rather that his very definition of fascism at once criticizes and *participates in* the rhetoric of virility. As with Gadda, what is at stake is the "salvation" of the masses — and here the camera — from the taint of complicity with fascism, and once again that salvation is possible only through a gendering that is itself complicit with a rhetoric of virility.

2 / Fascist Women and
the Rhetoric of Virility

Fascist Feminists, or *les Hoministes*

Perhaps no discursive regime so energetically enforced compulsory heterosexuality as did the fascist regime. Prolific mothers and virile men people
its imaginary, while its rhetoric of virility collapses gender and sex, bi-
ologizing both. As do all such naturalizations of gender and sex, the
fascist rhetoric of virility requires that virility be the property of the male
and femininity the property of the female. Any redistribution of properties, any mixing and matching of terms — a feminine man, a masculine
woman — is counted as an unnatural monstrosity, perversion, or aberration. Fascism as discursive regime is, in this sense, merely a particularly
feverish example of a more general formation. One might even suggest
that its eroticization, which inspired Susan Sontag's influential essay "Fascinating Fascism," is less an eroticization of a political regime than an
eroticization of the very compulsoriness of heterosexuality that the political regime makes so palpable.[1] Sadomasochism decked out in SS uniforms
would in that case be not so much "a response to an oppressive freedom of choice in sex," as Sontag argues, as the mastery through parody
of an oppressive regime of necessity, a substitution of choice for necessity that recalls the compulsion to repeat of the sufferers of war trauma
in Freud's *Beyond the Pleasure Principle*.[2] The trauma for these sufferers
would be the imposition and enforcement of heterosexuality; that its re-
peaters should be, as Sontag claims, gay men would therefore mark them

34

not as somehow politically suspect (which Sontag's essay homophobically does) but rather as survivors of a war repeated in every social formation governed by the "heterosexual matrix." Fascism comes to be a figure for that war and the trauma it produces; sadomasochism functions as the parody that theatrically denaturalizes the necessity of the heterosexual regime itself.[3]

Fascism offers a particularly virulent example of a more general discursive formation, then, but it is its particularity that interests us here — what precise forms it takes on during the "black twenty years." In the fascist topography of gender and sex, stepping out into the public sphere "masculinizes" and "sterilizes" women, while the loss of a position in the public sphere necessarily "devirilizes" men. Production and reproduction are strictly, and asymmetrically, linked for men and women: only men involved in economic production are figured as capable of sexual reproduction, whereas involvement in economic production is presumed to destroy the woman's ability to reproduce. Thus, as we have seen in chapter 1, the adjectives "masculine" and "virile" were applied to women as terms of abuse meant to ridicule the intellectual, "feminist," and hence supposedly sterile woman neglectful of her reproductive mission, and the "feminine" as applied to men named first the soldier returning from the barracks to find himself jobless and later the taxed "celibate" who produced no offspring.[4] The representation of the devirilized man dipped into homophobic fantasy to produce the "pederast" of Marinetti's manifestos and the limp-wristed "gagà" of Asvero Gravelli's *Vademecum dello stile fascista* (Vademecum of fascist style).[5] The representation of the "virile woman" for the most part skirted the historical association of the virilization of women and lesbianism (the nonreproductive woman is, in Gravelli's caricatures, still a mother, but mother to a dog) and concentrated on more overtly political connotations, for women's entry into the public, economic sphere threatened the very reproduction of the means of production. This threat was recoded as a threat to women's own reproductive equipment, and its political force retained in the repeated association of the "masculine woman" and feminism. This is not, of course, an innovation on the part of the fascist regime or even of the fascist movement but has roots in the reaction of late nineteenth-century medico-legal anthropology and sociology to women's suffrage and emancipation movements. Scipio Sighele, sociologist and popularizer of Weiningerian notions about women, neatly summarized the ideologeme of the sterile feminist in his 1910 *Eva moderna* (Modern Eve):

Coloro che aspirano ad emanciparsi, coloro che per l'ingegno, per l'attività, per la volontà si sono acquistata una reputazione più o meno legittima, hanno nell'aspetto fisico come nella fisionomia morale qualche cosa di mascolino. Si direbbe che in loro viva e si agiti un'anima maschile. Si direbbe che esse si sentano quasi uomini, e che sia appunto questa coscienza maschile che le costringe a chiedere la liberazione spirituale. Oggi, il rifiorire del feminisimo è dovuto in massima parte all'aumento del numero di donne maschili, les *hoministes,* come le chiama con espressivo neologismo Remy de Gourmont.

[Those who aspire to emancipate themselves, those who through intelligence, activity, or will have acquired a more or less legitimate reputation, have something masculine in their physical persons as in their moral physiognomy. One would say that in them a male soul lives and moves. One would say that they feel as men and that it is precisely this male consciousness that forces them to ask for spiritual liberation. Today, the reemergence of feminism is due in great part to the increase in the number of masculine women, the *hoministes,* as Remy de Gourmont calls them with an expressive neologism.][6]

In a move characteristic of turn-of-the-century antiegalitarian politics, Sighele translates a demand for political equality into a diagnosis of physical similarity: the notion of emancipation of women is so unthinkable that the woman who requests equality is, in body and in soul, a man. Once women have entered, and been forced to exit, the workforce during and after World War I, the threat of the substitution of women for men becomes more concrete and more immediate, and the discursive prohibition on entry into the public sphere becomes more urgent, more explicit. Women should not "take on masculine attitudes and invade the male sphere of action," reads the 1921 statute of the Gruppo Femminile Fascista Romano, and the propaganda of the regime will spread the Mussolinian word that work masculinizes women and robs their husbands of their virility.[7]

This is familiar territory, surveyed by Piero Meldini's selection of rank and file writings on the subject of the fascist woman and mapped by the works of a growing number of historians, including Victoria De Grazia, Marina Addis Saba, and Elisabetta Mondello, to name only a few.[8] What I would like to do in this chapter is to build upon the work of these historians and, as a literary critic, probe the ideological ramifications of the adoption of the fascist rhetoric of virility by women themselves. Does the rhetoric of virility swerve from its intended course when adopted by unintended users? The underpinnings of this question can be traced to Foucault's theorization of the "tactical polyvalence" of discourses in *The History of Sexuality.*[9] Against the notion that the world of discourse can be divided into dominant and dominated discourse, Foucault argues for a conception of discourse as "a series of discontinuous segments whose tactical function is neither uniform nor stable." This instability means that the beginnings of an opposing strategy are located not "outside" a discourse of control, repression, or prohibition but rather are produced by that same discourse. Foucault offers as an example the nineteenth-century psychiatrization of homosexuality, which at once extended social control of the "perversion" that it established and made possible the emergence of a "reverse discourse" that used the same vocabulary and categories to argue for the legitimacy and "naturality" of homosexuality. Is it possible that the rhetoric of virility, when wielded by women, produces a similar "reverse discourse"? Or does their adoption of the rhetoric simply recirculate the same strategy, leaving intact the logic of its exclusions and prohibitions?

I hope to begin to answer those questions by examining the works of two of what Sighele would have called *les hominisaes:* the prefascist futurist Valentine de Saint Point and the properly and devotedly fascist Teresa Labriola, both women who flaunt the prohibition against virilization.

Valentine de Saint Point, *Virilis Femina?*

Valentine de Saint Point's 1912 "Manifeste de la femme futuriste" is explicitly a response to the "scorn for women" trumpeted in Marinetti's founding manifesto. In women's defense, de Saint Point seems to argue for a mixing and matching of gender and sex that makes possible a virilization of women:

> *Il est absurde de diviser l'humanité en femmes et en hommes.* Elle n'est composée que de *féminité* et de *masculinité.* Tout surhomme, tout héros, si épique soit-il, tout génie, si puissant soit-il, n'est l'expression prodigieuse d'une race et d'une époque, que parce qu'il est composé, à la fois, d'éléments féminins et d'éléments masculins, de féminité et de masculinité: c'est-à-dire qu'il est un être complet.

> [*It is absurd to divide humanity into women and men.* It is composed only of *femininity* and *masculinity.* Every superman, every hero no matter how epic, every genius no matter how powerful, is only the prodigious expression of a race and an epoch insofar as he is composed at once of feminine and masculine elements, of femininity and masculinity: that is to say, insofar as he is a complete being.][10]

Though prefascist, the passage nicely illustrates the way in which fascist ideology will bind together ideologically incompatible elements, both progressive and reactionary, left and right, in order to appear, as Zeev Sternhell puts it, neither left nor right.[11] The binding mechanism at work in Marinetti's and D'Annunzio's texts operates here to yoke recognizably Weiningerian concepts — masculinity and femininity as characteristics loosened from their supposed, biological moorings — to an argument for androgyny foreign to the xenophobic Weininger, for whom the combination of masculinity and woman was abhorrent. While, on the one hand, such a discourse begins to glimpse, however obscurely, what we would now call the social construction of gender, on the other, it also produces an argument for a very problematic kind of bellicose androgyny.[12] Indeed, by turning Marinetti's argument against him, de Saint Point succeeds in turning it back against women as well; while Marinetti argued that men had become too feminine and women too masculine, de Saint Point finds women not virile enough: "Ce qui manque le plus aux femmes, aussi bien qu'aux hommes, c'est la virilité" [What women as well as men lack most is virility].[13] Is such a call for a virile woman merely the recirculation of the logic according to which the only good woman is a good man, or can we, as Foucault's example suggests, find in its polyvalence the beginnings of a reverse discourse?

The logic is certainly a familiar one and points to precedents in the literature of defense or praise of women. As Juliana Schiesari has argued in her work on the humanist discourse of *virtù,* one of the highest "compliments" that phallocentric discourse can pay to women is to efface their difference and laud their approximation of a masculine ideal. Such is the case in the Renaissance notion of the virago, in the praise of learned women such as Christine de Pisan as *virilis femina* and "beyond their sex," and in the underlying classical notion of self-sacrificing women such as Lucretia as *virilis.*[14] Beyond their sex, but still firmly implanted within phallocentric discourse, for the suggestion is that the only subject is a virile one and that equality can be attained only at the price of the erasure of sexual difference. The self-sacrificing woman sacrifices her difference from man. (This is, parenthetically, the reasoning at the bottom of the refusal of equal rights on the part of contemporary Italian philosophers of sexual difference: as Sandra Kemp and Paola Bono put it, "The polis is open only to women who agree to neuter themselves. Outside the polis sexual difference is recognized, but only in the form of a sexual role which implies inferiority. Becoming equal thus means becoming like a man.")[15] De Saint Point's sister futurist, Enif Robert, provides a vivid example of this topography of virility:

> Vi sono donne che una felicissima corrispondenza, una perfetta adesione, d'anima e di sensi, rende deliziose quando si concedono in una stanza "di profumi e d'ombre" ma che sanno poi, a tempo opportuno, essere an-

che vive, coraggiose, forti, VIRILI, INTELLIGENTI, a fianco del loro maschio.

[There are women whom a most felicitous correspondence, a perfect adhesion of soul and senses, renders luscious when they give themselves in a room "shadowy and perfumed" but who, at the right time, know how to be lively, courageous, strong, VIRILE, INTELLIGENT, at the side of their man.][16]

Deeply ensnared within the discourse it aims to refute, this declaration describes a movement that takes women out of the bedroom and into the public sphere, a virile public sphere that can only be imagined as "at the side of their man." Yet at the same time Robert seems to offer a variation, rather than simply a repetition, of the notion that the woman who enters the public sphere is masculinized, for here virilization appears to be the effect of contiguity ("a fianco del loro maschio") rather than a question of similarity and substitution, as it was for Sighele. But in either case, going out means going virile.

De Saint Point goes even further when she produces from among a list of viragos, amazons, and other women who went "beyond their sex," yet another invocation of Caterina Sforza:

Les femmes, ce sont les Erynnies, les Amazones; les Sémiramis, les Jeanne d'Arc, les Jeanne Hachette; les Judith et les Charlotte Corday; les Cléopâtre et les Messaline: les guerrières qui combattent plus férocement que les mâles, les amantes qui incitent, les destructrices qui, brisant les plus faibles, aident à la sélection par l'orgueil ou le désespoir, "le désespoir par qui le coeur donne tout son rendement."

Que les prochaines guerres suscitent des héroïnes comme cette magnifique Caterina Sforza, qui, soutenant le siège de sa ville, voyant, des remparts, l'ennemi menacer la vie de son fils pour l'obliger elle-même à se rendre, montrant héroïquement son sexe, s'écria: "Tuez-le, j'ai encore le moule pour en faire d'autres!

[Women: they are the Furies, the amazons, the Semiramises, the Joan of Arcs, the Jeanne Hachettes, the Judiths and the Charlotte Cordays, the Cleopatras and the Messalinas, the women warriors who fight more ferociously than the males, the women lovers who incite, the women destroyers who, demolishing the weakest, help in natural selection through pride or despair, the "despair by which the heart gives its all."

May the next wars give rise to heroines like that magnificent Caterina Sforza who, besieged in her castle, seeing from the battlements the enemy threaten the life of her son to force her to surrender, heroically showing her sex, cried out: "Kill him, I still have the mold to make others!][17]

If de Saint Point meant to provide an example of the self-sacrificing mother who would give her sons to the state, she picked the wrong lady. As we have seen in the first chapter, Caterina does not sacrifice herself for the sake of her sons and does not sacrifice her sons for the sake of the state; rather, she sacrifices her sons for the sake of her own political power. But unlike D'Annunzio, who characterizes Caterina's womb as "heroic" and her gesture as a "crude response," de Saint Point explicitly characterizes the *gesture* as heroic. The exposure of her "sex" is thus at once an exhibition of virility — a making public of what should remain private — and an affirmation of femininity, of her sexual difference from men. She points to "her sex," her genitals, but also to her sexual difference from men, in the very moment in which, in true virago fashion, she goes "beyond her sex." The "impropriety" of her gesture thus can be read as figuring the threat she poses not only to property relations but also to the "proper" relations of gender and sex, both understood as relations of reproduction.[18]

These are the beginnings of a "reverse discourse," both in the sense that they reverse the Aristotelian underpinnings of the essentialization of gender and sex and in the sense that they use the rhetoric of virility in defense rather than scorn of women. But just as a mere reversal remains governed by the oppositions it overturns, so is the "antimother" of de Saint Point's text governed by the antifeminist, antiegalitarian, pronatalist ending of the manifesto, in which de Saint Point calls for mothers to provide heroes for humanity. The critic Rita Guerricchio, in fact, argues that despite its apparently polemical form, de Saint Point's manifesto in reality corroborates the image and ideology of woman promoted by Marinetti.[19] As a strategy for dealing with the coexistence of progressive and reactionary elements in fascist ideology, the model of appearance versus reality employed by Guerricchio is well worn, perhaps even worn out; versions can be found in notions of a *paese reale* or of collective nicodemism and in explanations of the way in which fascism is supposed to have appeared to be on the left when in fact it was on the right.[20] An alternate to this (ultimately apologetic) use of the appearance/reality paradigm is the approach we have been adopting, according to which fascist discourse works precisely by binding together the progressive and the reactionary.[21] This latter approach allows us to discover the glimmerings of opposing strategies even within fascism as discursive regime and is, I find, particularly useful in understanding the contradictory position of women within fascism both as discursive and as juridico-political regime. With its contradictory strategies, de Saint Point's manifesto already participates in the fascist matrix.

Teresa Labriola and the Regendering of Virility

Indeed, fascism issues a contradictory interpellation to those it constitutes as women: as Marina Addis Saba has observed, it at once excludes women, depriving them of rights they never had and fixing them in the role of wife and mother, and calls them loudly to participate in political life.[22] It thus at once rigidly enforces the boundary between private and public spheres and calls for its transgressive crossing. One response to this divided interpellation produces what Emma Scaramuzza, and Marina Addis Saba after her, have called *la donna muliebre,* the active, intellectual, and fascistically feminist woman.[23] Borrowed from the Alleanza Muliebre Culturale Italiana, a women's organization active from 1930 to 1939, the term itself is a coinage that responds to and refashions the rhetoric of virility. "*Muliebre,*" writes Scaramuzza, transfers onto the feminine the "high moral tone attributed to *virile.*"[24] One such *donna muliebre,* Teresa Labriola, was not deaf to the contradictory interpellation; indeed in 1929 she described the position of Italian women as "con un piede nel passato e con un piede nel presente, con un orecchio teso alla 'internazionale' e con un altro viso a 'giovinezza'" [with one foot in the past and one in the present, with one ear cocked to the "Internationale" and another to "Giovinezza"].[25] Labriola's position as fascist feminist and ex-suffragist turned antiemancipationist theorist awkwardly straddles the worlds of past and present, and, though the stereophonic mixing of left and right often produces noise one would rather not hear, it also produces unexpected chords and discords. I will concentrate here on a small sampling of her extremely prolific activity — in particular, on the 1918 *Problemi sociali della donna* and on her frequent contributions to the periodical *La donna italiana* in the years from 1924 to 1939.

The daughter of the Marxist philosopher Antonio Labriola and the first woman to hold a university chair in Italy, Labriola was named one of the "ten most famous women alive" in a 1923 referendum in *L'Almanacco della donna italiana;* the word chosen to pinpoint her special "essence" was *maschilità.*[26] As the virile woman, however, Labriola is neither a Lucretia who sacrifices her difference to a patriarchal code of honor nor an Ines Donati, the woman *squadrista* whose dying words, "Volli essere troppo virile e dimenticai che, alla fine, ero una debole donna" [I wanted to be too virile and forgot that, in the end, I was a weak woman], were all too easily enthroned by the regime.[27] Both of those representations work to maintain the propriety of gender and sex. Labriola, on the other hand, exploits a disjunction already operative in the rhetoric of virility itself to produce a

notion of the woman who could be virile yet not masculine. That disjunction is created by elevating the term "virility" to the status of universality
and consequently occluding its relation to masculinity. By exploiting this
disjunction, Labriola inadvertently denaturalizes the relation between sex
and gender and ends up denaturalizing maternity itself.

I describe this exploitation as inadvertent, as the result of a logic not entirely under Labriola's control, for the paths taken by her reasoning are, to
use the two adjectives most used to describe fascist ideology, confused and
contradictory. In Labriola's case, the confusion results from a collision of
two competing ideological imperatives, one the "feminist" strain left over
from a barely audible "Internazionale," and the other the nationalist strain
that is dominant.[28] Labriola's "Latin feminism" brings with it a defense of
women's qualities (rather than of their rights) and a rejection of the over-
valuation of male qualities in what she refers to as "masculine society."[29]
Hers is (at least in part) an antiegalitarianism that argues against equality
not on the grounds that it collapses a hierarchy that should be maintained
but rather on the grounds that it masks a hierarchy that remains undisturbed. In the 1918 *Problemi sociali della donna* (Social problems of woman),
she argues, for example, not that women should be barred from the workplace or university but that the workplace itself is modeled on masculine
qualities and needs, and that the new postwar, fascist workplace should be
reformed to accommodate women and feminine qualities. Insofar as the
aim of her arguments is the reconciliation of maternity and work, she
opposes the rhetoric of virility that excludes women from the workforce
on the grounds that production and reproduction are antithetical. Her nationalism, on the other hand, comes to her bound up with a rhetoric of
virility, for, as George Mosse has convincingly shown, the ideal of manliness accompanies the development of nationalism itself.[30] Labriola's goal
is to nationalize women, educate them as fascists, and bring them into the
workplace without sacrificing their "feminine qualities." But how does one
bring about such a nationalization without betraying the "Latin feminist"
imperative and accepting a masculinization of women that Labriola repeatedly condemns? Labriola's solution is to split off "virility" from masculinity
by exploiting the ambiguity of "virility" as a universalist moral category
available to "all humanity." In so doing, she exploits a structure analogous
to what the contemporary feminist philosopher Adriana Cavarero has called
"the monstrosity of the subject": the monstrosity, that is, of the universal
subject who is at once neuter and male.[31] The so-called neuter universal
is, Cavarero argues, a male-gendered subject who, by universalizing him-

self, disavows yet retains his own gendered and sexed being. It — he — is thus at once gendered and ungendered, sexed and unsexed (though never, of course, gendered female). Labriola inserts herself into the space of such a disavowal when, making the words of an anonymous (and anomalous, in such a fiercely nationalistic text) Frenchman her own, she writes that "è da augurarsi che le donne conservino sì le qualità femminili, ma che al medesimo tempo acquistino qualità virili" [it is to be hoped that women will retain their feminine qualities but at the same time acquire virile qualities] in order to achieve her goal of forming "un'anima nazionale nella donna italiana" [a national spirit in the Italian woman].[32] Those virile qualities consist in the awareness of a sense of belonging to a race and to a nation. Rather than exposing its gender-neutrality to be an ideological mystification, Labriola makes the mystification work to her advantage, severs masculinity from virility, and installs femininity in its place.[33] Yet because "virility" can never entirely be cleansed of its relation to "masculinity," the attribution of virility to women implies the detachability of gender from sex.

Lest this sound more radical an operation than it is, it should be said that the qualities she works with are not redefined, but merely recombined; Labriola can produce a fascist women "con cuore materno, sì, ma ancora con mente virile" [with a maternal heart and yet with a virile mind] but cannot imagine womanhood apart from motherhood; indeed, she rejects egalitarianism also because it does not take into account "l'infante che galoppa dietro ad essa" [the infant that gallops behind the woman].[34] But as the (merest) beginnings of a strategy that adopts the categories and terms of the discourse it opposes, Labriola's strategy at once accepts the logic of identity that posits the male term as unmarked and refuses the erasure and denigration of feminine difference that the logic requires.

This paradox would be more manageable if it described a chronology, a position adopted and then superseded by another. But at least in the materials at hand, the paradox persists from 1918 till the late 1930s. As both practitioner and refuter of the rhetoric of virility, Labriola is at war with herself. Thus in the 1924 essay "Il femminismo italiano nella rinascita dello spirito" (Italian feminism in the rebirth of the spirit), she posits a (fascist) realm of values beyond sexual difference:

> La stessa comunione in cui noi viviamo, sia essa religiosa, sia essa nazionale, implica l'esistenza di valori che non sono maschili, ma sono spirituali. Essi hanno radici e nascimento in quella naturale esistenza che è sessuale. Ma su-

perano di continuo e di continuo negano nella brutale naturalezza, ciò che di istintivo è nella differenziazione dei sessi.

[The very communion within which we live, whether religious or national, implies the existence of values that are not masculine but spiritual. They have roots and origin in that natural existence that is sexual. But they continually rise above and continually negate that which is, in its brutal naturality, instinctive in the differentiation of the sexes].[35]

In a 1930 article, she exposes the underlying masculinity of the erasure of difference, which she labels "egalitarian":

Sembra che ogni virtù sia nell'uomo ed ogni manchevolezza sia nella donna, tanto che ogni particolaristico atteggiamento dell'uomo, in quanto essere di sesso maschile, viene considerato indice di umanità completa e assunta a punto di culminazione della emancipazione della donna. . . . No, mie amiche avversarie, no, io combatto l'errore di identificare maschio ed umanità.

[It seems that every virtue is in man and every lack in woman, so much so that every individual attitude of man, as a being of the male sex, is considered an index of complete humanity and raised up as the culmination of the emancipation of woman. . . . No, my adversarial women friends, no! I fight against the error of identifying male and humanity].[36]

And in a 1934 response to the essentialization of the relation between gender and sex in Julius Evola's *Rivolta contro il mondo moderno* (Revolt against the modern world), Labriola reaffirms the existence of "qualità razionali, asessuali, delle verità in sè, asessuali, che la donna possiede non in quanto donna ma in quanto partecipe della indifferenziata natura umana" [rational, asexual qualities, asexual truths that woman possesses not as woman but as participant in an undifferentiated human nature].[37] The paradox has her trapped in a cage whose bars are binary oppositions, as she scrabbles to refute the "antifeminism of so many fascists" and yet to remain the "fascist of the first hour" that she paints herself to be.[38]

Thus, on the one hand, her "feminism" is characterized by an anti-mimetic impulse with respect to male standards of values, assumed to be universal. Labriola bases her criticism of Anglo-American emancipationist feminism on a rejection of *mimetismo:* "imitazione esteriore e direi servile delle attività maschile" [the external and servile imitation of masculine activities].[39] This position allows her to be remarkably astute when it comes to the ways in which femininity is constituted as a defect according to a male symbolic order and women are bound to failure in masculine cultural institutions. Thus in a 1932 article "La donna nella cultura e nelle professioni" (Woman in culture and the professions), Labriola writes:

Il tipo maschile è prevalente nella società civile e — riconosciamo! — è quello che ha dato l'impronta principale alla storia umana. E non contano amiche di Re ed ambasciatrici d'amore! Le donne se ne stettero nei giardini chiusi di fronte dai cancelli! Così fu!... dato il tipo maschile considerato "specimen" dell'uman genere, alle donne restava una scelta ben limitata, ed era: "o perire o imitare."

[The masculine type is prevalent in civil society and, face it, is what has given the principal form to human history. The lady friends of kings and ambassadors of love don't count! Women stayed locked away in gated gardens! That's the way it was!... Given the male type considered the "specimen" of the human race, women were left with a very limited choice: either perish or imitate].[40]

To argue for women's equality on the basis of successes obtained in imitating such a model is, Labriola argues, the mistake made by egalitarian feminism.[41] Women are set up for failure and only rarely succeed in becoming honorary men. More often than not, they resort to a strategy that resembles Joan Rivière's notion of "womanliness as masquerade," an exaggeration of femininity designed to mask a competitive threat:[42]

Partendo dal tipo maschile, essendo esso norma di concezione e di condotta negli alti istituti di coltura, è ovvio che il mezzo per giungere alla mèta è stato ed è tuttora di intensificare fino al massimo, in una vera esasperazione, le qualità nudamente intellettualistiche, mortificando lo spirito nella sua lussuriosa ricchezza, e di simulare i caratteri della aggressività, oppure, cambiando rotta, di rendersi schiavo dell'uomo docente, esasperando l'abito del servilismo (come ha fatto gran parte delle studentesse), esagerando fino all'inverosimile i caratteri della femminilità.

[Since the masculine type is the norm of conception and conduct in higher institutions of learning and culture, it is obvious that the means for arriving at the goal was and still is to intensify to the maximum, in a true exasperation, nakedly intellectualistic qualities, thereby mortifying the spirit in its luxurious wealth, and to simulate the characteristics of aggressivity; or, in a reverse move, to make oneself into a slave of the male professor, exasperating the custom of slavishness (as most women students have done) by exaggerating beyond believability the characteristics of femininity].[43]

Coupled with a defense of women's intellectual abilities and directed against "la campagna che stan facendo molti uomini italiani contro le donne italiane e le giovani studentesse" [the campaign that many Italian men have launched against Italian women and young students], Labriola's argument champions the cause of the "diritti dell'intelletto femminile" [rights of female intellect] to a place within the university and cultural institutions, and

"non fuori ma dentro il vasto quadro della spiritual ascesa del popol nostro" [not outside but inside the vast panorama or the spiritual ascent of our
people].[44] That such a cause runs counter to the regime's policies and propaganda does not deter Labriola from finding the solution to the problem in
fascism, "in quanto questo intende ricostruire la tavola dei valori" [insofar
as it means to reconstruct the table of values].[45]

Among these values, Labriola would like to place an ideal of femininity, neither mimetic nor servile, that gradually takes shape as the sacerdotal,
spiritual mother.[46] One is tempted to argue that insofar as the ideal allows
her to mute the threat of substitution of men by women and to retain her
claim for women's place, as women, in the public sphere, its function is
primarily strategic, an adoption of "motherliness" as masquerade on Labriola's own part. Indeed, her own notion of femininity at once enables and
prohibits such a strategic use, for it at once posits femininity as "artificial"
and as "natural." That is to say that whereas Labriola condemns the exaggeration of "the characteristics of femininity in intellectual fields" because
"women [thereby] perform an antibiological function . . . because the characteristics of femininity must be sharpened only in order to arrive at the
natural destination of the female sex, which is maternity," her ideal of femininity requires the very disjunction that allows the strategic swerving and
"sharpening" of femininity.[47] Here the paradox that governs Labriola's work
produces its most interesting knots, for in order to maintain the paradox and
remain faithful to the nationalist rhetoric of virility, Labriola ends up constituting an ideal of womanliness whose logic mimes that of the ideal of
manliness.[48] The fortitude and forbearance shown by the virile subject in
relation to his own sensuality are matched in Labriola's ideal by the jet-
tisoning of female sexuality. As Labriola puts it, "Giardino sì è il nostro,
ma Armida ha da fare bagaglio" [Ours is a garden, but Armida has got to
go].[49] So drastic is the abjection of sexuality, here figured by the expulsion
of Tasso's enchantress from the fascist garden, that maternity (understood
as Italian and fascist) comes to be an exclusively spiritual, nonbiological
operation. In other words, in order to give to femininity the moral form
that would correspond to degendered virility, Labriola must denaturalize
maternity itself.

The denaturalization of the fascist mother is possible, however, only on
condition that other women be figured as the nature and sexuality that she
has overcome. Here the rhetoric of virility replicates its genealogical precedent, the humanist discourse of (virile) *virtù*, for as Juliana Schiesari argues,
the concept of *virtù* may "work at times in an emancipatory fashion, . . . but

it may also function to 'castrate' women, to deny their feminine sexuality in such a way that the discourse of virtue keeps the 'exceptional' woman separate from other women."[50] Indeed, banished from the garden of Italy, Armida has a destination all picked out: the land of Bolshevik biologization, populated by "amoral" proletarian women. Women must be educated to be mothers and nationalists, Labriola argues in the 1918 *Problemi sociali della donna,* because the winds of socialism have passed over the masses of peasants and proletarian women and wiped from their heads all sense of moral judgment in sexual matters.[51] Left alone, such women "si abbandonano ad utopismi folli" [abandon themselves to crazy utopianisms] and nonreproductive sex — they'd rather be commies than mommies.[52] Hence the need for "preparazione alla maternità per le donne" [training for motherhood for women] that includes "il desiderio e l'attitudine ad operare per fini nazionali" [the desire and aptitude to work for national ends].[53] Whereas Labriola changes many of her positions, sometimes simply reversing them (most dramatically, from suffragist to antisuffragist, but also from a position that sees a covert subordination in protectionist measures to one that recommends them on the basis of women's "physical inferiority"), she retains and bolsters this notion of a Bolshevik state of nature until 1938 (she stops writing in 1939).[54] In a 1930 article, "Problemi morali del femminismo" (Moral problems of feminism), Labriola argues against the recognition of "natural maternity," invoked as a legal category: mothers have rights and duties insofar as they occupy a juridical position, claims Labriola, not insofar as they may have physically given birth; faithful to Roman law, that juridical position is dependent upon marriage.[55] In fact, Labriola's fascist mother appears to be a revival of the social fiction that was Roman motherhood, in which maternity was limited to motherhood within marriage, and the *materfamilias* was such not because she had children but because she was the wife of a *paterfamilias.*[56] Mothers are legally constructed as mothers but do not exist in nature; "natural maternity" refers instead to the unwed genitrix who, for Labriola, exists in Bolshevik nature.[57] Labriola gives it specific geographical coordinates in the 1938 article "Il pericolo latente" (The latent danger): "La concezione biologica, intendo dire semplicemente biologica della maternità . . . ha sede geografica in Russia" [The biological conception, I mean the merely biological conception, of maternity . . . is located geographically in Russia].[58]

Labriola thus ends up turning women over to the state, reimprisoning them in the patriarchal family, and condemning them to compulsory heterosexuality if they are to have "rights and duties" in the fascist state. Yet in spite of this congruence between Labriola and the ideology of the regime, the notion of motherhood as legal and social fiction has a certain demystificatory force in relation to the fascist naturalization of motherhood. Thus in 1938, she once again argues against the rhetoric according to which entry into the public sphere masculinizes women. Renewed in the 1930s in reaction to the involvement of women in sports, the charge was rebiologized by practitioners of sports gynecology, eager to show the physical effects of "masculinization"; it is in this context that Labriola takes another shot at the opponents of the "new woman":

> Tu, lettrice, tu credi forse che il pericolo latente sia dell'immaschilimento della donna. Se ne è parlato di codesto famoso immaschilimento; se ne parla tuttora, e Dio sa, quanto se ne parlerà. La opposizione alla donna nuova o, a dir meglio, ad una ipotetica quasi fantastica donna nuova, deriva da pregiudiziali che sono . . . pregiudizi.
>
> [You, reader, perhaps believe that the hidden danger is of the masculinization of women. Much has been said about this famous masculinization; it is still bandied about and will continue to be for God knows how long. The opposition to the new woman, or better, to a hypothetical, almost phantasmatic new woman comes from prejudicial questions that are . . . prejudices].[59]

The latent danger turns out to be a different one: "una materialistica concezione di una maternità spogliata degli attributi spirituali" [a materialistic conception of a maternity stripped of spiritual attributes] that Labriola attributes to "troppo del materialismo bolscevico . . . in noi donne ed uomini nel momento presente" [an excess of Bolshevik materialism . . . in us men and women at the present moment]." Fascist discourse here turns against itself, the pot calling the kettle red, as it were. This is indeed a "reverse discourse," for by recirculating the terms of the rhetoric of virility Labriola comes to reject (by repudiating as "Bolshevik") the grounds of her own fascist idealism, which like all idealisms necessarily posits women as matter and strips them of "spiritual attributes."

As in de Saint Point's manifesto, however, the dominant fascist tone in Labriola's work drowns out the dissonant note, and the discourse proceeds undisturbed by its own implications. If we can hear it now, it is because the context has changed, and feminists have begun not only to reverse but also to rewrite the terms that constitute the rhetoric and politics of virility. That rewriting makes it possible, and necessary, to hear the dissonant notes within fascist discourse both as the product of the contradictory ways in which women accommodated themselves to the gendering of power and as a reminder of the tangled ruses of the rhetoric of virility itself.

3 / Mafarka and Son: Marinetti's Homophobic Economics

Fascism in the Text

In his essay "Fascist Ideology," the intellectual historian Zeev Sternhell has little trouble in characterizing the essential ideological import of F. T. Marinetti's futurism as fascist from start to finish, from 1909 to 1943:

> As early as 1909 the Futurists' Manifesto had set out the essentials of what subsequently became the moral ideals of fascism, to which the twenties and thirties made no new contribution:
>
> 1. We want to sing the love of danger, the habit of energy and rashness.
>
> 2. The essential elements of our poetry will be courage, audacity and revolt.
>
> 3. ... We want to exalt movements of aggression, feverish sleeplessness, the forced march, the perilous leap, the slap and the blow with the fist....
>
> 9. We want to glorify war — the only cure for the world — and militarism, patriotism, the destructive gesture of the anarchists, the beautiful ideas which kill, and contempt for women.
>
> 10. We want to demolish museums and libraries, fight morality, feminism and all opportunist and utilitarian cowardice.
>
> Marinetti remained faithful to fascism to the very end, and became an enthusiastic supporter of Salò Republic.[1]

In the space between item number 10 of the cited manifesto and the final sentence of the quotation lie several of the most basic questions dogging attempts to link literary texts to fascism: Where and how do we locate the ideology of the text? Is it determined, or overdetermined, by the declared affiliation of its author? Sternhell answers some of these questions in that same empty space: in the final sentence, the place where we would expect explication and commentary glossing the cited passage, we find biography, as though Marinetti's biographical affiliation with the fascist regime supplied the meaning of the passage. For Sternhell, biography glosses the text; biographical continuity guarantees ideological continuity. Implicit as well, in this framing of a text, is a definition of ideology and of the literary text's relation to ideology. The manifesto, which already has the structure of a list, is edited in order to resemble even more a checklist of fascist "elements" (and perhaps to eliminate articles of futurist faith not so univocally "fascist"). Offered in proof of the assertion that futurism is fascist to the core, the text becomes a repository of ideas whose ideological valences are presumed to be self-evident. In other words, the literary work is treated not as a text — as network of relations — but as a storage bin of ideas easily stripped of their rhetorical dress. And from this practice emerges a notion of ideology: the assumption seems to be that it is possible to tag some ideas — say militarism and antifeminism — as fascist, to attribute to certain elements an essential and stable meaning independent of the context from which they are pried.

Sternhell is, of course, an intellectual historian whose work has been both controversial and groundbreaking in arguing for the recognition of fascist ideology as "neither less homogeneous nor more heterogeneous than that of liberalism or socialism."[2] It would be more than a little unfair to take him to task for failing to be a good literary critic (after all, good intellectual history often makes for bad literary criticism). I have introduced him as straw man, however, because his approach stands in stark contrast to my own and to those of the theorists whose work has shaped my thinking. The question I want to ask is not so much *whether* Marinetti's texts can be considered fascist but rather *how* it is that we locate fascist ideology *in the text*.[3]

A first and fundamental difference in approach has to do with the function of biography. The passage I cite from Sternhell nicely illustrates the kind of metonymical blurring common to writing on authors with "fascist connections": while at one moment the proper name may function as a metonym for the work, at the next it may return to refer properly to the biographical individual. Such blurring often results in slurring: slurring over the complexities of reading texts, passing lightly over the sort of theorization that would be necessary to establish a causal relation between life and work, and hence slurring, in the sense of disparaging, the literary or critical production of the guilty author. Metonymy, in this operation, becomes causality. Discussions of the so-called Heidegger and Paul de Man affairs have been rife with metonymical slurring that, perhaps not coincidentally, allows accusers to bypass the task of reading and assessing difficult texts. The topic of fascism seems to cause even the most sophisticated of critics to fall back on a critical assumption — a resuscitation of the author function, a reclaiming of the intentional fallacy — that they would find untenable in a different case. In the wake of Michel Foucault's and Roland Barthes's theorizations of "text" and "author," I assume a disjunction between biography and text and reject any untheorized, immediate causal relation between the two. That "Marinetti" was biographically a fascist does not guarantee that "Marinetti" as a body of work is similarly fascist.[4]

A second and no less fundamental difference in approach turns upon the notion of ideology and varying conceptions of the way in which ideology can be located in a text. For Sternhell, "ideology" refers to sets of ideas, rationally conceived and articulated, "by which men explain and justify the ends and means of organized social action."[5] Such ideologies are best perceived in their "pure state"; Sternhell writes:

> Where the history of ideas is concerned, it is the political movement [as opposed to fascism as regime] which is of greater interest. It can be traced with advantage back to its origins, to the source which, being more pure, illustrates an outline as yet unmuddied.... The true nature of doctrines, and the differences between them, are always more clearly seen in the shape of their aspirations than when put into practice.[6]

The distinction between fascism as movement and fascism as regime, first advanced by Renzo De Felice, is a useful and historically accurate one, but Sternhell here gives it a narrative structure absent in De Felice: at the source of the river that is a political movement, the waters of ideology are purer, more transparent, more easily seen than when muddied by concrete realization in a regime (or, for that matter, by concrete realization in a text). The river metaphor handily solves a problem Sternhell has elsewhere described as fascism's "fundamental weakness: it lacks a source comparable to Marxism"; it has no founding text but appears as many fascisms, many concrete realizations from which the historian abstracts a "fascist minimum."[7]

Such a concern with the purity of ideologies is the object of Ernesto Laclau's critique of Nico Poulantzas's book *Fascism and Dictatorship*. The "abstract postulation of pure ideologies" goes hand in hand, Laclau argues, with another notion we have noted as one of Sternhell's implicit assumptions: that the elements that constitute an ideology have an isolable and stable meaning (in the case of Poulantzas, that meaning is determined by "class belonging"). Labeling this a "metaphysical" approach, Laclau argues that the correct approach is precisely the reverse: that one should instead "accept that ideological 'elements' taken in isolation have no necessary class connotation, and that this connotation is only the result of the articulation of those elements in a concrete ideological discourse."[8] Underlying Laclau's simple but powerful formulation are the fundamental insight of Ferdinand Saussure into the nature of linguistic meaning as determined by the articulation of linguistic units and Louis Althusser's theorization of the function of ideology as interpellation of subjects. For Althusser, of course, ideology refers not to rationally conceived sets of ideas but to the imaginary way in which people live their relation to their real conditions of existence; not distorted by practice, it is constituted through practice; not rationally conceived, it is unconscious, contradictory, phantasmatic.[9] The task of analysis is thus not that of abstracting elements but rather that of discovering the "distinctive unity of an ideological discourse." The ideological specificity of a discourse or text is to be found not in the single ideas that circulate within it but rather in the relations and articulations among elements; the question put to the text is not, for example, "Do we find antifeminism and militarism?" but "How are antifeminism and militarism joined together?" Such an approach is crucial in dealing with fascist discourse, which, as Ernesto Laclau and Alice Y. Kaplan have argued, works precisely by binding together seemingly incompatible elements and polarities; its ideological specificity therefore lies not in the elements it gathers together but in the binding mechanism itself.[10] If I find this latter approach more convincing than Sternhell's, it is because it seems to me better suited to its objects: better suited to understanding the multiple and intertextual "sources" of fascist discourse and better equipped to deal with the way in which texts produce meaning, with their rhetorical "muddiness."

Muddy Waters

It would be difficult to imagine a text "muddier" than Marinetti's 1909 novel *Mafarka le futuriste*. A tale of rape, carnage, and futurist declamation set in Africa, *Mafarka le futuriste* takes as its theme the generation of a mechanical son born of male parthenogenesis. In the opening scene, its protagonist, Mafarka-el-Bar, an Arabian king with imperial ambitions to conquer all of Africa, has recently defeated an army of black Africans and dethroned his uncle, King Boubassa. The novel thus combines a number of elements that might be called fascist: a rhetoric of virility, imperial fantasies tied to the colonization of Africa, misogyny, a reproductive project, and an obsession with self-sufficiency. My project in this chapter is to map out the ideo-logic that binds these elements together and to suggest a parallel articulation of elements in fascist discourse.

If *Mafarka* is a futurist text that looks ahead to fascism, it also looks back to nineteenth-century Orientalism. Like Flaubert's *Salammbô,* to which it is often disparagingly compared, *Mafarka* is a novel immersed in an Orientalist world into which no self-identified Western narrator intrudes.[11] The only "Western" voice to be heard is that of Marinetti in the preface, where he identifies himself with his "barbarian" theme: "Ne suis-je pas, tout au moins, un barbare, aux yeux de ces faux dévots du progrès" [Am I not, at the very least, a barbarian for those false devotees of progress?].[12] Within the novel itself, the perspective camouflages itself as non-Western, even producing a reverse Orientalism in which the West, and Western women, are the source of exoticism. But unlike *Salammbô,* a novel resolutely without a future, *Mafarka* ends both with the obliteration of the earth and with the birth of a superhuman creature who will rule over a new world. The Orientalist notion that the West will be reborn, revitalized, by returning to the East, a notion that appears in the narrative setting of the "Fondazione e manifesto del futurismo" (Founding manifesto) and "Uccidiamo il chiaro di luna" (Let's kill the moonlight) as well, thus informs the narrative structure of the novel.[13] As Liz Constable has noted, at least one of the functions of the African setting is to invert but preserve the figuration of the Eastern/African other as belonging to a time period different from that occupied by the West.[14] The notion that African peoples are "primitive," that they presently occupy a place in the West's past, is simply overturned so that they now occupy the place of the West's future, with all the Orientalist notions about atrociously "primitive" qualities still intact.[15]

Into this setting is introduced a reproductive fantasy: the novel's project, in its own terms, is to bypass the "vulva" and impregnate the "ovary" that is the male spirit: "L'esprit de l'homme," proclaims Marinetti in the preface, "est un ovaire inexercé. . . . C'est nous qui le fécondons pour la première fois" (17) [The spirit of man is an unused ovary. . . . It is we who will fertilize it for the first time!]. The narrative impetus for this fantasy is provided by the death of Mafarka's beloved brother Magamal, who contracts rabies and dies after ripping his bride to shreds and reducing her to what the text pleasantly refers to as "scarlet mud." Gazourmah, the mechanical son, is to be the immortal substitute for the dead brother. A sort of futurist Geppetto (Mafarka in fact sculpts his son from a piece of oak), Mafarka has reasons for creating his own kin that are less than kind — to women. The transplant of the ovary to the male spirit is necessitated by the unabashedly misogynist desire for procreation without procreative sex: in his "discours futuriste," Mafarka jubilantly announces that "il est possible de pousser hors de sa chair, sans le concours et la puante complicité de la matrice de la femme, un géant immortel" (169) [It is possible to procreate an immortal giant from one's own flesh, without concourse and stinking complicity with woman's womb].

Of course this is not really "la première fois" that such a fantasy has been conceived; my use of the term "autarky" is meant, in fact, not only to anticipate its later fascist use but also to evoke its much earlier classical sources — the Greek *autarkeia* was used to refer to Jason's desire for self-sufficiency in a world without women. Marinetti's claim to originality may seem at least partially justified by the form that the son assumes, for Gazourmah takes shape as an airplane, and as part human flesh and part mechanical structure, thus qualifying as an early cyborg: "C'est avec mes mains que j'ai sculpté mon fils dans le bois d'un jeune chêne. . . . J'ai trouvé une mixture qui transforme les fibres végétales en chair vivante et en muscles solides" (166) [With my own hands I sculpted my son in the wood of a young oak. . . . I found a compound that transforms vegetable fibers into living flesh and firm muscles]. But unlike the cyborgs theorized by Donna Haraway — the transgressive, oppositional creatures who conjure up visions of a postmodern, postgender world — Marinetti's Gazourmah is born of a dream of male parthenogenesis that rests on philosophical foundations that are not quite so shiny and new.[16] Jean-Joseph Goux nicely encapsulates those foundations when he writes of philosophical idealism that it "is first of all a conception of conception."[17] That conception is one in which woman supplies matter, and man supplies form; its progeny is the philosophical opposition between matter and spirit; and its dream is that of immaculate conception or, as Goux also puts it, "scissiparous reproduction, sexless procreation," in which value reproduces itself, concepts spawn concepts, and fathers create sons, all without "mother" or "labor," "out of desire and form alone."[18]

Goux's formulation points to the way in which the sexual and the economic are necessarily intertwined in the fantasy of male autarky. But in acting out the fantasy of male autarky that underlies this project, an additional factor emerges, for the novel finds itself in the bonds — the double bonds — of the "homosexual panic" theorized by Eve Sedgwick. As mentioned earlier, Sedgwick has analyzed this double bind, and resultant panic, as the product of the prescription of homosocial behavior (male bonding) and equally strong proscription of homosexual behavior that characterize all patriarchal, heterosexual culture. Within such cultures, the boundaries between the homosocial and the homosexual are unstable, and that instability works to regulate, in more or less terroristic fashion, all bonds between men. In *Mafarka*, as in the manifestos, the elimination of woman brings into view this boundary dispute and its attendant panic. In *Mafarka*, woman is to be eliminated not only as *matrice, mater*, empty receptacle, but also as "vulva," as object of sexual desire. Indeed, the part of woman to be bypassed is more often referred to as "vulve" than as "matrice" or womb, thereby underscoring the sexual relation and producing the repeated, odd formulation "J'ai enfanté mon fils sans le secours de la vulve!" [I gave birth to my son without the aid of the vulva]. As we shall see, the form that the "homosexual panic" assumes in this novel is somewhat different from the form it takes in the manifestos, where the question of the correct proximity of man to man is figured as a question of the correct proximity of man to woman. In *Mafarka*, instead, it is the question of the correct proximity between male mother and son that causes panic and requires the reintroduction of the woman as mother. What does remain constant, however, is the question of proximity itself, now overcoded so that it is a question not only of the correct proximity of man to woman and man to man but also of the proximity of futurist Europe to its once and future colonies. In both cases, what is at stake is the transfer of properties: from women to men (a transfer figured in the "male ovary") and from Africa to a (linguistically) Franco-Italian West. Not surprisingly, this latter transfer is figured on the model of the dominant pair: Africa is introduced metonymically in the first chapter, "Le viol des négresses" (The rape of negresses), as the racialized, sexualized body to be raped.

Male Mothers

Here in his "African novel" the "lyrical obsession with matter" of Marinetti's later "Manifesto tecnico della letteratura futurista" (Technical manifesto of futurist literature) appears instead as a lyrical obsession with *mater* — both with deanimating whatever is animate and gendered female, turning mother into matter, and with becoming a "male mother." Both transformations are already internal to the project of idealism, as Goux describes it in his chapter titled "Sexual Difference and History": the role of the mother is that of lifeless, formless matter, and the father's role, insofar as it is the purely ideological (as opposed to physiological) one of "cultural gestation," is that of "social mother."[19] It is as though *Mafarka* were the literalization of its philosophical underpinnings: Mafarka's own beloved mother, Langurama, is a mummy — lifeless flesh preserved as object of veneration — while Mafarka himself becomes the "social mother" and cultural gestator of futurism when he pronounces his "discours futuriste." As I have suggested, in *Mafarka* these transformations are bound up with "homosexual panic"; we might say, in fact, that becoming a male mother is the (however baffling) solution to the problem at the heart of the novel: How can one remain a heterosexual male once sexual relations with women have been eliminated? As it turns out, of course, all mothers, including Mafarka himself, end up deanimated, and all mothers, including Mafarka himself, end up having sexual relations with men. But the logic of this exchange of question (how to remain heterosexual) and answer (become a male mother) is the structuring (and unconscious) ideo-logic of the novel.

The deanimation of female matter does not, however, imply its elimination from the text. One of the conditions of being able to procreate without the complicity of "the vulva" appears to be that "the vulva" must paradoxically be everywhere present; as Alice Y. Kaplan has noted, "femininity" is attributed to almost everything in the novel: landscape, objects, Mafarka's brother Magamal, even Mafarka himself by the end, after he has embraced his mummified mother and become a mother himself.[20] Mafarka finds himself immersed in what Edward Said has called the "deep rich fund of female sexuality" characteristic of a certain Orientalism that here functions to make his repeated refusals of women's propositions seem all the more "heroic."[21] More importantly, though Mafarka rails against the debilitating effect of sexual relations with women, he is everywhere surrounded by scenes of rape. The "vulva" must be not only everywhere present but also everywhere and always open to violence: the relation to matter is almost always figured as heterosexual rape, as sexual violence against feminized matter or against female characters. Indeed, rape remains the relation to matter even for Gazourmah, Mafarka's mechanical son, who begins to spout the rhetoric of rape at birth and soon after finds himself some yielding breezes to violate. My analysis of the rhetoric of virility in the manifestos has suggested to me why this should be so: in the homophobic logic of the text, female "matter" must always be available, open to violence, in order to maintain the border between virility and what Marinetti slurringly refers to as "pederasty."[22]

But what happens when a male becomes a mother, becomes matter in relation to a mechanical son? The novel gives us two examples of possible relations between mother and son: Mafarka's own relation to his mummy, and the relation of Coloubbi, Mafarka's former lover, to Gazourmah. In the first case, reverence of the dead is combined with a strange surrogacy, for by constructing Gazourmah, Mafarka aims to give his mother a replacement for her dead son Magamal: he becomes his mother's surrogate mother. Langurama is the only female character in the novel not to be presented as a body to be raped, but it should be noted that she is *already* inert matter. This might suggest not that the mother is exempt from the sexual relation, but that it has already taken place (at least phantasmatically), and had the consequence consistent with the logic of the text. This suggestion is shored up by Langurama's literary precedents (in Théophile Gautier's *Roman de la momie,* for example, it is the object of desire who is mummified) and borne out by Mafarka's reaction to Coloubbi's attempt at seduction, which Mafarka rebuffs because it reminds him of mom:

> D'un mouvement très lent de son bras soyeux et terrible, Coloubbi atti-rait encore vers ses seins la bouche de Mafarka.... Brusquement il sursauta d'horreur, en criant: — Oh! ne fais pas le geste de ma mère!... Tes mamelles sont maudites et taries!... Va-t-en! (193)

> [With a very slow movement of her soft and terrible arm, Coloubbi again drew Mafarka's mouth to her breast.... Suddenly he started, horrified, and cried: Oh! Don't make the gesture of my mother!... Your breasts are cursed and dried up!... Go away!].

Coloubbi's own claim to be Gazourmah's mother provides further confirmation of the sexual nature of the relation between mother and son. Thus, while in relation to the "futurist discourse" of the novel, Coloubbi clearly stands for the passatist nostalgia for "amour" and "clair de lune" that the futurist Mafarka must overcome in order to give birth to his son, in relation to the economy outlined here, her importance lies in her sudden appearance as competing mother. She claims to be Gazourmah's true mother precisely because she is his lover:

> C'est mon fils, tu le sais, du moment que son premier regard fut pour moi!... Je fondais de plaisir sous la rude caresse de ses yeux!... C'est aussi mon amant, et je me suis livrée à tous ses caprices dans ce premier regard!... Tu vois: je jouis affreusement toute seule sous sa force de mâle, qui rêve déjà de me tuer en vidant ses veines dans les miennes! (216)

> [He is my son, you know, since his first glance was for me! I melted with pleasure beneath the rough caress of his eyes! And he is also my lover, and

I abandoned myself to his caprices in that first glance! You see: I take my pleasure horribly, by myself, beneath his male strength that already dreams of killing me, by emptying his veins into mine!]

Mother-love, it would seem, is inseparable from annihilating incest. Alice Kaplan has noted that both Mafarka and the narrative break down at this point: Coloubbi's claim causes Mafarka to dissolve into tears and sends the narrative off on a detour. Kaplan argues that the breakdown signals an involuntary return to the maternal, occasioned by the threat of total feminization; I would argue that the narrative stalls as it attempts to figure out a way to figure the male mother's incestuous relation with the son as heterosexual. After all, according to the heterosexual imperative of the text, Gazourmah should rape his mother, should rape Mafarka; the homophobic ideo-logic of the text cannot permit this, however, because Gazourmah's "mother" is his "father": father-son incest cannot be staged. This conundrum occasions the return to the maternal, which takes place in the form of Mafarka's search for his "momie maternelle" (218) [maternal mummy], Langurama, who then issues an order: "Mafarka, embrasse aussi pour moi ton fils, sur sa bouche!...N'oublie pas!" [Mafarka! Kiss your son for me too, on the mouth!...Don't forget!]. The order is clearly a relief to Mafarka: "Alors un cri de joie souleva la poitrine de Mafarka. Il bondit vers son fils comme le jet d'une fontaine" (221) [Then a cry of joy swelled Mafarka's breast. He leapt toward his son, like the gush of a fountain]. Made the bearer of an incestuous, but heterosexually incestuous, kiss, Mafarka can return to his son as a man turns from a wife to a lover; the rhetoric of justification is that of the supposedly unwilling adulterer, pushed into the arms of the "other woman": "Ô caressante haleine de ma mère! Tu me pousses dans les bras de mon fils! Tu m'ordonnes d'anéantir mon corps en lui donnant la vie!" (221) [Oh caressing breath of my mother! You push me into the arms of my son! You command me to annihilate my body, giving him life!]. It is at this moment in the novel that Mafarka is most clearly, and culturally, a mother, at the same time as he most clearly exhibits the forbearance marked as virile: "O mon fils! ô mon maître!...J'ai tout donné pour toi! C'est à force de jeûnes, de sacrifices sanglants et de prières que j'ai préservé ma volonté de dépendre d'un breuvage, d'une couleur fascinante ou d'un parfum de femme" (221) [Oh my son! Oh my lord!...I have given everything for you! By dint of fasts and bloody sacrifices and prayers, I saved my will from dependence on a potion or on a fascinating color or on the perfume of a woman]. Alice Kaplan quite correctly glosses the first three exclamations of this passage as marking a failure of will: Mafarka is the martyred mother, a "total woman."[23] But the second half ("By dint of fasts . . . ") introduces a rather different element, for this is a rhetoric of virility that quite specifically marks this mother as a male who can withstand the distraction women's perfume can cause to the "olfactory imagination of the male."[24] In other words, Mafarka is both the sacrificing, devoted mother who gives all to her child and the male who succeeds in maintaining both will and virility, for as we know from the later manifesto "Contro il lusso femminile" a mere whiff of a woman's perfume, a touch of a fine fabric, may sometimes lead to "pederasty." And by bearing the mother's kiss, Mafarka is able to give life to his son not through the lips of the vulva but through those of his own mouth. Gazourmah comes to life under the kiss of his male mother: "Voici mon âme! . . . Tends-moi tes lèvres et ouvre ta bouche à mon baiser! . . . Il sauta au cou de son fils et il colla sa bouche sur la bouche sculptée. Le formidable corps de Gazourmah sursauta aussitôt violemment et ses ailes puissantes se déclenchèrent" (222) [Here is my soul! . . . Give me your lips and open your mouth to my kiss! . . . And he threw himself on the neck of his son and pressed his own mouth onto the sculpted mouth. Immediately the formidable body of Gazourmah started violently, and his powerful wings sprung open]. A page later, of course, Mafarka meets the fate of all that is feminine in the text, as he, too, is reduced to inert matter. But here the homoerotic kiss is stolen under cover of familial relations, through the mother's interposed kiss, and as a same-sex version of Pygmalion, who, like Mafarka, was driven to sculpt out of a scorn for women. As in *Come si seducono le donne,* where the futurist male can *inculare* neutralists' wives while fighting for the nation's borders, here the homoerotic fantasy is smuggled in *as* heterosexual.

The narrative introduction of a competing incestuous mother (Coloubbi) and its detour to Mafarka's own mother (who gives permission to commit incest) were thus motivated by a requirement of what Luce Irigaray has called the male hom(m)o-sexual economy. By male hom(m)o-sexual economy, Irigaray means the patriarchal, exogamic economy in which women are exchanged among, and serve as the mediation and alibi for relations (economic as well as sexual) between, men. It is important to distinguish this double-*m*-ed hom(m)o-sexuality from homosexuality, now with a single *m,* which refers instead to male same-sex relations that are at once required by and yet subversive of that economy. This is a familiar formulation, for it recalls Eve Sedgwick's notion of the double bind whereby male homosociality is prescribed but male homosexuality is proscribed. For

Irigaray, male same-sex relations are subversive insofar as they forgo the pre-scribed mediation through women and put into circulation the phallus that serves as (excluded) universal equivalent, and thus deprive the economy of its "money." In other words, male same-sex relations would bankrupt the hom(m)o-sexual economy. Within that economy, then, neither male homo-sexuality nor father-son incest may be openly avowed, for, as Irigaray writes, "they openly interpret the law according to which society operates."[25] In *Mafarka,* the evocation of mother-son incest is thus the displacement and alibi of father-son incest, of the pederastic relation (and at this point I take "pederasty" out of the quotation marks that contained it as Marinetti's slur on all male same-sex relations). Within the economy of the text, the open-ness of this particular scene is paid for by the final pages of the novel, where the mediation through women is less than delicately restored in the dialogue between Gazourmah and the (linguistically feminine) "Mocking Breezes." I quote at length to show how "costly" the scene has been:

> LES BRISES NARQUOISES: Tu ne pourras jamais voler au ciel, ô bel amant trop lourd!
> GAZOURMAH: Vous me jugez trop lourd...Ah! ah!...Vous désireriez peut-être me rouler à votre gré comme une plume légère?...Eh bien, non! C'est de force que je m'ouvrirai un passage parmi vos hanches moelleuses, et mon poids me permettra de garder mon équilibre sous vos caresses rudoyantes! ...Pour humer encore mon odeur de mâle, vous vous précipiterez toutes dans le vide que je laisserai derrière moi en fendant votre foule désirante. Je volerai à contre-courant dans le ruissellement de vos nudités, et ce seront vos bras qui presseront mon corps et le feront gicler en avant.
> LES BRISES NARQUOISES: Nous te culbuterons dans nos lits orageux!... Nous te culbuterons pour t'embrasser partout!...
> GAZOURMAH: Je m'allongerai sur vous, pour mordre vos lèvres, les jambes complètement repliées en arrière et je vous dépucellerai toutes ô Brises charmantes et narquoises, fougueusement, en traversant l'espace! (227–28)

> [THE MOCKING BREEZES: But you won't be able to fly to the sky, handsome and too heavy lover!
> GAZOURMAH: Do I seem too heavy to you?...Ha! Ha!...You'd like to sweep me along at your will, like a light feather?...Well, forget it! By force I will open a passage between your soft thighs, and my weight will allow me to keep my balance beneath your rude caresses!...To catch yet another whiff of my male odor you will all cast yourselves down into the void that I will leave behind me as I cleave your lustful crowd. And I will fly against the current in the streaming of your nudity, and it will be your arms that will embrace my body and make it spurt ahead.
> THE MOCKING BREEZES: We will tumble you in our tempestuous beds! ...We will tumble you about to kiss you all over!...

GAZOURMAH: I will stretch out on you, with my legs completely folded back, and I will bite your lips, and I will deflower all of you, oh lovely mocking breezes, impetuously, as I move through space.]

Surely there are other ways to imagine the relation between an airplane and the clouds through which it flies, but even as airplane, the transcendent male spirit needs to negate matter *as* female. The by now tedious insistence upon rape as even the superhuman Gazourmah's relation to feminized matter serves both to reaffirm the heterosexual imperative and to throw into high relief the anomaly of the tender kiss exchanged between Mafarka and son. The "cost" of this reaffirmation is the success of Mafarka's project, for this is the relation to the "vulva" that Mafarka had railed against throughout the novel and that Gazourmah's vulva-less birth was meant to bypass. The narrative, however, plays itself out in a triumphant, futurist mode as though oblivious to the loop in which its own project has been caught. This is no send-up of idealism, but rather a rehearsal of its foundations.

That rehearsal is repeated in the "apocalyptic" scenes in the novel. In both cases those scenes are apocalypses of heterosexuality. The first is the "débauche végétale" (200) [vegetable orgy] that immediately follows Mafarka's close call with Coloubbi; he almost gives in to the temptation of nostalgia and in the place of surrender makes a burnt offering to the Hurricane that arises inexplicably to threaten Gazourmah. The "offering" is the vegetable orgy; male tree trunks and virile bowsprits are consumed by naked female flames; ships tossed by the sea become "tartanes en chaleur" [tartans in heat]; Mafarka as pimp races about preparing his own personal holocaust: "Et Mafarka ne se lassait pas de courir ça et là comme un proxénète lugubre, préparant des lits de volupté pour les amours de ces déesses rouges! Il disposait les jeunes troncs sur des matelas de feuilles, et les troncs centenaires aussi" [And Mafarka did not tire of running here and there like a lugubrious pimp, preparing beds of lust for the loves of these red goddesses! He arranged both young and centenarian trunks on mattresses of leaves]. No noun enters this description without being both personified and gendered, and there is no relation that is not a (hetero)sexual one. Even the night during which the orgy takes place is personified as a woman in labor, giving birth to an unknown world: "La Nuit gonflait son ventre en gésine. Quel monde allait-elle donc enfanter?" [The Night swelled her laboring belly. To what world would she give birth?]. The question thematizes the function of the apocalypse itself; it seems to want to mark the death of the sexual relation to woman and in its place put the parturition of the male mother:

"Oh! la joie de t'avoir enfanté ainsi, beau et pur de toutes les tares qui viennent de la vulve maléfique et qui prédisposent à la décrépitude et à la mort!... Oui! Tu es immortel, ô mon fils!" [Oh! The joy of having given birth to you thus, handsome and pure of all the defects that come from the maleficent vulva and predispose one to decrepitude and death!... Yes, you are immortal, my son!]. The implicit reference to Pandora, whose birth not only inaugurated sickness and death but also introduced the "damnable race of women" to mankind, makes it clear that the world about to be born reinaugurates a pre-Pandoran state, yet that pre-Pandoran state cannot be imagined except through mediation by women or the feminine. Similarly, the pages that follow the dramatic dialogue quoted above describe the earth convulsed by quakes and engulfed in volcanic eruption as Gazourmah flies off to dethrone the sun.[26] The destruction of the earth is one with the destruction of Coloubbi: "C'est la Terre que tu as tuée en me tuant!" (229) [By killing me you kill the Earth!]. Male spirit once again deanimates female matter as the condition of its very existence.

The kiss between male mother and son is not entirely unprecedented in the novel, however, for Mafarka's relation to his brother Magamal similarly appears to smuggle in homoerotic relations under the cover of the proximate relations of the family and within the sheltering boundaries of the so-called Sotadic Zone. Given the Orientalist context, it seems appropriate to adopt this term coined by Richard Burton, the Orientalist and translator of the *Arabian Nights,* in order to refer to a topography of "Pederasty." Burton considers "pederasty" to be "geographical and climatic, not racial";[27] within the Sotadic Zone, Burton writes, "the Vice is popular and endemic, held at the worst to be a mere peccadillo, whilst the races to the North and South of the limits here defined practise it only sporadically amid the opprobium [*sic*] of their fellows who, as a rule, are physically incapable of performing the operation and look upon it with the liveliest disgust." When Burton mentions the "limits here defined" he refers not to some vague geographical region but rather to very precise coordinates, as follows:

> 1. There exists what I shall call a "Sotadic Zone," bounded westwards by the northern shores of the Mediterranean (N. Lat. 43 degrees) and by the southern (N. Lat. 30 degrees). Thus the depth would be 780 to 800 miles including meridional France, the Iberian peninsula, Italy and Greece, with the coast-regions of Africa from Marocco [*sic*] to Egypt.
> 2. Running eastward the Sotadic Zone narrows, embracing Asia Minor, Mesopotamia and Chaldaea, Afghanistan, Sind, the Punjab and Kashmir.

3. In Indo-China the belt begins to broaden, enfolding China, Japan and Turkistan.

4. It then embraces the South Sea Islands and the New World where, at the time of its discovery, Sotadic love was, with some exceptions, an established racial institution.

From a narrow Mediterranean strip, the zone expands to "embrace" and "enfold" an area so great as to encompass nearly the entire globe and, moving steadily eastward from North America, seems to be encroaching upon even the place from which the Englishman speaks.

In Marinetti's geography, then, where Egypt, Morocco, and central Africa seem to coexist, we are safely within the zone — but not so safe as not to require that "Sotadic love" be figured as brotherly love. Magamal is blatantly feminized: he has "grâces féminines" [feminine graces] (29) and, with his "corps de caoutchouc" (29) [body of rubber] makes his appearance for the first time in the novel as if in response to Mafarka's desire for "une vierge ardente, élastique" [an ardent, elastic virgin] (28). But the more interesting case is recounted in the tale that Mafarka tells the African king, Brafane-el-Kibir, as part of his strategy to conquer him and take his lands. Ironically, the story turns out to recount Mafarka's previous and recent success in precisely such an endeavor; introduced as the story of the horse trader, the stuffed fish, and the devil, it is also the story of Mafarka's usurpation of his uncle King Boubassa's power. Indeed, the tale can be read as a mise-en-abyme of the entire novel, for, like Mafarka, Gazourmah's ambitions are imperial; he aims to dethrone not an uncle but the Sun itself, and become king not of Africa but of the firmament. Briefly, the story recounts how Mafarka the horse trader sells a marvelous horse to the devil, disguised as a rich merchant (in obvious counterpoint to Mafarka, who is disguised as a poor beggar as he tells the tale). The wondrous stallion, whose red mane and tail ignite in the wind and whose purple, sapphire-encrusted *zeb* is the dream of all the girls of the city (*zeb* is in fact slang in Arabic for "dick"), turns out not to be a reliable means of transportation, for he cannot resist an opportunity to copulate: "Tout grisé par l'odeur de la vulve humide, il agitait sa crinière fouettante contre les flancs de la femelle, qui sursautait à la brûlure en déchaînant des ruades terribles. Trois fois le démon fut ainsi désarçonné, bien qu'il fut excellent cavalier" (61) [Completely drunk from the smell of the moist vulva, he tossed his whiplike mane against the flanks of the female, who started at the burning sensation, delivering terrible kicks. Thus was the devil, even though an excellent horseman, thrown from the saddle three times]. Enraged, the devil decides to get his revenge by castrating the horse and serving up its *zeb* to Mafarka as a stuffed fish, delicately prepared with curdled milk, violets, and cinnamon. Unaware, Mafarka eats the stuffed penis and immediately exhibits the same behavior as the horse, copulating with everything female in sight. As his violence grows, so does his own penis until it eventually reaches its maximum length of eleven meters, is mistaken for a rope curled next to him as he sleeps, and then, as it is tied to a sail, becomes the mast of the ship that is his body.[28] In this way Mafarka sails to Tell-el-Kibir, where King Boubassa hears the story and insists upon personally experiencing the virtues of such a miraculous *zeb*. The *zeb* in question is of course Mafarka's own at this point, and he hastens to comply with the king's request:

> Le roi Boubassa, aguiché par ces aventures merveilleuses, voulut expérimenter personellement les vertus d'un zeb aussi miraculeux. Mafarka-el-Bar s'empressa, dit-on, de satisfaire le roi, et profitant de la posture soumise qu'avait prise ce dernier, il le bâillonna, l'enchaîna et lui ravit le sceptre! (64)

> [King Boubassa, titillated by such marvelous adventures, insisted upon personally experiencing the virtues of such a miraculous *zeb*. Mafarka-el-Bar, it seems, hastened to satisfy the king, and taking advantage of the submissive posture that the king had assumed, gagged him, chained him, and stole his scepter!]

This single exception to the femaleness of the object of sexual violence goes unremarked in the text, as Brafane-el-Kibir breaks in to ask about the fate of the castrated stallion, still wandering about looking for its lost *zeb*. The final scene (to which I shall return) is important, however, not only as the culmination of the story of how Mafarka comes to power but also as the last exchange in what I will argue is a fable of phallic economics.

The fabular and fabulous character of the story recalls tales of both Scheherazade and Boccaccio. Mafarka's strategy, like Scheherazade's, aims to gain power through storytelling;[29] as in Boccaccio's tales of the eating of hearts, the object that serves as the catalyst of the story's plot is consumed. When hearts are eaten in the *Decameron* (in, for example, the tale of the two "Guglielmi," Tale Nine of Day Four), they are eaten as signs of nobility (the gentle heart) and as the consummation of a love for which the heart is the metaphor. The consumption of the heart is not an act of cannibalism but rather the culinary consummation of a prohibited sexual relation. In the context of the (homophobic) homoerotics of Marinetti's text, it seems all too easy to read the consumption of the *zeb* as yet another thinly disguised (homo)sexual act. But what is different about eating a stuffed penis is that, within a phallic economy, you are eating the general equivalent; you are, in other words, eating the gold standard of your libidinal economy, gobbling up your own capital.

It may help to translate the tale into more explicitly economic terms, in the wake of Marx, Goux, and Irigaray. Goux in fact points to what would seem to be an analogous example of eating in Marx: as their empire declined, the ancient Romans were given to eating pearl salads during their orgies. The intertwining of the sexual and the economic in the ingestion of pearls is what particularly interests Goux: What does it mean to eat pearls, and why do so within the context of an orgy? Why is it so economically and sexually "perverse"? The economic perversion, Marx tells us, lies in treating wealth as though it had a direct use value. Yet pearls, of course, have no known nutritional value, and it is therefore blatantly not their use value that is consumed; rather, they are consumed *as* exchange value. As a quasi-money, pearls are consumed insofar as they stand as general equivalent and hence as "the abstract potential of all *jouissances.*"[30] The pearl-eating Romans, Goux concludes, found *jouissance* in the general power of *jouissance,* imaginary satisfaction in the fetishism of exchange value. The price of this imaginary satisfaction is great (and not only for one's digestive tract), for in order to find *jouissance* in the use of the general equivalent, one must renounce all exchange; the economy falls apart. Now, Goux has no difficulty (perhaps too little difficulty?) translating this into the libidinal economy: for the penis to be the phallus, that is, to be the general equivalent, it must be prohibited from immediate use value, which Goux identifies as masturbation, and from immediate relative exchange value, which Goux identifies as incest. As an analogy, or isomorph, to those pearl salads, Goux offers an example from Sade of masturbation before piles of gold; our own example from Marinetti works perhaps even better, for not only does it represent a similar entwining of the sexual and the economic, but it makes visible, via Irigaray, a blindness in Goux's argument. Irigaray's analysis of the hom(m)o-sexual economy also addresses the consequences of treating the general equivalent that is the phallus as use value: when, as she writes, the "penis itself becomes merely a means to pleasure, of pleasure among men, *the phallus loses its power.*"[31] Short-circuiting the commerce that is the exchange of women, male homosexuality, as we have said, eats the capital of hom(m)o-sexuality. Goux is thus both right and wrong when he points to incest as the equivalent of eating pearls: right insofar as what is at stake is the violation of exogamy, but wrong insofar as he seems to assume that it is only mother-son incest that is at issue. In Mafarka's story, the use of the penis as relative exchange value is figured as uncle-son incest, and the loss of phallic power that it entails is fantasized instead as its explicit reversal; that is to say, Mafarka *gains* the power of the king, the general equivalent in the political realm, in precisely the moment that he, in theory, loses phallic power by using the general equivalent in the libidinal realm for pleasure between men. The lubrication for this reversal is supplied by a recoding that takes place within the scene itself: what happens is that what is initially represented as the consensual sexual relation between men (the king asks and Mafarka complies) is, necessarily for the hom(m)o-sexual, homophobic economy, recoded as a political rape: "lui ravit le sceptre."

Mafarka's story of the *zeb* is not, however, only or even principally a sexual fantasy; as in the Romans' orgiastic consumption of pearls, the sexual fantasy is bound up with an economic fantasy. The story also tells the tale of an increasingly "primitive" economy; it begins with an exchange that takes place within a money economy, as Mafarka sells the horse to the devil, and then moves quickly to what we might call a barter economy, as the devil takes his revenge. Revenge, after all, seems to be based upon the principle of barter: the exchange of an eye for an eye, a tooth for a tooth, is in principle no different from the exchange of a horse for a pig. From revenge, the tale seems to move to hoarding, and from hoarding to theft. In this economic fantasy, the fantasy of the eating of the *zeb* and the consequent growth of Mafarka's own penis appears to be based upon the notion that grounds the fantasy of hoarding: to accumulate something is to increase it. This notion is, of course, faulty with respect to money, since money must circulate. As Marx explains, the independence of wealth is "a mere semblance; its independence of circulation exists only in view of circulation, exists as dependence on it."[32] Wealth is dependent upon exchange, so that what appears to be, in hoarding, an increase in wealth is in fact its decrease. The notion of hoarding is foundational to the fantasy of male autarky in the novel, for it proposes to hoard the penis, multiply the stores of virility by withdrawing it from the economy of the exchange of women. Its economics are equally faulty, however, and the declaration of independence of the male organ exposes its dependence upon women in the (hom[m]o-)sexual economy. Wealth — in this case, virility — is, in that economy, dependent upon the exchange of women, upon their circulation both as commodities and as the "paper" representatives of the phallus. Once women are no longer exchanged, another economy must be envisioned. But as we have seen, the narrative can imagine that other economy only as the decrease of phallic power; indeed, Mafarka describes his years of powerlessness as those years in which he was trapped within the uncle's bowels. The narrative starts and stalls at each attempt as ideological closure (here in the form of homophobia) moves in to choke it in order to secure the value of the phallus. Hoarding thus seems to stand as another (still baffling) solution to the dilemma of how to remain heterosexual without having sexual relations with women: it is an economy without exchange, Midas preferred to Medusa.

This petrified economy of no exchange is also an economy of pillage — there is take, but no give. It makes (ideological) sense, then, that the consequence of the eleven-meter (hoarded) penis should be figured as the "rape" of the king/uncle by his usurping nephew, for the final stage in this series is an economy of theft and rape. And the same sense might allow us to suggest that the economy of theft and rape is here not coincidentally set in Africa, for this is also a colonialist economic fantasy.

Future Salads

Outside of the tale within the tale, the economic fantasy in the novel appears in the series of what Alice Kaplan has suggested are "uneven exchanges": as technological qualities are attributed to humans (largely, males), human qualities are distributed onto the landscape. As we have seen, those "human" qualities are largely "feminine" qualities. But what happens to the (female) bodies from which those qualities have been borrowed? The novel seems to offer two possibilities, which often make up a sequence rather than an alternative: the body becomes the bearer of "new" properties, and/or it is reduced to paste. In the first case, the body in question is the black African woman's body, and as Liz Constable has noted, the properties in question are those desired not so much by an individual male as by a nation: with "hanches sucrées, couleur de belle vanille" [sugared thighs, the color of vanilla] and "mamelles couleur de café brulé" (40) [breasts the color of roasted coffee], African women appear "suspendues, telles des bananes, à la tige savoureuse de sa voix" (102) [suspended, like bananas, on the savory stem of his voice].[33] Even Magamal, with his "corps de caoutchouc," fits into this series. Rubber, sugar, vanilla, coffee, and bananas are fantasized colonial products that become properties of the body to be raped, so that possession of the woman becomes possession of the products as well:

> On voyait des ventres lisses et luisants des jeunes femmes et leurs petites mamelles couleur de café brûlé se tordre de douleur sous les poing lourds des mâles, dont les reins de bronze se levaient et s'abaissaient indéfatigablement parmi le flic-flac dansant des pourritures vertes. (40)

[One saw the smooth and shining bellies of the young women, and their small breasts the color of roasted coffee squirm with pain beneath the heavy blows of the men, whose bronze loins rose and fell indefatigably, in the dancing flicflac of green putrefaction.]

This rape, which takes place in the green paste produced from the grinding of African bodies by a "fantastique pressoir," is, within the terms of the novel, color-coded racially: the bronze rapists are, like Mafarka, Arabs, while the women raped are black Africans.[34] And the relation between Arabs and black Africans is, through that putrefaction, figured as an economic one:

> Tous ces monceaux de cadavres noirs, lustrés, fumants et presque liquéfiés sur la verdeur poudreuses des prairies, ne vont-ils pas se transformer bientôt en des flaques de purin aux riches reflets d'ébène, pour réjouir les yeux ladres du Soleil propriétaire . . . et les tiens, mon premier ministre! (27)

> [Will not all these piles of black corpses, shiny, smoking, and almost liquefied on the dusty green of the prairies, soon be transformed into pools of liquid manure, with rich ebony reflections, to cheer the proprietary eyes of the owner, the Sun, . . . and yours, my prime minister!]

What is striking about this passage is not so much its interest in putrefaction — Flaubert's fascination, in *Salammbô*, with the differing rates of putrefaction of bodies according to their national and ethnic identities provides a powerful and perhaps more shocking literary precedent — but rather the nature of that interest. Flaubert's interest seems detached, almost hyperintellectual, in relation to Mafarka's very proprietary interest, which is underlined by the possessive adjectives in the passage: the Sun owns the land to be enriched by the rot; the prime minister owns the eyes that like those of the Sun are proprietary; and Mafarka owns the prime minister. It is this relation that authorizes us to say that there is indeed a Western perspective in the novel and that this perspective is colonial. Mafarka the Arab is to the black Africans what the white man is to all Africans; the position of the subject in the fantasy is found not in this or that character but in the relation between characters (or, as Laplanche and Pontalis put it, in the "syntax" of the fantasy).[35]

Putrefaction transforms and transfers properties. Mafarka's interest is in the future usefulness of such transformations:

> D'ailleurs, le Soleil suffit à bien travailler la terre. . . . Mais regarde donc, imbécile! Ses doigts de rayons interminables plongent bien avant dans le sillon fécondé, pour cuire d'une caresse vive les germes impatients. . . . Laisse donc ses doigts méticuleux soigner nos salades futures dans les entrailles pourries

des nègres! Aie confiance en ce bon Soleil agricole qui embrasse tous ses domaines d'un regard brûlant et paternel. (27)

[Besides, the Sun is enough by itself to work the earth. . . . But look, imbecile! Its fingers of interminable rays plunge ahead into the fertilized furrow to cook the impatient germs with a lively caress. . . . Let its meticulous fingers cultivate our future salads in the putrefied entrails of negroes! Have faith in this good peasant Sun who embraces all his territory with a burning and paternal gaze.]

The fantasy at work here posits a self-sufficient Sun, able to reap crops without interference of the "natives," indeed, by puréeing the natives into part of the inanimate raw material necessary in order to produce those future salads.[36] (The culinary, colonial logic of this process brings to mind Helen Bannerman's story "Little Black Sambo," in which tigers race after each other so fast that they are finally turned into butter, puréed into a useful product.) A most convenient transformation, for it sidesteps all the various problems posed by the very existence of "natives" and clears the field for the possibility of the self-sufficiency of the emperor that is the Sun.

At this point we might leap from the economics of this transfer of properties to the fantasized economics of fascism, but as a literary critic one must stop to note that a "transfer of properties" is also a rhetorical operation. Yet another series of questions needs to be asked, and answered, before arriving at the payoff: How, rhetorically, are properties transferred in the text? How does the animate come to be inanimated, and vice versa, and how does that animation allow or, in terms of the ideology of the novel, require gendering? How, rhetorically, does the ovary become male? An analysis of another scene of putrefaction will begin to offer some answers.

In a scene that brings to mind the scenarios of Klaus Theweleit's *Male Fantasies,* a male protagonist stands transfixed before a bloody mass that had been a female body:

Mafarka s'avança dans l'obscurité de la chambre nuptiale. Tout autour, sur les colonnes, des sphinx et des chimères de granit s'acharnaient immobiles, empêtrés dans leurs barbes nattées. Et Mafarka crut entendre le han formidable de leurs poumons dilatés par l'effort, car ces monstres sculptés se hissaient sur le levier des pattes crochues, tâchant de se délivrer, à coups de reins, de leurs entraves, pour bondir en avant.

Mafarka glissa sur de la pâte molle et ne comprit pas. Mais une odeur chaude et sucrée de sève humaine et de pourriture le mordit aux narines, et ses yeux, peu à peu habitués à la pénombre, devinèrent les lambeaux d'un cadavre féminin, partout, autour de lui, par jonchées sinistres, comme après une flagellation.

Alors, tressaillant d'angoisse, il appela à grands cris l'esclave, qui s'avança
en portant sa cage de résine flambante.

La couche apparut toute souillée d'une boue écarlate et comme défoncée
par une lutte diabolique. De son creux inondé de sang émergeaient, pêle-
mêle avec des touffes de cheveux, des vertèbres et des os qui semblaient avoir
été mâchés par des dents de tigre en rut.

Et Mafarka, le coeur flottant et comme en rêve, fixa longtemps ces déchets
lamentables qui suaient une odeur noire de luxure. C'étaient bien les restes
lamentables de la divine Ouarabelli-Charchar! (135)

[Mafarka went forward into the darkness of the nuptial chamber. All around,
on columns, sphinxes and chimeras of granite struggled immobile [*s'acharnaient immobiles*], entangled in their braided beards. And Mafarka thought he
heard the tremendous grunt of their lungs dilated by the effort, for these
sculpted monsters rose up by the lever of their hooked claws, trying to free
themselves of their chains through the force of their loins, and leap forward.

He slipped on some kind of soft paste, and didn't understand. But a warm
and sweet odor of human semen and of putrefaction bit his nostrils, and his
eyes, having little by little adjusted to the semidarkness, made out the shreds
of a female cadaver, spread everywhere, all around him, in sinister scatterings,
as after a flagellation.

Then, trembling with agony, with loud cries he called the slave, who came
forward carrying his flaming resin torch.

The bed appeared all soiled with a kind of scarlet mud, and as though
broken down by a diabolical struggle. From its hollow inundated with blood,
emerged, pell mell with tufts of hair, vertebrae and bones that seemed to
have been chewed by the teeth of a tiger in heat.

And Mafarka, with a wavering heart and as in a dream, stared for a long
time at these miserable remains, from which oozed a black odor of lust. These
were indeed the lamentable remains of the divine Ouarabelli-Charchar.

Like Theweleit's soldier males, Mafarka enters into a trancelike state before
the "bloody miasma" that had been his brother's fiancée, Ouarabelli-
Charchar. Such a reduction of the female body to paste allows Theweleit's
subjects to differentiate their own bodies and psyches from those of others.
But the interest of the passage lies not only in the information it might
give us about a particular psychology.

Why, first of all, should the scene of "scarlet mud" be overseen by
chimera and sphinx, struggling to free themselves of stone? What underlies
this combination of animation and deanimation? An answer can be found
by juxtaposing the passage to one of its unmistakable subtexts. Any reader
of fin de siècle French literature will recognize in Marinetti's interior dec-
oration another bedroom, that in which Huysmans's Des Esseintes instructs
a female ventriloquist to project the dialogue between the chimera and the

sphinx from Flaubert's *Tentation de Saint Antoine* into stone statuettes of the monsters that he, Des Esseintes, has had placed in the corners of the bedroom:

> Il fit apporter, un soir, un petit sphinx, en marbre noir, couché dans la pose classique, les pattes allongées, la tête rigide et droite, et une chimère, en terre polychrome, brandissant une crinière hérissée, dardant des yeux féroces, éventant avec les sillons de sa queue ses flancs gonflés ainsi que des soufflets de forge. Il plaça chacune de ces bêtes, à un bout de la chambre, éteignit les lampes, laissant les braises rougeoyer dans l'âtre et éclairer vaguement la pièce en agrandisssant les objets presque noyés dans l'ombre. Puis, il s'étendit sur un canapé, près de la femme dont l'immobile figure était atteinte par la lueur d'un tison, et il attendit.
>
> Avec des intonations étranges qu'il lui avait fait longuement et patiemment répéter à l'avance, elle anima, sans même remuer les lèvres, sans même les regarder, les deux monstres.[37]

> [One night he had a miniature sphinx brought in, carved in black marble and couched in the classic pose, its paws stretched out and its head held rigidly upright, together with a chimera in coloured terra-cotta, flaunting a bristling mane, darting ferocious glances from its eyes, and lashing flanks as swollen as a blacksmith's bellows with its tail. He placed one of these mythical beasts at either end of the bedroom and put out the lamps, leaving only the red embers glowing in the hearth, to shed a dim light that would exaggerate the size of objects almost submerged in the semi-darkness. This done, he lay down on the bed beside the ventriloquist, whose set face was lit up by the glow of a half-burned log, and waited.
>
> With strange intonations that he had made her rehearse beforehand for hours, she gave life and voice [*elle anima*] to the monsters, without so much as moving her lips, without even looking in their direction.][38]

This passage, too, is about animation and, like the Marinetti passage, is inlaid with intertexts. In the passage from *A rebours,* it is a woman who animates the chimera and sphinx: *elle anima.* A first contrast between the passages may be noted here, for in the Marinetti passage the woman is quite definitely no longer capable of animating herself or anything else, while the chimera and sphinx appear to be self-animating: "des sphinx et des chimères s'acharnaient." In the Huysmans passage, the woman serves as a vehicle for literature, for poetic discourse, as she projects Flaubert's dialogue into the statues. Indeed, as I have argued elsewhere, this particular scene stands as a figure for decadent poetics as a kind of ventriloquism in which the body spoken through is necessarily a woman's.[39] I would argue here that the Huysmanian intertextual frame suggests that the Marinetti passage may also be about poetics, and specifically about a disjunction between poetic "animation" and the figure of woman. That it is similarly about poetics is signaled in the struggling of the statues: like that of Michelangelo's slaves or of Mallarmé's swan stuck in the ice, the immobilized struggle is the struggle of form to emerge from matter, the artistic struggle of at least a certain poetics. The imagined sound of the statues' breathing refers to a kind of self-inspiration (compared to the "inspiration" of the woman breathing words into the statues in the Huysmans passage). The disjunction between this animation and the figure of woman is marked linguistically, first by the paronomasia embedded in "s'acharnaient immobiles," and then by the phrase "une odeur noire de luxure," which appears at the end of the passage. The stone statues "s'*achar*naient," struggle to become flesh (*chair*), in the same scene in which the woman's flesh (and note her name, "Char-char") is torn to pieces, chewed into scarlet mud. The "odeur noire de luxure" that overhangs the scene further calls up decadentism by evoking the synesthetic poetics of, for example, Baudelaire; one might argue, in fact, that this specific synesthesia evokes Baudelaire through an allusion to the Jeanne Duval poems, where the blackness of the woman's body becomes the master trope of the poems. If that is so, then the "shreds of a female cadaver" are also the remains of the corpse of a feminized decadent poetics.

But if this remnant, the "odeur noire de luxure," recalls a repudiated poetics, it also persists, transformed, in futurist practice. This is not the first time that such a figure appears in *Mafarka,* where the landscape is dotted with "bushes of thorny envy," "slopes of steep desperation," and "red cries of sailors." In decadent texts, the figure combines the senses; in this futurist text, it combines human and nonhuman properties. Known in aestheticized terms as synesthesia, the figure is more properly called hypallage and, according to Heinrich Lausberg, refers to the grammatical and semantic displacement of the relation of an adjective to a substantive; an adjective is referred grammatically not to the substantive to which it should be linked semantically, but rather to another substantive in the same context. It is a figure particularly linked to Latin and Greek, insofar as it is a change in the relation of adjective and noun in which an adjective does not agree with the case of the word it logically qualifies but agrees grammatically with another case. The interest of this figure rings out from the definition: What does it mean to say that an adjective *should* refer to a particular noun? What imperative does the figure go against? If you look up the figure in other manuals, you discover that rhetoricians don't like it. Eighteenth-century rhetoricians, for example, were vehement in trying to ban hypallage from French, calling it a vice of style, denying that it is a figure at all, and campaigning for its de-motion to "misapplication of epithet."[40] Gérard Génette begins his essay on "Métonymie chez Proust" with examples of hypallage but soon moves to a discussion of diegetic metaphors.[41] But hypallage is not a diegetic metaphor: thorny envy and steep desperation are not metaphors produced on the basis of a metonymical transfer from the spatio-temporal world of the *récit*. Nor does the transfer take place on the basis of analogy; it is not, that is to say, a metaphorical substitution based on an analogy between known properties. Hypallage is produced rather on the basis of proximity within the same sentence; it is indeed a metonymical transfer of properties, but one based on the properties conventionally associated with one of the nouns, not on properties associated with the experience of a character or the consistency of a fictional world. In other words, hypallage acts upon the linguistic code itself — this is what is called "logic" (or sometimes "natural order") in the definitions of the figure, and it is the linguistic code itself that is violated by the redistribution it effects. This is a "subversive" operation, as Fredric Jameson reads it in his analysis of Wyndham Lewis's use of hypallage: it is "an implicit repudiation of that valorization of metaphor, from Aristotle to Proust, as the 'hallmark of genius,' a fundamental subversion of that still organic aesthetic ideology for which the very essence of the poetic process consists in the perception, or better still, the invention, of analogies."[42] Marinetti's theoretical pronouncements in his "Manifesto tecnico della letteratura futurista" are very much in line with that aesthetic ideology; his practice in *Mafarka*, perhaps not so.

If hypallage rhetorically shakes up the linguistic code, the ideological uses to which it may be put can be defined only by concrete instances. The anarchic free-for-all that Jameson describes — "substances, like marbles in a box, have been rattled so furiously together that their 'properties' come loose and stick to the wrong places" — is reined in by the limits that ideologies impose on this rattled semiosis. In *Mafarka*, as in the manifestos, the principal limit concerns the feminine. The thematic problem posed by women is, in fact, one of proximity: get too close to them and the dreaded feminine rubs off on you. This problem is also a rhetorical one: women devirilize, they feminize, they *adjectivize*. The solution in *Mafarka* is to eliminate woman as *matrice, mater,* and vulva and attribute the ovary to the male, thereby producing the principal hypallage of the novel, the male ovary; in the "Manifesto tecnico," adjectives are eliminated entirely. Puréed and putrefied like Ouarabelli-Charchar, woman must be eliminated over and over. But because this virility threatened by the feminine can, in the homosocial economy, maintain itself only by negating that feminine, her attributes must be redistributed, spread around, as it were, again and again to landscape, to cars, to matter itself. In *Mafarka* as in the manifestos, female "matter" must always be available, open to violence, in order to maintain the border between virility and what Marinetti slurringly refers to as "pederasty."

It is here that we may return to the questions with which this chapter began, and posit a point of articulation between the fantasy of male autarky as it is played out in *Mafarka* and another fantasy of autarky that will be played out on the stage of fascist Italy decades later: that of the cultural autarky of the nation and later of the economic autarky of the *impero*. I would like to suggest that these fantasies are interstructuring, intercontaminating. As we have seen, the fantasy of male autarky is built upon misogyny, comes to be threatened with bankruptcy by same-sex relations, and therefore requires the reintroduction of the other in the form of the woman (to be raped). Might we also say that the fantasy of national autarky, which is built upon nationalist xenophobia, comes to be threatened with bankruptcy by the erasure of difference within and therefore also requires the reintroduction of the other in the form of the colony (to be raped)? Does the structure of Marinetti's homo(phobic) economics also inform the structure of fascism's fantasized "home economics"?

This is the moment of articulation most subject to narrativizations of the sort found in Sternhell — source and muddy deltas, roots and branches, and so forth — so I want to be very clear about how I see the relation between literary text and fascist discourse. I am not suggesting that proponents of national autarky, having happened upon *Mafarka* one rainy afternoon, found in it a blueprint for their policies. Nor am I suggesting that Marinetti was possessed of clairvoyant powers by means of which he foresaw future policy. I am suggesting, rather, that Marinetti's novel and fascist discourse both construct economic and cultural fantasies that share not only individual elements but an overall structure, a syntax that I have been calling an ideo-logic.

In other words, Marinetti did not "act alone." The notion of social fantasy, of fantasy as structuring a community's relation to reality, allows us to address ideological structures as they manifest themselves in and across the most diverse of texts. Just as the fantasy of male autarky does not originate with Marinetti, so the cultural materials that his novel binds together can be found already joined, at least partially and in varying configurations, in texts roughly contemporaneous with Marinetti. A case in point would be an 1898 political tract entitled *La virilità nazionale e le colonie italiane* (National virility and Italian colonies) and written by one Pasquale

Turiello. National virility and Italian colonies are, Turiello argues, "del tutto correlativi, avendo mutua ragione di causa e di effetto" [completely interdependent, having a mutual relation of cause and effect].

Turiello spells out that interdependence: Italy has suffered from "muliebrità politica" [political womanliness] since the Risorgimento, he argues, a womanliness that consists in a languid weakness that has caused the nation to give in too easily to other nations, in particular to France, and to have passed up the opportunity to acquire colonies.[43] After 1870, Turiello claims, Italy thought of Africa only "supinamente" [on her back]. Now is the time to begin to take "virile action," he announces, and here virility is linked to anti-parliamentarism, an expanded program of physical education in schools, discipline, and demographic colonialism:

> A tutto ciò [political womanliness] non v'ha rimedii definitivi che questi due: maggior concitazione operosa (che in pace non può derivarci se non da un'educazione più maschia) e favore e campi nuovi all'emigrazione dignitosa, apparecchiandole sedi proprie. Non potendosi desiderar che questa cessi, anzi urgendo all'Italia che cresca, sorge subito il dilemma, che o questa emigrazione sia affidata solo alle convenienze mutabili di stati stranieri, sicchè vi vada ospite a testa bassa, e finchè ad altri piaccia riceverla; o vada a testa alta in terre nostre, conquistate ed aperte.[44]

> To all this [political womanliness] there are only two definitive remedies: more industrious activity (that in peacetime can only derive from a more masculine education) and new fields and favor for dignified emigration, by providing new locations for it. Since we cannot desire that emigration stop, but rather urge that Italy grow, we are faced by a dilemma: either this emigration will be entrusted to the changing conditions of foreign states, so that it goes as a guest with head hung low, and only as long as others are willing to receive it, or it will go with head held high to our own lands, open and conquered.]

Several pages later, Turiello writes: "La soluzione del problema africano rimane anche oggi un problema più di virilità che di finanza italiana" [The solution to the African problem is still today a problem more of Italian virility than of Italian finance].[45] These arguments are similar to those that Mussolini will make. Here I cite Turiello in order to point to the way in which the fantasies of virility and colonialism that Marinetti's novel elaborates are already part of the cultural matrix.

It should not be so surprising, then, to find that two fantasies of autarky share an ideological structure. Most vigorous in the 1930s, the project of cultural autarky consisted in the effort to expel all that was foreign — linguistically, literarily, cinematically — in order that Italian culture might produce itself as authentically Italian and fascist. The campaign against the

Lei,[46] decrees against the use of words from foreign languages and dialects, protectionist measures in the cinema as well as the practice of dubbing all films into Italian, and literary movements like *Strapaese* were all among "autarchic" measures and proposals. As Giuseppe Carlo Marino notes, the project remained elusive and dependent upon "la norma del negativo"; "italianità" could define itself only as that which was not foreign.[47] But if the "foreign" is expelled culturally, it makes a necessary reentry economically. In force during the early 1940s, the project of economic autarky aimed to make the nation, and then the empire, economically self-sufficient (this "policy" became something closer to a necessity after sanctions were imposed upon Italy as a result of the Ethiopian campaign in 1936). A paradox is produced in the encounter between cultural imperative and economic reality, for as it turns out, the nation çan be self-sufficient — can survive economically — only if it depends upon others, if it annexes new markets and assures itself of sources of raw materials not available in the "metropolis." The paradox is solved by expanding the "nation" into "empire," for as empire, the nation can declare itself autarchic by taking into itself the foreign upon which it depends culturally for definition and economically for survival.[48] If, then, the homophobic fantasy of male autarky can do without women only through the mediation of women, the xenophobic fantasy of cultural and economic autarky can do without the foreign only by annexing it.

4 / D'Annunzio and the Antidemocratic Fantasy

Reading Splits

Like Marinetti's *Mafarka le futuriste,* D'Annunzio's 1895 *Le vergini delle rocce* takes as its theme the generation of a superhuman son.[1] Claudio Cantelmo, the novel's protagonist, sets out to choose, from among three sisters, a genitrix who will bear him an exceptional son. The theme in itself makes the novel an easy target for quick identifications of pseudo-Nietzschean *superuomismo* with protofascism, but surrounding the fairy-tale princesses are politically explicit declamations that make it all the easier for intellectual historians and literary critics to find the literary roots of fascism in this fin de siècle text. A text about the making of a precursor has itself been made out to be a precursor. My task in this chapter is to rethink the precursory relation, to ask to what extent we may find protofascism rooted in a fin de siècle literary text, and to compare the ideological implications of D'Annunzio's reproductive fantasy to those of Marinetti's parthenogenetic dream.

As with *Mafarka,* my strategy will be to posit points of articulation among the elements that make up the narrative. In the case of *Le vergini,* those elements come already split neatly apart by D'Annunzio criticism: the political declamations contained in book 1, and those of the old prince, have been lifted like a clouded gem from the intact and antiquated setting of the decadent fairy tale in which we find the virgins Anatolia, Massimilla, and Violante. This splitting makes it possible to isolate what are almost unequivocally protofascist statements and connect them, in precursory fashion,

77

to D'Annunzio's own political activity during the Fiume takeover. A particularly brutal example appears in Paolo Alatri's inaugural address from the symposium on D'Annunzio held at Yale in March 1987. Alatri cites the loci classici of Nietzscheanism, antiegalitarianism, and antiparliamentarism from the novel and then concludes brusquely that "the fact that two or three years after the march on Rome, D'Annunzio posed or could appear as an antagonist to Mussolini rather than one of his followers or collaborators detracts nothing from the common belonging of both men to the same cultural, ideological, and political root."[2] Alatri's essay is surely not an example of subtle literary analysis (nor even less of subtle historical analysis since he cites a historical fact only to discount it), but all the same one must grant that even without metonymical slurring or wholly retroactive reading, *Le vergini* does indeed contain political orations whose constitutive elements can be found on a checklist of protofascism. Let us then, for the moment, follow a "split" reading of the text and examine both a definition of protofascism and the incriminating passages.

In *Fables of Aggression,* Fredric Jameson offers a persuasive description and diagnosis of protofascist discourse in the form of just such a checklist of four elements. The first of these constitutive elements of protofascism concerns its relation to Marxism; Jameson writes that protofascism "remains a reaction to and a defense against the continuing ideological threat and presence of a (defeated) Marxism, which thus occupies that taboo position around which the various fascist ideologies must organize themselves." If the Marxist, and later Bolshevik, threats function as catalyst, they must be accompanied by the weakening of other political forces: the elaboration of protofascism "as an ideology is, however, determined less by the practical dangers of Marxism or Communism than by the disintegration and functional discrediting — even after the failure of revolution on the Left — of the various hegemonic and legitimizing ideologies of the middle class state (liberalism, conservatism, Catholicism, social democracy, and so on).[3] Or, as Alice Kaplan puts it, both left and right must be weakened in order for fascism to be both left and right (or, again, as Sternhell would say, neither left nor right): "All standard systems of political representation must be on the blink."[4] Jameson elaborates on this second element:

> If therefore as a reaction-formation it defines itself against Marxism as the fundamental enemy, protofascism grasps itself consciously as the implacable critique of the various middle class ideologies and of the parliamentary system in which they find representation. (3) The structural inconsistency of these first two features opens up an ambiguous space in which a critique of

capitalism can be displaced and inflected in the direction of the characteristic features of classical petty-bourgeois ideology.

From within this ambiguous space arise what have been called fascism's "two souls," its anticapitalist thrust and its anticommunist stance. Jameson adds a final characteristic:

> (4) Finally, these various free-floating attitudes must be given practical embodiment in a mass ideological party which can stand as a figure for the new collectivity at the same time that it serves as the vehicle for the seizure of power. In this, protofascism distinguishes itself from Caesarism — the *coup d'état* of the isolated charismatic hero — and once more affirms its reactive stance towards Marxism, insofar as the original model of the party apparatus is a Leninist and Bolshevik innovation.[5]

A part of this last characteristic, and a necessary component of protofascism, as of fascism itself, is a strong populist element. Indeed, Ernesto Laclau has argued that fascism is not so much an expression of "the most conservative and reactionary sectors of the dominant classes" but rather "one of the possible ways of articulating the popular-democratic interpellations into political discourse."[6] Nationalism is left out of these constitutive elements, I suspect, because it is part of a number of political movements at the turn of the century, and its inclusion here would only blur what is already a portrait painted in broad strokes. Without entering into a discussion of varieties of nationalisms, however, one might safely say that insofar as protofascism is a reaction formation against Marxism and communism, it is resolutely anti-internationalist.

Some points of comparison with the texts under examination are obvious. We have already seen several of these features functioning in the Marinetti texts examined in chapter 1: the organizational function of the reaction against communism is in evidence in *Al di là del comunismo;* futurism's critique of the parliamentary system and various middle-class ideologies (love and marriage chief among them) fits into the schema; even the drive of futurism to become itself a political party would seem to correspond to these basic characteristics. There are, as well, some obvious differences: the populist component is missing in Marinetti, as it is in D'Annunzio, for as surely as D'Annunzio is aristocratic, Marinetti is "artocratic."[7] The political tirades of book 1 of *Le vergini* are antipopulist and anti–social democratic, and unlike that of Wyndham Lewis, D'Annunzio's stylistic practice, with its archaisms and elaborate Latinate hypotaxis, is anything but populist.[8] Indeed, D'Annunzio's project in *Le vergini* seems rather to fit the description of Caesarism since what we have in Claudio Cantelmo is precisely a charismatic hero whose very isolation is the precondition for his political theorizing.

With these differences marked, however (and we will return to the question of the absence of populism), we should point to what, according to this definition, are the strongly protofascist elements in the novel. These appear in several oft-quoted passages from book 1, the sort that Alatri feasts upon, as, for example, in the argument against equality and parliamentarism:

> Bollate voi sino all'osso le stupide fronti di coloro che vorrebbero mettere su ciascuna anima un marchio esatto come su un utensile sociale e fare le teste umane tutte simili come le teste dei chiodi sotto la percussione dei chiodaiuoli. Le vostre risa frenetiche salgano fino al cielo, quando udite gli stallieri della Gran Bestia vociferare nell'assemblea. Proclamate e dimostrate per la gloria dell'Intelligenza che le loro dicerie non sono men basse di quei suoni sconci con cui il villano manda fuori per la bocca il vento dal suo stomaco rimpinzato di legumi. Proclamate e dimostrate che le loro mani, a cui il vostro padre Dante darebbe l'epiteto medesimo ch'egli diede alle unghie di Taide, sono atte a raccattar lo stabbio ma non degne di levarsi per sancire una legge nell'assemblea. Difendete il Pensiero ch'essi minacciano, la Bellezza ch'essi oltraggiono![9]

> [Brand to the bone the stupid foreheads of those who would wish to put upon the human soul an exact mark like a social utensil, and to make all humanity to resemble nail-heads under the percussion of the nail-hammer. Your frantic laughs ascend to heaven when you hear the stablemen of the Great Beast cry aloud in the assembly, therefore proclaim and demonstrate for the glory of Intelligence that their sayings are as low as those indecent sounds with which the peasant expels from his mouth the wind from a stomach gorged with beans. Proclaim and demonstrate that their hands to which your father Dante would give the same epithet that he bestowed upon the nails of Thais, are adapted to pick up manure, but unworthy to be raised for the sanction of a law in the assembly. Defend the Thought that they menace, the Beauty they are outraging!][10]

The "Great Beast" in question is the parliamentary system against which D'Annunzio had already railed in an 1892 article entitled "La bestia elettiva" (The elective beast). The invective against it here takes on what will be a recurrent form in protofascism: political equality is figured as physical or spiritual equality, and thereby ridiculed and discredited.[11] As the basis of the parliamentary system, egalitarianism is rejected because it collapses a hierarchy that the ridiculers deem natural. The simultaneous translation of egalitarianism into the spiritual realm (all souls with the same mark) and into physical, "natural" form (all heads the same shape) thus eclipses the political. The passage also translates political inequality into stylistic terms as D'Annunzio, observing the rules of an obsolete literary decorum, employs a low style to speak of workers figured as peasants (the *stallieri*) and the lower part of the body politic (the epithet that Dante used to refer to Thaïs's fingernails was "shitty") and a high style to speak of aristocrats. (The English translator, out of a different sense of decorum and desire for stylistic homogeneity, effaces this difference and renders the passage into the dominant linguistic register — the aristocratic one — of the novel). This is not a "leftist" antiparliamentarism motivated by outrage at the corruption, through kickbacks and bribes, of a system whose worth is unquestioned, nor a radical antiparliamentarism that sees in bourgeois liberalism a mystification of true democracy, but rather an antiparliamentarism motivated by a refusal to grant the "mediocre" masses access to the political process (that is, a "rightist" antiparliamentarianism with roots in theorizations of the relation between the masses and the "elite" in the works of Vilfredo Pareto, Sighele, and others). Nothing could be less ambiguously protofascist.[12]

Yet protofascism is itself ambiguous, neither left nor right, both left and right, located in that "ambiguous space" described by Jameson. There is another way to read this passage that preserves this shiftiness: that is, to read it as a protest against commodification, against the kind of identity produced by commodity fetishism that was Adorno's obsession. Marx himself authorizes this connection when, in the first chapter of *Capital,* he links the commodity form to notions of political equality. In a famous paragraph, Marx explains why it is that Aristotle, great thinker though he was, could not understand how exchange was possible. Aristotle had tried to explain the secret of value, to understand how qualitatively different things, for example, five beds and one house, could be compared and exchanged. "Exchange," Aristotle reasoned, "cannot take place without equality, and equality not without commensurability."[13] This is as far as Aristotle is able to go, however, and the philosopher concludes that it is impossible that such unlike things as five beds and one house could be made equal; exchange is impossible, and yet it takes place, "a makeshift for practical purposes."[14] Marx, of course, can explain why Aristotle was stumped. The notion of equality was inaccessible to Aristotle, Marx argues, because of the material conditions of thought, because, that is, he lived in a society founded on slavery. The equality of human labor, that which is "really equal" in the five beds and one house, was, for Aristotle, unthinkable. Exchange can be thought of and the notion of value deciphered, Marx writes, only when "the notion of human equality has already acquired the fixity of a popular prejudice. This, however, is possible only in a society in which the great mass of the produce of labour takes the form of commodities, in which, consequently, the dominant relation between man and man, is that of owners of commodities."[15] The commodity form and notions of political equality thus develop dialectically, one thinkable only alongside the other, one the condition of possibility of the other. Arguments for or against one should, I would argue, therefore be read alongside arguments for or against the other. In the case of D'Annunzio's text, the argument against political equality is part of an aristocratic argument against the parliament, and yet if we read it dialectically, it may also be a protest against commodity fetishism, a protest against the reification of social relations, here literalized as souls are treated as social "utensils."

Less ambiguously and hence more stereotypically protofascist is another of the most often quoted passages in the novel:

> Per fortuna lo Stato eretto su le basi del suffragio popolare e dell'uguaglianza, cementato dalla paura, non è soltanto una costruzione ignobile ma è anche precaria. Lo Stato non deve essere se non un instituto perfettamente adatto a favorire la graduale elevazione d'una classe privilegiata verso un'ideal forma di esistenza. Su l'uguaglianza economica e politica, a cui aspira la democrazia, voi andrete dunque formando una oligarchia nuova, un nuovo reame della forza; e riuscirete in pochi, o prima o poi, a riprendere le redini per domar le moltitudini a vostro profitto. Non vi sarà troppo difficile, in vero, ricondurre il gregge all'obedienza. Le plebi restano sempre schiave, avendo un nativo bisogno di tendere i polsi ai vincoli. Esse non avranno dentro di loro giammai, fino al termine dei secoli, il sentimento della libertà. Non vi lasciate ingannare dalle loro vociferazioni e dalle loro contorsioni sconce; ma ricordatevi sempre che l'anima della Folla è in balìa del Pànico. (30–31)

> [Fortunately the State erected on the basis of popular suffrage and equality, and cemented by fear, is not only an ignoble construction, but also a precarious one. The State should be only an institution perfectly adapted to favor the gradual elevation of a privileged class towards an ideal form of existence. Upon the economical and political equality to which democracy aspires, you will go ahead forming a new oligarchy, a new kingdom of strength, and though in few, you will succeed sooner or later in retaking the reins, to command the multitudes to your advantage. It will not be greatly difficult to you in truth to reconduct the masses to obedience: plebeians remain ever slaves, having a native need of extending their wrists for the manacles; until the termination of centuries they will never have within themselves the sentiment of liberty. Do not let yourselves be deceived by their vociferations, and unseemly contortions, but remember that Panic controls the soul of a Crowd.] (46)

Lifted from D'Annunzio's 1892 "La bestia elettiva," parts of which were themselves lifted from an essay by Jean de Néthy, which in turn popularized notions from *Thus Spake Zarathustra*, this passage is part of the circulation and translation of Nietzschean notions in the fin de siècle.[16] As J. T. Schnapp notes, D'Annunzio's essay gives historical concreteness to what, for Nietzsche, was an atemporal philosophical allegory and thus aligns itself with that interpretation of Nietzsche that may be called the "fascist Nietzsche."[17] Some of that concreteness has been eliminated from the version that appears in *Le vergini:* in the essay, for example, it is not simply "democrazia" but "democrazia socialista e non socialista" [socialist and nonsocialist democracy]; the plebes are condemned to suffer "tanto all'ombra delle torri feudali quanto all'ombra dei feudali fumaiuoli nelle officine moderne" [as much in the shadow of feudal towers as in that of the feudal smokestacks of modern workshops]; historical anecdotes and personages, monarchs in particular, are offered as examples. But the editing is certainly not extensive enough to warrant recuperation by appealing to a more informed understanding of Nietzsche's texts, which might then be refound and completed in D'Annunzio's texts.[18] Indeed, that this is a fin de siècle ideologeme is marked in the novel itself by the attribution of this passage not to the protagonist Claudio Cantelmo but to one of many anonymous patricians puzzling over their fate in the modern world.

A third incriminating passage appears at the beginning of book 1:

> Il mondo è la rappresentazione della sensibilità e del pensiero di pochi uomini superiori, i quali lo hanno creato e quindi ampliato e ornato nel corso del tempo e andranno sempre più ampliando e ornandolo nel futuro. Il mondo, quale oggi appare, è un dono magnifico largito dai pochi ai molti, dai liberi agli schiavi; da coloro che pensano e sentono a coloro che debbono lavorare. (12)[19]

> [The world is the representation of the sensibility and the thought of a few superior men, who have created it and in the course of time broadened and adorned it and who will continue to amplify and adorn it in the future. The world, as it appears today, is a magnificent gift granted by the few to the many, from the free to the slaves, from those who think and feel, to those who must work.] (17)

Here again we can read the shiftiness of protofascist discourse. If, for example, *superiore* is taken in a physical rather than moral sense, as indeed it may in Italian, then the first sentence of this passage might even sound leftist: the world as the representation of a few men in high places could be the starting point for a critique of ideology. As Lucia Re writes in one of the best essays on the novel, "Had it been spoken from the perspective of the underdog (the slave or the son), it would have curiously coincided with Marx's diagnosis of the mechanisms governing the formation of ideologies."[20] The very possibility of this reading points to the way in which protofascism seems to oscillate between left and right; critiques of liberal bourgeois ideology and of capitalism come from both sides and cross wires as they do. But such a reading of the passage is, as its grammatical form suggests, contrary to the facts; the declaration comes not from the perspective of the underdog but from that of the exiled aristocrat. Re argues as well that the passage is "Nietzschean, in the spirit of the *Genealogy of Morals*," and attributes to it the force and function of the Nietzschean critique: "It points to the intrinsic violence of all ideologies (the *inventions* of superior, or stronger men), which are passed off as truths embedded in language."[21] But again, if the passage begins in a Nietzschean vein, by putting into play the question of the relation between political and moral "superiority," it ends by taking a detour to the right:

> Il mondo, quale oggi appare, è un dono magnifico largito dai pochi ai molti, dai liberi agli schiavi: da coloro che pensano e sentono a coloro che debbono lavorare. — E riconobbi quindi la più alta delle mie ambizioni nel desiderio di portare un qualche ornamento, di aggiungere un qualche valor nuovo a questo umano mondo che in eterno s'accresce di bellezza e di dolore. (12)

> [The world, as it appears today, is a magnificent gift granted by the few to the many, from the free to the slaves, from those who think and feel, to those who must work. And I recognized consequently the highest of my ambitions, in the desire to bring likewise some ornament, to add some new value to this human world that is eternally increasing in beauty and in grief.] (17)

The few give liberally, with largesse (*largire*), the "gift" of their representation of the world; Claudio would add "ornament" and "value," not, as with Nietzsche, call into question "the value of these values themselves."[22] Claudio's is not an investigation into the origins of values or ideologies as much as an imaginary institution and embellishment of those values. Book 1 contains in fact a fictional genealogy of the protagonist, as well as a literary genealogy of the text, in which "genealogy" brings with it none of the demystifying, epistemological force of the Nietzschean text but rather serves as the legitimating foundation of Claudio's project and of the literary *auctoritas* — in the language of Dante, Leonardo, and Bandello — of D'Annunzio's prose. From the Renaissance ancestor Alessandro, Cantelmo receives "la tavola delle mie leggi" (41) [the table of my laws], the authorization of political and reproductive project alike. There is no *pudenda origo* here: origins are, in the political narrative at least, illustrious ones, and Claudio's task is to perpetuate the lineage and values represented by the demonic ancestor Alessandro.

And yet again, in support of the "Nietzschean" hypothesis (and in illustration of the "shiftiness" of protofascism), we find force among the values represented by Alessandro: "Il mondo non può essere constituito se non su la forza" [The world can be constituted only upon strength] (44), opines another of the anonymous patricians. In illustration of his dictum, the patrician tells the story of the Scythians who, having spent twenty-eight years away from their homeland as they held Asia in their power, returned to find an army blocking their access. The army was, it turned out, formed of the children of their wives who, in the intervening years, had given themselves to their slaves; aware of their origins, the soldiers fought fiercely. When the Scythians realized that they could not defeat them with arms, one of the Scythians advised the others to put down their bows and arrows and approach their former slaves carrying only a whip. The mistake, he argued, was to have fought with arms, for in that way the slaves' sons felt they were equals and sons; seeing the nobles unarmed, he reasoned, the slaves would at once realize their station, surrender, and flee — which, of course, they did. The nobles' only remaining arm, in fact, is a *scudiscio,* a flexible wooden or leather whip used for whipping horses, whose etymology leads us from the Latin *scuticium, scuticus,* back to the Greek *skythikós,* from *skythai:* Scythian. The Scythians thus put down their arms and keep only their namesake, only the etymological emblem of their proper name, of their property as Scythians. Their force is, in other words, a moral quality not yet unmasked for the violence a truly Nietzschean critique would read in it. In the ideological fantasy that structures this fable, relations of domination and servitude are presented not as the result of violent appropriation and imposition but rather as positions or qualities intrinsic to the individuals themselves. Nobles are nobles because of their noble properties, and slaves are slaves because of their slavish properties; each recognizes those properties as such in the other. Violence is instead presented as the correlate of relations of equality.

To put it another way, and recalling again the opening chapters of *Capital,* social relations are fetishized in the fable: properties that are the effect of a network of social relations appear to the actors instead as "natural." The misrecognition proper to fetishism is nicely staged in the fable, for the slaves misrecognize the actual relations of force; they, after all, are winning in terms of physical force at the very moment in which they surrender and flee. Their interpretation — what is narrated as their "recognition" — of the nobles' gesture *inverts* the actual state of affairs, and it is this inversion that is characteristic of the structure of fetishism as Marx analyzes it. While Marx's analysis is devoted to solving the "mystery of money" and the secret of the fetishism of commodities, Marx adds a note that begins to solve the mystery of another kind of fetishism: "One man is king only because other men stand in the relation of subjects to him. They, on the contrary, imagine that they are subjects because he is king."[23] Slavoj Žižek explains the inversion thus:

> "Being-a-king" is an effect of the network of social relations between a "king" and his "subjects"; but — and here is the fetishistic misrecognition — to the participants of this social bond, the relationship appears necessarily in an inverse form; they think that they are subjects giving the king royal treatment because the king is already in himself, outside the relationship to his subjects, a king; as if the determination of "being-a-king" were a "natural" property of the person of the king.[24]

This fetishism is, Žižek argues, one that can occur only in precapitalist societies and is incompatible with the commodity fetishism of capitalist ones; in the transition from one society to the other, the "place of fetishism has just shifted from intersubjective relations to relations 'between things.' The crucial social relations, those of production, are no longer immediately transparent in the form of the interpersonal relations of domination and servitude."[25] As Marx might say, the "mystical character" of the king becomes the "mystical character of gold and silver."[26]

D'Annunzio's text brings together these two moments by binding together a protest against commodity fetishism, a protest that is part of the leftist heritage from Marx to the Frankfurt School, with a longing for a refetishization of social relations that emerges not only in the fable of the Scythians but in Cantelmo's longing for a charismatic leader: the "Re di Roma" [king of Rome] who would be the product of his reproductive union. This is the point at which, I would argue, we leave the checklist of protofascist "elements" behind and enter into a different ideological arena. It is also, of course, the point on which the critics of *superuomismo* stake their arguments for the precursory nature of D'Annunzio's text in relation to fascism. The question, to put it bluntly, is whether this "king" is the precursor of those "supermen" to come, Hitler and Mussolini, or whether he belongs to a different cultural field.

Claudio's "king" would be one whose kingly properties are intrinsic to him: "*natura ordinatus ad imperandum, dalla natura ordinato a imperare*" [ordered by nature to command] (39), writes D'Annunzio, citing Dante. It is essential that such a king appear outside of any relation to the subjects, for that relation, Claudio declares, debilitates him, restricts him to "l'officio umile e stucchevole assegnatogli per decreto fatto dalla plebe" (20) [the humble and annoying office assigned to him by decree of the people] (29). In the chapter devoted to Claudio's discussion with the old prince, this axiom is articulated again:

> Sia un Borbone o sia un Sabaudo sul trono, il Re è pur sempre assente; poiché non si chiama Re un uomo il quale, essendosi sottomesso alla volontà dei molti nell'accettare un officio ben determinato e angusto, si umilia a compierlo con la diligenza e la modestia di un publico scriba che la tema d'esser licenziato aguzzi senza tregua. (150)

> [Be it a Bourbon or a Savoyard who is upon the throne, the king is always absent, for one cannot call the man a king, who, submitting himself to the will of the people, in accepting a well-determined but hampered duty, humiliates himself to fulfill it with the diligence and modesty of a public scribe, whom the fear of being dismissed stimulates without respite]. (233)

D'Annunzio's formulation, "il re è pur sempre assente," recalls by negation the formulas associated with the medieval doctrine of the "king's two bodies" — "Imperium semper est" [Empire is eternal] and "Dignitas non moritur" [The office does not die] — and its sixteenth-century descendant, "Le roi ne meurt jamais" [The king never dies].[27] The sempiternity of the medieval king has been replaced by the sempiternal absence of modern kings. In other words, the problem with modern times, in this *deprecatio temporum,* is that the king is no longer truly a king, is absent even when he is present, because his relation to his subjects is defetishized, made visible as an office, a position in the social network to which he may be hired or fired, to which he might "freely" sell his labor, as it were. The solution offered by the narrative aims to restore the power of the king, to refetishize social relations, by severing the king's ties to his subjects. Claudio's model, the only king worth the name, is thus Ludwig of Bavaria: "Luigi di Baviera è veramente un Re; ma Re di sé medesimo e del suo sogno. Egli è incapace di imprimere la sua volontà su le moltitudini e di curvarle sotto il giogo della sua Idea" (152) [Louis of Bavaria is truly a king, a king of himself and of his dream; he is incapable of imprinting his will upon the multitude, and of bending them under the yoke of his idea] (236). Claudio's own exile and goal of internal sovereignty are motivated by this same desire to restore "intrinsic value" to the kingly. That this refetishization boomerangs as the kingly king is no longer capable of "impressing his will on the multitude" is not so much a philosophical failure of D'Annunzio's political project as it is the result of a second-order fetishism on the level of the ideological fantasy of the text itself.

Žižek's intertwining of Marx, Hegel, and Lacan in his notion of ideological fantasy is helpful in conceptualizing this second-order fetishism. For Žižek, ideological fantasy "consists in overlooking the illusion which is structuring our real, effective relationship to reality." Žižek translates Octave Mannoni's formulation of the fetishist's oscillation between knowledge and belief, the "je sais bien, mais quand même . . ." [I know very well, but all the same . . .], into the sphere of ideological analysis by combining it with Marx's formulation in the first chapter of *Capital* — "Sie wissen das nicht, aber Sie tun es" [They do not know it, but they do it] — in order to produce a description of ideology as fetishistic disavowal: "They know that, in their activity, they are following an illusion, but still they are doing it."[28] This overlooked illusion is the ideological fantasy; thus, in one of Žižek's most frequent examples, the anti-Semite knows very well that Jews "are guilty of nothing" but nevertheless will act as though they are, finding in the apparent innocence of his good Jewish neighbor only the confirmation of Semitic deviousness, and so on. In the case of the literary text at hand, we might say that the *text* knows very well that a sovereign's power exists only as the result of a network of social relations (and not as the expression of divine right or intrinsic qualities), but nevertheless it, the text, acts as though regality were an internal quality that could exist outside of any relation to subjects, as though it were possible to propose a refetishization of social relations. In other words, the narrative knows very well that it is no longer possible to be a king, and yet all the same it proposes a king as the goal of the political and reproductive project alike. The result of this ideological fantasy, itself a fetishistic structure, is a blockage of the novel's own ideological project, exemplified in the figure of Ludwig of Bavaria: the only true king is also a king incapable of exerting the sovereignty his solitude makes possible.

The oscillation between the text's knowledge and its disavowal of that knowledge accounts for a "splitting" of the text, just as fetishism accounts for what Freud calls *Ichspaltung,* or splitting of the ego. Critics have, in various ways, mimed rather than read this split. Hence the "splitting" apart of the political elements from the virgins' narrative that we have been addressing in this "split" reading is in fact a displaced symptom of a split internal to the text itself, a split that we are calling fetishistic.

Carlo Salinari, who also follows a "split reading" of the novel, has a rather different name for the blockage discussed above and for the internal splitting of the text.[29] He calls it *velleitarismo,* a state produced by a dispro- portion between one's goals and one's real abilities, and finds D'Annunzio's *superuomini* "stranamente divisi" [strangely divided] between their dreams and their capacities. Thus for Salinari, Claudio Cantelmo simply shoots too high when he sets out to generate a new king of Rome *and* find a woman so extraordinary that none of the three virgins could possibly mea- sure up. Similarly, D'Annunzio the writer shoots too high, and his work remains flawed by a disproportion between his modest roots and his as- pirations toward a position of prominence as a European writer. Writer and characters alike are *velleitari.* For Salinari, D'Annunzio's texts act out, apparently unconsciously, their author's failure, the disproportion between his own capacities and his performance. Oddly, this does not prevent Sali- nari from attributing to D'Annunzio powers of prophecy on a rather grand scale. He pokes fun at the critic Alfredo Gargiulo who, in 1912, ridiculed the character of Claudio Cantelmo — this aspirant to an ideal Latin type, reader of Nietzsche, tyrant of barbaric energies with plans for conquer- ing Rome — as completely and historically implausible. Salinari thinks he gets the last laugh when he writes of Gargiulo: "E non si accorgeva . . . del turbine che stava per travolgere l'Europa e dei superuomini violenti, tiran- nici e distruttori che stavano per apparire sulla scena politica" [And he was unaware . . . of the whirlwind that was about to devastate Europe as well as of the violent, tyrannical, destructive supermen who were about to appear on the political scene].[30] Though D'Annunzio's character does not man- age to produce a king of Rome, Salinari suggests that his literary text still manages to prophesy the coming of a Duce or a Hitler. If this is so, then D'Annunzio's artistic failure is his text's prophetic success. This backhanded compliment marks the strange division of Salinari's criticism that takes the failure of a character to be the failure of the text and yet attributes to the text a (prophetic) knowledge that it elsewhere vehemently denies. That di- vision might in turn be explained by an ideological fantasy of the leftist critic himself, who "knows very well that Mussolini was a ridiculous buf- foon à la Fellini, whose virility was a sham," and so on, and yet all the same acts in his criticism as though Mussolini were the fierce and sexually potent tyrant he imagines D'Annunzio — or his characters, no matter — to be.

The implications of my own reading are, I think, rather different. The fetishistic blockage is not a measure of failure (as though the novel would have been a "better one" had Cantelmo generated a son) but rather a knot that holds together an ideological oscillation between a knowledge and a disavowal of that knowledge. If these two are split apart (within the "split reading"), then we end up with failure coupled with prophecy, the failed D'Annunzio and the triumphant Duce. If read together (read *as* a fetishistic splitting), we get an ideological fantasy that imagines not the totalitarian leader, whose rule is legitimized through underlining the defetishization of social relations, but rather a king whose rule is possible only without subjects. The Duce, on the other hand, insistently and throughout the regime presents himself as the embodiment and conduit of the people's will. His persona in the 1920s tends to underline his common bond with the "people" and his essential Italianness: he is, in his own words, "un uomo come voi, con le vostre qualità, con i vostri difetti, con tutto ciò che costituisce l'elemento essenziale di quella speciale natura umana che è la natura italiana" [a man like you, with your qualities, with your defects, with all that constitutes the essential element of that special human nature that is Italian nature].[31] Even in the late 1930s, however, after the imperial rhetoric has taken a firm hold, Mussolini is still painted as "interprete del suo popolo" [interpreter of his people].[32] In this he fits Žižek's description of the totalitarian leader who says to his subjects not " 'You must follow me because I'm your Leader' but quite the opposite: 'In myself, I'm nothing, I am what I am only as an expression, an embodiment, an executor of your will.' "[33] These are not the words that would explain the functioning of D'Annunzio's king; one might imagine him rather saying: "I am what I am only in your absence; your presence unmasks me, reveals the secret of my mastery, makes me no longer a king." "Il re è pur sempre assente."

This is not to say that the Duce is not fetishized throughout the *ventennio*. Here Žižek's analysis of the fetishism operative in totalitarian (communist) regimes is of use in reconceptualizing the notion of the "charismatic leader" so important to studies on fascism. Žižek argues that through this defetishization of himself, the totalitarian leader accomplishes a refetishization of sorts: what is fetishized is not the leader, but the "people" as support of the "party." The people, in other words, come to be the repository of intrinsic value. A totalitarian (communist) regime can therefore be subverted not by exposing the leader's dependence upon the people but by revealing that "the instance to which he is referring to legitimize his rule (the People, the Class, the Nation) *does not exist* — or, more precisely, exists only through and in its fetishistic representative, the Party and its Leader."[34] This, it seems to me, describes the functioning of the totalitarian, fascist leader as well: the refetishization of the Duce that occurs in fascism is a fetishization of the people/nation *in* the leader. It is therefore not so much an attribution of value to the Duce as "superman" as the attribution of value to him insofar as he represents the Italian nation and people. His is the charisma of a nation, a people, a "race."

This hypothesis runs against the grain of studies on fascism that insist upon and perpetuate the notion of a charismatic leader and that focus on the elitist-superman-who-scorns-the-masses strand of fascist ideology. In fact, it makes visible the critics' own ideological fantasy, the illusion that structures their relation to reality. I would suggest that critics and historians who refetishize the "charismatic leader" do so because they *share* in the fetishization of the people. (This applies as well to the debunkers who aim to strip the Duce of charisma by revealing him to be an uncultured hooligan; the strategy attributes charisma to the Duce precisely in order to take it away, oscillating endlessly between attributions of magical power and revelations of brutal stupidity).[35] If, as Žižek writes, it is possible to subvert totalitarianism by showing that the people do not exist, critics and historians have been blocked in their attempts to accomplish such a subversion by their own belief that the people *do* exist outside of their relation to the leader. The dominant postwar strategy has been, in fact, to insist upon splitting the "people" off from the "Duce." The result of this splitting is a double-layered Freudo-Marxian fetishism of the left, in which both leader and people are fetishized. In one layer, the people occupy the position of the (Marxian) fetish whose intrinsic value is unrelated to the social network in which it finds itself; the Duce is "fool's gold," but the people are the real thing. The "people" are, in this sense, the fetish of both leftist and fascist populism, and salvaging the "people" becomes a principal goal of "consensus" studies: notions of "collective nicodemism," a *paese reale,* or a "fascism without fascists" all work to save the fetishized people from fascism itself. Yet critics and historians know perfectly well that this "people" antiseptically separate from the leader doesn't exist ("Ils savent bien, mais . . . "); in order to maintain their own populist position as separate and distinct from that of fascism, they must disavow that knowledge. Thus it happens that, in the other layer, the leader is refetishized: the charismatic leader functions as the (Freudian) fetish who stands in for and covers over the "lack" that is the nonexistence of the People-as-distinct-from-the-Duce (in this case the people would be analogous to the maternal phallus, and the leader, the fetish that stands in the place of its absence). The result of this doubly layered fetishism is a disavowal on a grand scale of the importance that populism plays in fascism. This is where D'Annunzio becomes important in maintaining the fantasy: critics *need* the antipopulist D'Annunzio because Mussolini brings them too close to the populism whose presence they disavow. D'Annunzio's "superman" texts allow critics to overlook the fetishization of the people, allow them not to recognize the absence that the fetish covers over, and allow them to substitute for it a refetishization of the leader that mimes the refetishization that D'Annunzio's Ludwig represents.

To return to Le vergini, then, we might say that just as the text is not prophetic but looks backward (impossibly), it also looks forward (impossibly). The precursor relation is thematized in book 1 when Claudio calls his ancestor Alessandro a "precursor of himself":

> Tu non fosti, in quel tempo, se non l'annunciatore e il precursore di te medesimo, dovendo riapparire su dal tuo ceppo longevo nella maturità del secoli futuri, alla soglia di un mondo non anche esplorato dai guerrieri ma già promesso dai sapienti: riapparire come il messaggio l'interprete, e il padrone d'una vita nuova... Ed esca il tuo eguale dalla mia genitura! (39)

> [Thou at that period wert but the announcer and precursor of thyself, destined to appear again from thy long-lived stock in the maturity of future centuries, at the threshold of a world not yet explored by warriors, but already promised by the sages: to reappear as the message, the interpreter, the master of a new life... that thy equal may be begotten by me!] (60–61)

At least two moments are necessary to make a precursor: an old testament and a new, a promise and its fulfillment, an event and its retrospectively established origin. Only Claudio's action makes Alessandro a precursor of himself; that is, Alessandro's reappearance in Claudio's narrative constitutes his "second moment." But neither Alessandro nor Claudio can truly be a precursor if there is no son, no "He is who to come," to acknowledge retroactively the precursor. One cannot chose to be a precursor; one is chosen. To understand what the novel has to say about the precursory relation, however, I must put an end to the "split reading" of the "political" narrative and join it to the fairy tale of the virgins, for it is the question of "choice" that constitutes the point of articulation between the two.[36]

Medusa and Rhetoric

How then are the "political" narrative and the narrative of the virgins bound together? It seems to me that the question of choice, as it is articulated through an interchangeability of the crowd and woman, forges the link between the two. Possessed of the "table of his laws," Claudio heeds the voice of Alessandro as he dispenses Machiavellian advice: "Non t'indugiare; non ti lasciar contaminare dalla folla, né ti lasciar prendere da una femmina.... Bisogna che tu non dimentichi mai questa sentenza del

tuo Leonardo, e che tu possa sempre rispondere superbamente come Castruccio: — Io ho preso lei non ella me" (41–42) [Do not delay; be neither
contaminated by the multitude nor taken by a woman.... Never forget
this sentence of thy Leonardo's, and mayst thou always be able to answer proudly, like Castruccio: "I took her, not she me!"] (63–64). Woman
and the crowd are inserted into identical and parallel syntactic structures.
Rhetorically an example of isocolon, the parallel constructions suggest that
the terms can be exchanged one for the other: Don't let yourself be contaminated by the crowd, nor taken by a woman; and vice versa: Don't let
yourself be contaminated by a woman, nor taken by the crowd. But if
woman and the crowd can be exchanged, the "I" here should precisely not
be exchanged with either of those terms: "I chose her not she me." What is
at stake is the blockage of an exchangeability, grammatical as well as ideological: the male, aristocratic "I" should only be the subject of the choice,
and not its object, while "she" should only be "her" and not "she," the
object of the choice but not its subject. And just as "she" should not be
the subject of the choice but only its object, so the crowd should not be
the subject of choice. Yet choice, in the form of suffrage and democracy
(the targets of attack in book 1), is precisely what the crowd wants. The
crowd wants choice and has infected the city. The subsequent paragraphs
describe the *contagio* that the crowd brings with it, destroying the state, civilization, and beauty from within. This crowd has made a king impossible —
that king who is absent even when he is present is so because of the crowd,
because the crowd's choice has turned him into an employee of the state.

The crowd's choice is, in the *deprecatio temporum,* countered by another
choice, or, to pay closer attention to the language of the text, their *elezione*
is countered by another sort of *elezione,* one election pitted against another.
The Dantesque meaning of "election," the free choice of God in select-
ing souls for eternal glory ("credevi a una virtù di stirpe la qual potesse
per gradi, d'elezione in elezione, elevar l'uomo al più alto splendore di sua
bellezza morale" [26] [Thou believdst firmly in a virtue of races, that could
by degree, choice after choice elevate man to the highest splendor of his
moral beauty] [38]), is opposed to the "elections" that universal suffrage
would bring; the *vóto* of the old prince ("Il Re delle Due Sicilie finirà i
suoi giorni sul suo trono legittimo. E mi conceda Iddio che questo si com-
pia prima ch'io chiuda gli occhi! Ecco l'unico mio vóto" [83] [The king of
the Two Sicilies will finish his days in glory upon his legitimate throne, and
my only prayer is that God may permit this to be accomplished before my
eyes are closed] [129]), where *vóto* has the nonsecular meaning of "prayer"

and the nonpolitical sense of desire or wish, is counterposed to another vote, the political vote of the masses; the *officio* of the poets ("Difendete la Bellezza! E' questo il vostro unico officio" [28] [Defend Beauty! This is your sole office] [43]), their sacred duty and calling, is contrasted with the *officio umile* (20) [humble office] (29), the humble political office that reduces the king to a functionary. To the secular term is opposed its non-secular homonym as if to combat the "contagion" caused by the crowd. This contagion within the *deprecatio temporum* spreads to the narrative of the virgins: Claudio's "choice" is not a *scelta* but an *elezione;* he sets out not to choose in a banal secular way, as the verb *scegliere* would have suggested, but rather to *eleggere,* to elect one from among the three women. Reading the two narratives together thus necessarily politicizes the narrative of the virgins, forces us to read it as a meditation on the possibilities and impossibilities not only of spiritual election but of political election as well.

The two narratives share not only a double-edged lexicon; they are also structurally parallel. Both the state, in the political narrative, and the family, in the narrative of the virgins, are being destroyed from within: the state by the crowd, the family by the mother. And both participate in logics of fetishism: in the political narrative, fetishism surrounds the figure of the monarch; in the narrative of the virgins, it is around the mother that the narrative stages a fetishistic moment of revelation. For the moment at least, those fetishisms can be named separately: a Marxian fetishism in the former case, and a Freudian fetishism in the latter.

This is not as much of a leap as it may seem. Freud himself suggests a political parallel to the "moment of revelation" that turns the little boy into a fetishist. The scenario is a familiar one: the little boy refuses to "take cognizance of the fact perceived by him that a woman has no penis. No, that cannot be true, for if a woman can be castrated then his own penis is in danger." Immediately after these phrases, in the essay titled "Fetishism," Freud writes that "in later life grown men may experience a similar panic, perhaps when the cry goes up that Throne and Altar are in danger."[37] Throne and altar are surely in danger here: like Claudio, the "anima senile" [senile soul] who occupies a Trasteverine "cupola solitaria" [solitary dome] and the "Re di stirpe guerriera" [king of a warrior race] who inhabits "un'altra dimora inutilmente eccelsa" [that other dome above, uselessly sublime] (29) have been disempowered (19). But the connection to *Le vergini* runs much deeper than this superficial similarity. There is, within Freudian fetishism, an important link to the question of choice. The fetish itself functions to suspend a decision — the decision between castrated and not castrated — in an infinite oscillation that Jacques Derrida and Sarah Kofman, among others, have called undecidable.[38] The fetishist simultaneously affirms and denies castration through the fetish that stands in for the presence and absence of the maternal phallus. The subtlest fetish, according to Freud's essay, accomplished precisely this: the *Schamgürtel,* or "suspensory belt," allowed the possibility that a woman could be castrated, or that she might not, or that a man might be castrated, or might not. The English translation as "suspensory belt" neatly names the function of the fetish for the fetishist and of the logic of fetishism for *Le vergini.* Indeed, the only "suspense" one could speak of in this novel is that of the "suspension" of a decision, of the choice among three women.[39] The necessity of that suspension, for the fetishist, lies in the possibility of an exchangeability: if woman can be castrated, then a man can be castrated; what applies to the little girl could apply to the little boy. We can thus say that fetishism is a strategy that blocks a certain exchangeability: as D'Annunzio might put it, it makes sure that I choose her, not she me.

The little boy's story, as recounted in three of Freud's essays from the 1920s pertaining to the "moment of revelation" ("Fetishism," "Medusa's Head," and "Some Psychological Consequences of the Anatomical Distinction between the Sexes"), returns again and again to "the terror of castration that is linked to the sight of something": sister, mother, Medusa. That "sight" is a double vision. The revelation is structured as taking place in two moments: a first moment in which "nothing is seen," the child seeing nothing or disavowing what he has seen, and a second moment in which what is seen is seen *as* nothing, as an absence.[40] Freud's infantile theorist does not ever see "castration" but rather "sees" an interpretation of an earlier perception. The narrative of the virgins also returns again and again to the taboo sight of the mother. Antonello, the less sickly of the brothers, promises Claudio that he will be spared the sight of her:

> Quando posi il piede su la soglia, l'imagine fantastica della demente mi ri-apparve così viva e così fiera ch'io n'ebbi un segreto brivido. Tutto il luogo mi sembrò tenuto dalla sua dominazione sinistra, attristato e atterrito dalla sua onnipresenza....
> — Non vorrei che temeste...Voi non la vedrete...Ho potuto fare in modo che non la vediate, in queste ore almeno. (70–71)

> [When I paused, with my foot on the threshold, the image of the insane woman reappeared to me so full of life and cruelty that I had a secret shivering at it. The whole place was as if under her sinister domination, saddened and terrified by her omnipresence....

I would not have you fear, you will not see her; I have arranged so that in these hours at least you will not see her. (110–11)

Even this first mention of the mother is, on closer examination, fetishistic: her fantastic presence ("l'imagine fantastica") is combined with her promised absence. But as Antontello promises, the first time Claudio sees not her but rather her empty sedan-chair, which Antonello hastens to explain is used "by no one of us." Claudio, who feels himself attracted by this "vecchia cosa che non anche pareva ben morta" (90) [old thing that did not seem quite dead yet] (139), examines and opens it to discover a particular odor: "La portantina odorava come un cofano di nozze" (90) [The sedanchair smelled like a wedding chest] (140). Freud would have little trouble in explaining the uncanny feeling ("un'inquietudine strana" [strange inquietude]) that Claudio experiences in the face of this maternal thing "not quite dead" that smells like marriage and appears in a "casket."[41] Here is the *pudenda origo* missing from the political narrative, the original maternal *pudendum*. This first moment, in which there is "nothing" to be seen, is followed by a second when the sedan chair is occupied by the mother herself:

A traverso l'apertura dello sportello, sul fondo di velluto verdastro, io vidi allora il volto della principessa demente: irriconoscibile, contraffatto da un gonfiore esangue, simile a una maschera di neve, con i capelli rialzati su la fronte in guisa d'un diadema. Gli occhi larghi e neri splendevano su la bianchezza opaca della pelle, sotto l'arco imperioso delle sopracciglia, mantenuti forse nel loro splendore straordinario dalla visione continua d'un fasto inaudito. La carne del mento s'increspava su i monili ond'era cinto il collo. E quella enormità pallida e inerte mi risuscitò nell'imaginazione non so qual figura sognata di vecchia imperatrice bisantina, al tempo d'un Niceforo o d'un Basilio, pingue e ambigua come un eunuco, distesa in fondo alla sua lettiga d'oro. (115)

[Through the opening in the door, against the background of greenish velvet, I then saw the face of the demented princess, unrecognizable, disfigured by a bloodless swelling, like a mask of snow, her hair, raised up in front after the manner of a diadem, while the great black eyes maintained, perhaps, in their extraordinary magnificence by the continual vision of unheard of and wonderful pageantry, glittered in the opaque whiteness of the flesh, under the imperious arch of the eyebrows. The flesh of the chin wrinkled over the necklaces with which the throat was girdled, and that pallid, inert enormity resuscitated in my imagination a dream figure, of some old Byzantine empress at the time of a Nicephorus or Basil, stretched within her golden litter, fat and ambiguous as a eunuch.] (178)

This moment of revelation is already a fetishistic moment (as indeed it is in Freud) as the narrative proceeds metonymically up to the "last thing seen": first the window, then the velvet, then the sight of the . . . face. The displacement upward puts on a disguise, for this is a face that is unrecognizable, disfigured, like a mask, and the "pale and inert enormity" of the mother's body (Lacan's Maternal Thing?) renders ambiguous the "thing" that was to have been revealed: "fat and ambiguous as a eunuch," she may be castrated and yet seems not to be. Even when he sees it, he can't really see it. But D'Annunzio says it better:

> Allora i miei occhi si armarono di una curiosità nuova; e m'assalì quasi una smania inquieta di riguardare, di considerare più attentamente le tre persone, come se non le avessi bene vedute. E notai anche una volta qual arduo enigma di linee sia ogni forma feminina e quanto sia difficile *vedere* non pur le anime ma i corpi. Quelle mani in fatti, alle cui dita lunghe avevo cinto i miei più sottili sogni come anelli invisibili, quelle mani mi sembravano già diverse apparendomi come i ricettacoli d'infinite forze innominate da cui potevano sorgere meravigliose generazioni di cose nuove. (110)

> [Then my eyes armed themselves with a new curiosity, and an uneasy, burning wish assailed me to examine, to consider the three persons more attentively; I noted once more what an arduous enigma of outlines every feminine form may be, and how difficult it is to *see* not even the souls, but the bodies. Those hands, in fact, around whose long fingers I had girdled like invisible rings my most subtle dreams, already seemed to me different, appearing like the receptacles of infinite, unnamed forces, from which would issue marvelous generations of new things.] (170–71)

What kind of difficulty in seeing the female body requires that Claudio arm his eyes? As if in explanation, the eyes of the narrative look away, to the "hands" that are the principal thematic fetish in the novel. More interesting than those hands, however, is the "strange analogy" that continues the passage:

> E imaginai, per un'analogia strana, l'ansia e il dolore di quel giovine principe che, essendo stato chiuso in un luogo oscurissimo con la necessità di eleggere il suo destino fra gli inconoscibili destini recatigli da messaggiere taciturne, passò tutta la notte palpando le mani fatali che si tendevano verso di lui nella tenebra. Le mani della tenebra: — v'è forse una più paurosa imagine del mistero? (111)

> [And, by a strange analogy, I imagined the anxiety and the pain of that young prince, who, being confined in a most gloomy spot, with the necessity of choosing his fate from among the unknowable destinies brought to him by taciturn messengers, passed the entire night feeling the fatal hands stretched

towards him in the darkness. Hands in the darkness — does there exist a more frightful image of mystery?] (171)

This "strange analogy" pulls a thread of the political narrative back into the fabric of the narrative of the virgins: the verb used is, once again, not *scegliere* but rather *eleggere* — Claudio's word of choice — and the situation described seems to imply that the young prince is receiving something like "votes" that will decide his destiny, one of which he must "elect" for himself. A strange "election" is taking place in this very dark place. But whence the horror, and what is the analogy? Clearly, the hands form the link: the prince only feels hands, but cannot see them; the narrator only sees hands, and they multiply before his armed eyes. The analogy seems to be that in both cases the hands seem to exist independently of the body, and the body, the rest of the body, is invisible, kept in the dark. Now that should be good for the fetishist, since after all what he wants is to keep castration in the dark and let his fetish stand in its place, out in the open. But the problem here — the horror, the horror — is that the prince is locked up in the dark with the necessity of choosing, the necessity of election. The horror is, in equal measure, sexual and political. Shortening the phrase, he is "chiuso in un luogo oscurissimo con la necessità," with none other than Necessity herself, who has already made an appearance in the text. Necessitas, the mother of the Fates, is named on the second page of the novel: "Dissimili alle tre sorelle antiche perché non figlie ma vittime della Necessità..." (4) [Unlike the sisters three of antiquity, because not daughters but victims of fate...] (2) — such are the three sisters, all victims of their mother. The prince, then, is locked up in the dark with the mother, in the dark with the castrated mother. And as if it weren't bad enough to be holed up with the castrated mother, he is also holed up with the necessity of election, with a phantasm of the very election that would turn him into an absent king. "Il re è pur sempre assente," fetishistically present and absent at one and the same time.

If the mother is Necessity, though, Claudio does not escape the fate of the prince by avoiding her. His fate lies with a trio of sisters, though not any of the trios that Freud mentions in "The Theme of the Three Caskets," the Freudian text that analyzes a man's choice among three women. The trio that Freud does not see in that essay, for no doubt very good Freudian reasons, is one that D'Annunzio can see with his own armed eyes, the Gorgons: "Come le Càriti, come le Gòrgoni e come le Moire, tre erano le vergini" (124) [Like the Charities, the Gorgons, and the Moerae, the virgins were three] (193). And, like mother like daughter: Violante, the third sister, is also the third sister Medusa. This is right there on the surface of the text for all to see: during her pregnancy, the mother wore a ring bearing a "ritratto di Violante" [portrait of Violante] whose "lineamento medusèo" (77) [Medusan lineaments] (120) Claudio admires. And Violante offers to Claudio "her secret" in the form of a landscape whose "Medusan iconography" Lucia Re has already pointed out:

> Il dirupo scendeva quasi a picco, sotto i contrafforti massicci da cui era munita la muraglia settentrionale, profondandosi fino a un aspro alveo biancastro che pur nella sua aridità minacciava le rovinose collere del torrente. . . . Tutte le più crude convulsioni e contrazioni dei corpi posseduti da energie demoniache o da spasimi letali, tutte parevano fisse in quella compagine orrida come la balza ove Dante ebbe l'indizio dei nuovi martirii prima di giungere alla riviera del sangue custodita dai Centauri. Tutti i modi delle materie pieghevoli e scorrevoli vi parevano finti a contrasto del duro sasso: i cirri delle capellature ribelli, i viluppi delle serpi azzuffate, gli intrichi delle radici divelte, gli avvolgimenti delle viscere, i fasci dei muscoli, i circoli dei gorghi, le pieghe delle tuniche, i rotoli delle funi. Il fantasma d'una turbolenza frenetica si levava da quella immobilità perfetta a cui il meriggio toglieva qualunque ombra. (78)

> [The precipice descended almost perpendicularly under the massive props with which the northern wall was furnished, sinking downward to the whitish, rugged bed of a river that even in its dryness still menaced with the ruinous wrath of a torrent. . . . The roughest, the rudest contractions of bodies possessed by demoniacal energies or by destructive spasms appeared transfixed in that horrid structure, like the precipice, where the new martyrs were indicated to Dante, before reaching the river of blood guarded by the Centaurs, and in it also every kind of material, flexible and fluid, seemed invented to contrast with the hard stone — curls of rebellious heads of hair, throngs of fighting serpents, intricacies of uprooted growths, twistings of entrails, bunches of muscles, circlings of whirlpools, folds of membranes, coils of rope. The specter of a frantic turbulence arose from that perfect immobility from which the noontide swept every shadow, and the palpitation of a vehement fever seemed compressed by that inert crust.] (123)

The allusion to Medusa's coiffure ("i cirri delle capellature ribelli, i viluppi delle serpi azzuffate") is not the only tip-off: the "duro sasso" recalls the effect of the Medusa (one hears Petrarch: "Medusa e l'error mio m'han fatto un sasso") as does the perfect immobility of the rocky landscape. The *gorghi* [whirlpools] paronomastically insert the name of the Gorgon herself into the petrified scene and once again quilt a strand of the political into the fabric of the narrative of the virgins: the *gorghi* are part of the landscape formed by the crowd:

— Voi vedete, mio caro padre, — io ripresi a dire, senza poter frenare i palpiti che mi sembravano ripercuotersi nella voce — voi vedete che da per tutto le antiche regalità legittime declinano e che la Folla sta per inghiottirle nei suoi gorghi melmosi. (153)

["You see, dear father," I went on to say, unable to restrain the palpitations that reverberated in my voice, "you see old, legitimate royalty declining every-where, and that the multitude, the masses stand ready to engulf it in their slimy abysses.] (237)

The crowd's relation to royalty is, again, parallel to that of Violante to Claudio. But what specifically is the double Medusan threat? Re reads the deathly threat of the Medusa in Violante's landscape to be the threat of death itself and, in an etymological footnote on the names "Castruccio" and "Castromitrano," alludes to the political and sexual castration implied. There is, I think, yet another threat nested within these threats of death and castration, a threat already contained in the intertextual network that forms the Medusa's genealogy and that appears in *Le vergini* through a Dantean allusion at the end of the description of Violante's landscape:

Ma, stando noi reclinati verso la roccia multiforme, eravamo congiunti l'uno all'altra da quel fascino che accomuna coloro i quali leggono insieme in un medesimo libro. Noi leggevamo in un medesimo libro affascinante e periglioso. (79)

[But standing, bent towards the multiform rock, we were drawn one to the other by that fascination that gives common enjoyment to those who read together in the same book, for we were reading together in a book at once charming and perilous.] (123)

The "book" refers to the landscape quoted above, though the intertextual citation is of course from canto 5 of the *Inferno* where the "book" is the "Galeotto" that brought together Paolo and Francesca; the first-person plural imperfect tense, "noi leggevamo," is forever marked by Francesca's plaintive and coy "Noi leggiavamo un giorno per diletto / di Lancialotto" [We read one day for pastime / of Lancelot]. On the one hand, this citation might be coupled with the other Dantean allusion in the passage; that other allusion is to canto 12, which describes the circle of the violent in which those who were violent against blood relations are immersed in a river of boiling blood, and their common element brought out: Francesca's adultery also violated blood relations. On the other hand, the citation can be cou-pled with a Medusan difficulty: the problem of interpretation as it led to adultery in canto 5, and the threat to interpretation that is Medusa's threat in canto 9.[42]

In order to articulate this Medusan threat in more specific terms, we need to take a detour through the Freud essay that Lucia Re reads together with *Le vergini*. The essay is the already mentioned "Theme of Three Caskets," which itself takes on a problem of interpretation: "Who are these three sisters and why must the choice fall on the third?"[43] Why, when cataloguing groups of three sisters, does Freud not see the Gorgons? The three goddesses from among whom Paris chooses Aphrodite, the three sisters of the Cinderella story and of *King Lear*, the Norns, the Horae, the Moerae, all might have led to the Gorgons. But instead, Freud begins to multiply: from stories about three women he switches to a fairy tale about twelve boys that, he notes, is the ninth story in Grimm's fairy tales, and from there to the story of the six swans, and then back again to the three sisters that are the Fates, and finally to Death herself. Why all the multiplication along what Freud refers to as a devious route? As Freud himself will later observe, the Medusa does indeed have something to do with multiplication. There is an easier explanation: the Gorgons do not supply a story of a man choosing among three women. What they do supply, however, is of more than a little interest for *Le vergini;* a narrative about seeing without being seen, about making sure to remain a subject rather than being turned into an object.

There are of course many versions of how Perseus slays the Gorgon: two in particular have to do with whether or not she sees you.[44] In one version, the Gorgons had but a single eye among the three of them and took turns using it; Perseus succeeds in beheading Medusa only because one of the other Gorgons has the use of the eye at that moment. In another version, Minerva gives Perseus a special mirror that makes all things visible but makes him invisible. In both cases, Perseus cannot be seen by Medusa, for being the object of her sight meant petrification; her threat, in other words, is not that you have to avoid seeing *her* but rather that you must make sure that she doesn't see *you*. Her threat is that she turns you into an object (of her sight): she sees you, or, as D'Annunzio might put it, she chooses you (if, that is, you are a man, since Medusa had no effect upon other women). These are versions that Freud does not see in his essay on Medusa: the terror of castration is a terror linked to the sight of something, but that something in the Medusa essay doesn't look back. Freud's Medusa is the object of sight, not its subject; his essay already wears the head of Medusa as an apotropaic against Medusa herself.

At least one reason for Freud's not seeing her in the "Three Caskets" essay has to do with the "magic wand" that he waves when he discards several versions of his theme in which the tables are turned and a *woman* chooses among men. The first two versions Freud mentions, an Estonian folk epic and the *Gesta romanorum*, tell not of a man's choice among three women but of a woman's choice among three men and/or three caskets. In these cases, writes Freud, "the subject is a girl choosing between three suitors." In the *Merchant of Venice*, however, an inversion takes place that allows Freud to strip "the astral garment from our theme" and "see that the theme is a human one, *a man's choice between three women*": Bassanio's choice between three caskets is, Freud argues, a choice among three women. (Freud's version is untroubled by the fact that there are three caskets in Shakespeare's play, one woman, and three men . . . , but that is only the first of several arithmetic problems that will arise.) If we reinvert his inversion, however, and consider the discarded versions, we may discover a different "human theme."

In the *Gesta romanorum*, an emperor puts a king's daughter to the test before allowing her to marry his son. Three caskets are made, one of gold, one of silver, and one of lead; the first and most beautiful contains bones of the dead; the second, earth; and the third, three precious rings. The story insists on a contrast between container and contents, a disjunction of metonymy that must be deciphered; this is the first hint that questions of rhetoric and interpretation are at stake. And that is not all that requires interpretation: each of the caskets bears an inscription. The girl's choice is thus above all a test of her interpretive skill.

Freud, however, does not mention the inscriptions and moves quickly on to the "inverted" truth of the story that he finds in the *Merchant of Venice*. In haste to show how psychoanalytic interpretation can strip the garments from the theme, Freud applies a kind of Catholic arithmetic to the plot so that three men become one, Bassanio, while one woman, Portia, becomes three caskets. What drops out of the picture as a result is the element of competition between men: three men compete at guessing the contents of the caskets from the inscriptions written on them. Once again, the story stages a contest in interpretation; Freud, who as we know was particularly prickly when it came to contests in interpretation, does not care to see the question of rhetoric and its interpretation as central even to Bassanio's winning speech. The passage is worth quoting in its entirety (no matter how far we may seem from fascism at the moment), for it is instructive to note what Freud left out when he waved his wand:

> So may the outward shows be least themselves —
> The world is still deceiv'd with ornament.
> In law, what plea so tainted and corrupt
> But, being season'd with a gracious voice,

Obscures the voice of evil? In religion,
What damned error but some sober brow
Will bless it, and approve it with a text,
Hiding the grossness with fair ornament?
There is no vice so simple but assumes
Some mark of virtue on his outward parts.
How many cowards, whose hearts are all as false
As stairs of sand, wear yet upon their chins
The beards of Hercules and frowning Mars,
Who inward search'd, have livers white as milk,
And these assume but valor's excrement
To render them redoubted! Look on beauty,
And you shall see 'tis purchas'd by the weight,
Which therein works a miracle in nature,
Making them lightest that wear most of it.
So are those crisped snaky golden locks,
Which make such wanton gambols with the wind
Upon supposed fairness, often known
To be the dowry of a second head,
The skull that bred them in the sepulchre.
Thus ornament is but the guiled shore
To a most dangerous sea; the beauteous scarf
Veiling an Indian beauty; in a word,
The seeming truth which cunning times put on
To entrap the wisest. Therefore then, thou gaudy gold,
Hard food for Midas, I will none of thee;
Nor none of thee, thou pale and common drudge
'Tween man and man; but thou, thou meagre lead,
Which rather threaten'st than dost promise aught,
Thy paleness moves me more than eloquence![45]

In a previous passage, the gold casket was chosen by another of Portia's suitors and found to hold a portrait of Death (in this, it is faithful to the *Gesta romanorum*); in this passage, gold is rejected as hard food for Midas, while the silver casket is described as "pale and common drudge." This should have posed a problem for Freud, since he quotes the final line of the above passage, "Thy paleness moves me more than eloquence!" as proof that the third casket — as pallor and dumbness — signifies death. But both the silver and the lead are described as pale, and the gold contains Death's likeness; if all three are death, how can one argue that only the meaning of the third is death? What is, for Shakespeare, the difference between the caskets? Bassanio's speech spells it out: an example of the "rhetoric of antirhetoric," it claims that the difference between the third casket and the previous two is that the third is without ornament, without eloquence;

the third is antirhetorical and stands for plain speech. What is at stake in the oppositions operative in the passage is hermeneutics itself: appearance ("outward shows") as it hides essence, cosmetics ("the weight which therein works a miracle") as they mask nature, falsehood ("a plea so tainted and corrupt") as it conceals the truth ("the voice of evil"), rhetoric ("ornament") as it disguises plain speech. Had Freud read his own footnotes, he might have seen this. He, not James Strachey (the translator), notes the variant "plainness" for "paleness" and writes that "in Schegel's translation this allusion to death is lost; indeed it is given the opposite meaning: 'Thy plainness speaks to me with eloquence.' "[46] Surely Freud, whose principal strategy in the essay is to assign to things an opposite meaning — women become men, beauty becomes death, and so on — should have entertained this antonymy as well, for Schegel's translation quite shrewdly captured Bassanio's strategy. Similarly, Freud might well have noticed a Medusa standing in for cosmetics and eloquence: like the "weight, / Which therein works a miracle in nature, / Making them lightest that wear most of it," the Medusan coiffure, "those crisped snaky golden locks," are often found upon a death's head and are yet another form of "seeming truth." And her petrifying effect sneaks in with her alliterative and stony relative, Midas.

Freud's second Shakespearean example, *King Lear,* similarly stages a competition: three women compete in oratorical display. Standard readings of Cordelia's "speech" are that sincere, truthful Cordelia won't play along, that, as Freud takes it, she will not speak, or speaks only unrhetorical truth. But as Paolo Valesio has shown, Cordelia's disavowal of "that glib and oily art / To speak and purpose not" is every bit as strategic, rhetorically speaking, as her sisters' more obviously "glib and oily" speeches: her "rhetoric of antirhetoric" adopts, as does Bassanio's, extremely sophisticated rhetorical strategies in the argument against rhetoric itself.[47] The two speeches, in fact, share not only a general strategy but also similar conceits:

> I yet beseech your Majesty —
> If for I want that glib and oily art
> To speak and purpose not, since what I well intend,
> I'll do't before I speak — that you make known
> It is no vicious blot, murther, or foulness,
> No unchaste action, or dishonored step,
> That hath depriv'd me of your grace and favor,
> But even for want of that for which I am richer —
> A still-soliciting eye, and such a tongue
> That I am glad I have not, though not to have it
> Hath lost me in your liking.[48]

In Bassanio's speech, it is weight that makes the wearer lighter; in Cordelia's, want that makes her richer. And, like the lead casket in Bassanio's speech, Cordelia threatens rather than promises aught: in her earlier response to her father, her threat is the threat of nothing:

> CORDELIA: Nothing, my Lord.
> LEAR: Nothing?
> CORDELIA: Nothing.
> LEAR: Nothing will come of nothing, speak again.

The "nothing" that she promises is, in Elizabethan English, also the "nothing" that the fetishist is loath to see: the female genitals. There is thus in Cordelia's answer, as in Bassanio's speech, a Medusan threat.

The link between Medusa and rhetoric that we have sketched out in these two Shakespearean texts can be confirmed by two other citations from the Medusan intertextual field: one that D'Annunzio quite surely knew, given the Platonizing of *Le vergini,* and another that he was quite likely to have known, given his erudition.[49] The first is from Plato's *Symposium:*

> Agathon's speech reminded me of Gorgias, and put me exactly in the posi-
> tion of the man in Homer; I was afraid that he would end by turning on
> my speech the Gorgon's head of Gorgias, that formidable orator, and thus
> reducing me to the speechlessness of a stone.[50]

The paronomasia "Gorgias"/"Gorgon" allows Plato to figure Agathon's eloquence as having the dazzling effect of the Gorgon: his oratorical display threatens to render Socrates speechless as a stone, deprive him of his oratorical gift. This move is opposite to Freud's: Freud interprets the speechlessness he finds again and again in folktales and literary examples of his theme as figures for death; Plato instead takes the petrification of the Medusa, literally death, to be a figure for a loss of speech or oratorical skill. This Platonic tradition is revived in the Renaissance, as Coluccio Salutati confirms: "Medusa is artful eloquence."[51] Salutati simply gives us in abbreviated form what we might have gotten more laboriously from a reading of the Medusa in Dante or Petrarch.

If Medusa is the third sister and a figure for rhetoric, why is it that the lead casket and Cordelia are figured as unrhetorical, as plain speech, truth, or speechlessness? Following Freud's lead, we may see in it simply another inversion: just as death could be figured by beauty, so rhetoric comes to be figured by truth. But this second reversal is one that Freud is not alone in overlooking, for it is not so easily explained as a wish fulfillment: it is one thing to say that rhetoric conceals truth, but quite another to say that truth conceals rhetoric. This is especially so if, like Freud (whose science is a science of interpretation), you are involved in a contest in interpretation. In the "Theme of the Three Caskets," what is at stake is the truth of psychoanalytic interpretation. That truth appears symptomatically as the desire to de-multiply (Freud does his multiplication tables backwards: 12 [boys], 9 [th story], 6 [swans], 3 [fates], rather than 3, 6, 9, 12), a desire to reduce things to One, to Death, to psychoanalytic truth.[52] But if truth is itself a trope, there could be no such reduction to singularity. If Medusa is the art of eloquence, and her oratorical display will strike you speechless as a stone, then her art — what Nietzsche might call her mobile army of metaphors — will silence your truth.

Where does D'Annunzio's novel stand in relation to this third sister? I want to suggest not that D'Annunzio anticipates Freud's conclusion that Beauty stands for Death, which as Lucia Re points out he does indeed, but rather that D'Annunzio's novel reads the Gorgon as a figure for rhetoric and her threat as a deprivation of rhetorical skill. The first hint in this direction comes in the prologue, as each virgin introduces herself with a speech, a display of oratorical skill. A second comes when Claudio imagines a version of the guessing game of the caskets:

> Un giorno — imagino — erano entrambi convenuti nella casa magnifica di Cecilia Gallerani; e Leonardo aveva rapito gli animi sonando quella nova lira fabbricata di sua mano quasi tutta d'argento in forma d'un teschio di cavallo. Nella pausa che seguì l'entusiasmo, la rinata Saffo si fece recare un mirabile cofanetto ricco di smalti e di gemme inviatole dal duca in dono; e mostrandolo chiedeva ai presenti quale oggetto tanto prezioso potesse a lor giudizio meritar d'esservi riposto. Ciascuno espresse un diverso parere. — E voi, Messer Alessandro? — domandò Madonna Cecilia, con dolci occhi. Rispose l'audace: — Di quello che fra i tesori di Dario fu trovato, del quale nulla fu visto che fosse più ricco, uno antico Alessandro volle far la custodia alla *Iliade* di Omero. (38)

> [One day — I imagine — they both met in the magnificent house of Cecilia Gallerani, and Leonardo had enraptured all souls present by playing upon a new lyre he had manufactured in the form of a horse's skull of almost pure silver, the reincarnated Sappho caused a wonderful small trunk, rich with enamel and gems, to be brought, which the duke had sent to her as a gift. Displaying it to all present she asked of each, what in his judgment could be a precious enough object to be deposited therein, each one expressing a diverse opinion. "And you, Messer Alessandro?" questioned Madonna Cecilia with sweet eyes, and the audacious youth replied, "An ancient Alexander wishes to make this coffer, found among Darious's treasures, and than which nothing richer has ever been seen, the keeper and guardian of Homer's *Iliad*."] (58)

This most precious casket holds, Claudio imagines, a text, just as Violante, the third sister, revealed as her "secret" a "book" in which she and Claudio read her Medusan truth.

The third example — and it is to the third that falls the choice, says Freud — returns us to the political narrative. The crowd becomes *gorghi*, becomes Gorgons who threaten speechlessness. The crowd is a figure for the Medusa of antieloquence (one thing represented by its opposite) and would reduce Claudio and all the poets to speechlessness because it itself is unspeakable:

> Chiedevano intanto i poeti, scoraggiati e smarriti, dopo aver esausta la dovizia delle rime nell'evocare imagini d'altri tempi, nel piangere le loro illusioni morte e nel numerare i colori delle foglie caduche; chiedevano, alcuni con ironia, altri pur senza: "Qual può essere oggi il nostro officio? Dobbiamo noi esaltare in senarii doppii il suffraggio universale? Dobbiamo noi affrettar con l'ansia dei decasillabi la caduta dei Re, l'avvento delle Repubbliche, l'accesso delle plebi al potere?" ... Ma nessuno tra loro, più generoso e più ardente, si levava a rispondere: "Difendete la Bellezza! ... Voi possedete la supreme scienza e la suprema forza del mondo: il Verbo. Un ordine di parole può vincere d'efficacia micidiale una formula chimica. Opponete risolutamente la distruzione alla distruzione!" (28)

> [In the meantime, the poets, discouraged and bewildered, after having exhausted riches of rhyme in evoking images of former times, in bewailing their dead illusions, and in numbering the colors of the fallen leaves, asked, some with irony, some without: "What shall be our duty today? Ought we to exalt universal suffrage in double-sixes? Ought we, with the anxiety of decasyllabics, to hasten the fall of the king, the advent of republics, the accession of the people to power?" ... But not one of them, more generous and more ardent, arose to reply: "Defend Beauty! ... Do not be disheartened, being few, you possess the supreme force of the world — speech. An order of words can surpass the murderous efficacy of a chemical formula. Resolutely oppose destruction with destruction!"] (43–44)

What is threatened is the possession of the science of the word, of this "supreme force" that we should take to be precisely what it says it is, the science of the word, which is rhetoric, and its constructions, which are Beauty. The threat is that the world might no longer be the representation of the sensibility and thought of a few superior men, to which, as was Claudio's goal and desire, one might add an "ornament," no longer the rhetorical construction of the few but the truth of the many. In short, the crowd's claims for choice, for political representation, are a threat to the poet's and aristocrat's means of self-representation.[53] If the threat of this Medusa is that choice falls to her, she — the crowd or the woman —

chooses you, then a preemptive strike may be in order. That strike can be accomplished by using her own tools against her. If Perseus could use a mirror in order to turn the Medusa's own gaze against her, then by using rhetoric even while disavowing its use, by seeming to embrace speechlessness before it falls to you, you might triumph over her. And once you have conquered that threat, cut off the Gorgon's head, you can wear it as a shield. Eloquence becomes your shield against all rivals. As Nancy Vickers writes, "The male rhetorician, both politician and artist, thus places the shield of eloquence between himself and the 'world of harms' that surrounds him."[54] Such is D'Annunzio's strategy: in order to "oppose destruction to destruction" his text produces a shield of rhetorical display to defend against the possibility that the poet and aristocrat might no longer be the subject of choice: that the crowd, or the woman, might do the choosing in his place. The result is a self-consciously antireferential text that produces rhetorical constructions to which truth might never be opposed. An example might be the following sentence: "Ah, come potrei dimenticare io quel silenzio ardente in cui palpitò l'ala invisibile d'un messaggiero che portava una parola non proferita?" (123) [Ah, how could I ever forget that ardent silence in which palpitated the invisible wing of a messenger who bore an unproferred word?] (192). Inaudible, invisible, never spoken, existing only in writing, what is described could never be exposed as untruthful. On a grander scale, this strategy sets "rhetoric" and "truth" oscillating in an overarching logic of fetishism that governs the novel itself. The move here is the opposite of the one suggested in Shakespeare; D'Annunzio does not oppose a nonrhetorical truth to a rhetorical lie but rather refuses to allow such a distinction to be made (just as the most subtle fetishist refuses to be inserted into the binary logic that turns diversity into difference). The question and answer with which the novel opens sets the oscillation going: "Tali io le conobbi nel tedio dei giorni comuni o sono esse le creature del mio desiderio e della mia perplessità? Tali io le conobbi nel tedio dei giorni comuni ed esse sono le creature del mio desiderio e della mia perplessità" [Did I know them thus in the tedium of our days together, or are they creatures of my desire and my perplexity? I knew them thus in the tedium of our days together, and they are creatures of my desire and my perplexity]. Refusing to choose between a binary alternative, between the virgins as rhetorical construction and the virgins as real, true beings, the text finds itself in a stasis that, however, constitutes its (decadent) poetic. The threat of the Medusan crowd is the source of the poet's eloquence: the crowd threatens to destroy Beauty, yet Beauty threatened with destruction is precisely what is valorized in the novel.

One final contrast can be drawn between the Freudian and D'Annunzian versions of the choice among three women, a contrast that points to ideological differences between the two. For Freud, the function of the narrative as wish fulfillment is to put choice in the place of necessity, a wishful reversal that allows "man" to choose what cannot be chosen, death: "Choice stands in the place of necessity, of destiny. In this way man overcomes death, which he has recognized intellectually."[55] And in this way he remains the subject of choice, rather than its object. Freud seems unaware that Necessity is the mother of the Fates who have dominated his discussion, but she asserts herself just as choice is made to stand in her place. Freud's fetish is choice; he knows very well that there is no choice, no choosing of death, and yet all the same he puts this nonexistent choice in the place of Mother Necessity. This we might describe as a "democratic fantasy." D'Annunzio, on the other hand, puts Necessity *and* the mother in the place of choice, in the place of Claudio's own choice among the three virgins as well as in the path of the choice of the crowd. (Claudio in fact does choose Anatolia — but Anatolia does not choose him, having already chosen the mother, chosen to dedicate herself to her mother's care.) The fetish of *Le vergini* is Necessity; the text knows very well, indeed all too well, that there is choice (and suffrage), yet all the same it acts as though there were not by putting Necessity, and the mother, in its place. This is the "antidemocratic fantasy" that blocks the choice of the protagonist who thereby cannot fulfill his destiny as precursor. There is no bypassing of the "vulva" for Claudio, no idealist fantasy of producing a son out of desire and form alone.

Precursing

The novel has been considered a "precursory" one on at least four levels: thematically, its protagonist and eloquent ideologue is a precursor to the son, "he who is to come"; formally, the novel was to have been the first of a trilogy whose third book was to have borne the title *The Annunciation;* ideologically, it is, as we have seen, a target for those who seek "elements" of protofascism in literary texts; biographically, it was written by the man who came to be known as the John the Baptist of fascism, the precursor himself.[56] A curious split divides these levels. On the first two levels, the precursor has no following: no genitrix is chosen, no son is conceived, no superman born, and no trilogy ever written; the precursory relation is announced only to remain unfulfilled. On the second two levels, the precursory relation is set up retrospectively and retroactively from the point of view of those who follow, from the point of view of the success of the fascist regime. The question we need to address here is whether it matters to the second two levels that the precursory relation is annulled on the first two levels.[57]

If being a precursor were only a matter of retrospective reading, we would be compelled to accept as precursors of fascism any of the many figures that the regime was eager to adopt as legitimating fathers: Dante, Machiavelli, Mazzini, Garibaldi, and a host of others. Perceiving the violence of such appropriation, most critics and historians are unwilling to grant it legitimacy. But if, on the other hand, the precursory relation were not at all a question of retroaction, then it would become a case of prolepsis, a relation of foresight and prediction. "Precursor" texts, in that case, are easily taken to be "prophetic" ones, as a "saying" of the future may be misunderstood as a "seeing" of the future. And indeed, Salinari, whose intent is to indict, attributes proleptic powers of prophecy to D'Annunzio's texts; Valesio, whose intent is to absolve, also finds D'Annunzio's works "brilliantly proleptic" and reads D'Annunzio as "the first, and very penetrating, *critic* of Italian fascism."[58] Though their evaluations differ, their strategy is the same.

The precursorial relation, however, is not a prophetic one but rather one that involves *both* a knowledge gained retroactively and a reading of the text that discovers or creates in it a "fore-knowledge." The precursory relation is thus necessarily a product of reading and interpretation.[59] Attributions of prophecy erase the role of retroactive interpretation and thereby also erase the hand of the critic: the ball is tossed, and the hand hidden. The "Old Testament," for instance, becomes the Old Testament, a precursor text, only as the result of an act of interpretation; as John Hollander puts it, "A previously nonexistent book called the Old Testament is created out of an old one, the Torah, by a hermeneutical fiat."[60] That this interpretation then attributes to it not only precursorial but also prophetic status is a matter for theologians (though there still must be a reader, in this case God, who knows the future and can retroactively read prophecy).[61] Both attributions of prophecy and the wholly retroactive appropriation of precursors cover over the act of interpretation, the first by erasing the function of retrospection and the second by eliding the difficulties and heterogeneities of the texts and figures in question.

How does D'Annunzio's novel, in which interpretation itself is a theme, read the precursor relation? I would suggest that by looking backward, impossibly, the novel ends up producing a father rather than a son, that, in fact, the ideological fantasy is not that of fathering a son but of fathering a father (hence the son is imagined as "king").[62] While the protagonist claims to desire a son, the text succeeds in producing fathers — the demonic Alessandro, the old prince, Socrates, and so on — but never in figuring a son, never in figuring the future from which point of view Claudio would become a precursor. This doubling back of the reproductive project is reflected in the description of Alessandro as "precursor of himself" in the passage we have already quoted:

> Tu non fosti, in quel tempo, se non l'annunciatore e il precursore di te medesimo, dovendo riapparire su dal tuo ceppo longevo nella maturità del secoli futuri, alla soglia di un mondo non anche esplorato dai guerrieri ma già promesso dai sapienti: riapparire come il messaggio l'interprete, e il padrone d'una vita nuova.... Ed esca il tuo eguale dalla mia genitura! (39)

> [Thou at that period wert but the announcer and precursor of thyself, destined to appear again from thy long-lived stock in the maturity of future centuries, at the threshold of a world not yet explored by warriors, but already promised by the sages: to reappear as the message, the interpreter, the master of a new life!... that thy equal may be begotten by me!] (60–61)

Alessandro becomes a precursor of himself only in the "maturity of future centuries" as brought back by Claudio, as "fathered" by him in the novel; this second Alessandro makes a precursor of the first. But the future necessary to Claudio's precursorship does not exist in this profoundly nostalgic novel whose desire proceeds backward on the genealogical tree; if he is a precursor at all, then he must be said to be a precursor of the past.[63] The only "future" that can be said to exist is found in the listing, at the end of the novel, of the next novel in the trilogy: "Qui finisce il libro delle vergini e incomincia il libro della grazia" (193) [Here finishes the book of the Virgins, and commences the book of Grace] (296). The second novel is necessary in order to make the first "the first," just as a second future moment is necessary in order to make the precursor truly a precursor. Whether or not D'Annunzio ever "really" planned to finish the trilogy, one might argue that it was ideologically necessary both that the trilogy be projected and that it not be completed. It is, as the text fetishistically knows, impossible to construct oneself as originary origin — an origin is so only secondarily — and yet the text persists in doing so; that is to say, disavowal manifests itself as the naming of the novel to come, and "knowledge" manifests itself in the failure of the protagonist to produce the child, "he who is to come" (which failure, in turn, makes it impossible to continue the trilogy). The naming of the novel to come repairs the failure to produce the child to come. This knowledge of impossibility and its disavowal are what make possible the narrative. As Žižek writes, "Fantasy is basically a scenario filling out the empty space of a fundamental impossibility, a screen masking a void."[64]

As in the case of the fantasy of the subject-less king, here D'Annunzio's text twists away, ideologically, from either fascism or protofascism. As in the earlier example, the text twists to the right and aligns itself with a "reaction" of a sort different from that of fascism. Historically speaking, the novel sits on a cusp between two kinds of "reactionary" politics. As Alexander De Grand writes, "Until the 1890s, the 'reactionaries' had been champions of some past aristocratic regime which had been swept away in one of the liberal or national revolutions of mid-century. After the decade of the 1890s, however, in France and in Italy 'reactionary' began to assume its modern meaning of rejection of mass or democratic society."[65] The meeting of these two "reactions" in the text results in the "looking forward, impossibly," that we have been describing. Any thinking of the future in this novel falls back into nostalgia.

For fascist discourse, for the discourse of fascism as regime, on the other hand, futurity is the condition of possibility of the present. As Pier Giorgio Zunino writes, "From whatever vantage point within the regime one contemplated the reality constructed by fascism, there was full awareness that neither the past nor the present furnished sufficient justification for the regime. Only things yet to be accomplished could provide the dictatorship with genuine legitimacy."[66] Fascism wanted precursors as well, of course, to prove its fundamental "Italianness"; as Zunino puts it, "In fascism there was, more than a desire for the past, a necessity of the past." But as a "revolution" it also painted itself as radically unprecedented, as precursor of itself, anxious for its glorious realization. Indeed, the status of "futurity" is, according to Emilio Gentile, the factor that distinguishes nationalism (as a political organization and its ideology) from fascism. While nationalism was a "mimetic" phenomenon, devoted to a myth of the past and to a notion of the nation as historical product and inheritance of values, fascism redefined the nation as continuous creation and will to power. The fascist future is a "continuous creation of new social and political realities," among them the nation itself.[67]

In relation to D'Annunzio's novel, we might say that fascism takes the disavowal without the knowledge, or rather takes the disavowal to be the knowledge. That Mussolini could baldly state that "I superuomini si eleggono" [Supermen elect — or choose — themselves] and betray no sense of the "failure" that D'Annunzio's text might predict for such an "election" is a measure of the distance between them.[68] Neither Mussolini nor fascism could be a token of a type; neither could have been produced according to a preexisting model. It is not by chance that fascism produced a reproductive fantasy in which Mussolini was depicted, perhaps not unhumorously, as giving birth to himself, at once both Zeus and Athena. As we shall see in the next chapter, only the Duce could conceive, and conceive of, himself.

5 / Fascism as Discursive Regime

Fascism, Rhetoric, Ideology

In the most important of several speeches given on the eve of the March on Rome, the 1922 "Discorso di Udine," Benito Mussolini paints the relation between fascism and rhetoric as antagonistic:

> Con il discorso che intendo pronunciare innanzi a voi, io faccio una eccezione alla regola che mi sono imposta; quella, cioè, di limitare al minimo possibile le manifestazioni della mia eloquenza. Oh, se fosse possibile strangolarla, come consigliava un poeta, l'eloquenza verbosa, prolissa, inconcludente, democratica, che ci ha deviato per così lungo tempo! Io sono quindi sicuro, od almeno mi lusingo di avere questa speranza, che voi non vi attenderete da me un discorso che non sia squisitamente fascista, cioè scheletrico, aspro, schietto e duro.[1]

> [The speech that I intend to make today is going to be an exception to the rule that I have imposed upon myself of limiting the manifestations of my eloquence, as far as I can. Oh! if it were only possible to do as the poets advise and strangle the verbose, prolix, inconclusive, democratic oratory that has side-tracked us for so long! I am certain, or at any rate I flatter myself in hoping, that you do not expect anything from me in a speech that is not eminently fascist, that is to say straightforward, hard, bare facts.][2]

Mussolini's disavowal of rhetoric is ambivalent at best. On the one hand, he claims that his speech must be antirhetorical, just as fascism is antirhetorical, nothing but the hard, bare facts. On the other, he admits both that this speech is an exception to his self-imposed rule limiting his speeches, and

114

therefore is guilty of the rhetorical excess banned by that rule, and that his personal rule is in any case impossible to enforce since it is not possible — it is contrary to the facts, given over to the optative subjunctive — to "do as the poets advise." It is as though the vain orator could only half heartedly assume an antirhetorical stance; indeed, in the midst of his disavowal, he is unable to resist "flattering himself" and hence slides momentarily in the direction of epideictic. Yet Mussolini's antirhetorical stance is nevertheless philosophically necessary and becomes one of the most basic commonplaces of fascist discourse.

If fascism presents itself as antirhetorical, antifascism occupies the position that is, predictably, precisely the opposite (which is to say, the same); antifascist discourse claims for itself the neutrality of a "nonrhetorical" language and finds not only fascist discourse but fascism itself to be irredeemably rhetorical or, even worse, "degenerated rhetoric," as Umberto Eco puts it.[3] Fascist and antifascist discourse join together in opposing their own nonrhetorical truth to the rhetorical lies of the other. While on the one hand this shared assumption is unremarkable, each claim for truth disowning rhetorical bombast and sharing similar assumptions about language, on the other it has had remarkable consequences in studies of fascism.

The question of the relation between rhetoric and fascism has been answered in a way that resembles, indeed comes to be implicated in, the answer given to the question of the relation between fascism and ideology: fascism has no ideology, the argument goes, but is instead sheer "rhetoric" — by which is meant bombastic, insincere speech that can be opposed to some nonrhetorical (antifascist) use of language. Onto this opposition is superimposed another opposition: rhetoric is identified with an irrational use of language, while the (antifascist) "nonrhetorical" use of language is dubbed a "linguaggio razionale" [rational language].[4] This is, of course, a strategic account whose reasoning goes as follows: there were no ideas, and hence no appeal to rational faculties, in fascism; there was only rhetoric, and behind that rhetoric, violence first illegal and then of the state. Supporters of fascism and, ultimately, reason itself (as well as the possibility of "nonrhetorical, rational" language) are thereby saved from the taint of complicity, for reason and rational belief had, according to this account, no part in fascism. This view opens the way to the various theories of bedazzlement according to which the supporters of fascism were hypnotized and spell-bound by the leaders' "rhetoric" and hence oblivious to the violence done to them and to reason.[5] Its strategic value is clear: if fascist ideology is irrational, the "institutionalized unconscious," as Julia Kristeva puts it, or the postmodern equivalent of evil, then we may still consider ourselves to be rational, good, and outside of that thing called fascism.[6] In other words, fascism is represented as a black box whose contents are unspecified but whose moral significance is given in advance.

There are, to be sure, a number of contradictions that nag at such accounts: time and again one reads that Mussolini's speeches are boring, his lexicon impoverished, his prose stultifying. The supposedly bedazzling rhetoric fails to bedazzle. And so, the reasoning goes, the irresistible attraction must have been something else, something outside of language and rhetoric, and that something else becomes variously pure force, the personal charisma of the Duce, as constructed and communicated by a demonized technology, or "aesthetics" broadly conceived and located in mass spectacle and ritual.[7] This is the bind consensus studies get themselves into; reason is rescued through the "rhetoricization" of fascism, yet "rhetoric" fails (or cannot be allowed?) to account for fascism's success. The term "rhetoric" thus comes to name both an ideological void and the means by which it is filled in.

The effects of this bind can be found even in the analyses of those who take most seriously questions of rhetoric and language in the study of fascism: the group of scholars, linguists for the most part, who, in the early 1970s in Italy, began studying Mussolini's language and rhetoric, on the one hand, and the linguistic politics of fascism, on the other.[8] There is among them general agreement that fascism attempted to become a "regno della parola" [reign of the word], that a study of Mussolini's rhetoric, imposed as official linguistic model during the regime, may contribute to our understanding not only of the "verbal revolutionism" of the regime but of its political revolution as well.[9] Implicit (though ambivalently so) in their studies is the notion, with which I agree, that a study of fascist rhetoric can bring us closer to the core of fascism itself.[10] Yet the more minute the analyses become, the more the tendency to slide away from language and rhetoric to "something else" asserts itself. An excerpt from Erasmo Leso's important work on Mussolini's rhetoric illustrates the way in which what is termed empty, repetitive rhetoric quickly becomes "irrational" and then "magical." In speaking of Mussolini's dialogues with the crowd, Leso writes:

> It is clear to me that to organize a speech in these terms and around these themes means to renounce immediately, and a priori, any possibility that language offers of communicating arguments, knowledge, data, problems — and solutions to problems, if you want, but rationally argued. Here language is exploited only for emotional ends in order to determine an emotional con-

sensus: an unconditional consensus of a religious sort. The relation that is set up between Mussolini and his listeners is a relation of faith, or even better, it is a magical relation: I am in the presence not of a political leader and ordinary citizens, but of a charismatic head and his faithful followers.[11]

"Magic" and charisma are the products of a particular use of language and are opposed to another possibility of language that would allow its employment to argue rationally, present data, expound upon knowledge, and so on. The radical implication of Leso's description is that both rationality and irrationality are equally possibilities of language and that both are equally rhetorical. And while Leso is, on the whole, careful to maintain the distinction between "magic" as constructed rhetorically and an essentialized "magic" emanating from the Duce's person, in at least one moment he seems to fall victim to the slippage between the two that is typical of other, less exacting analyses. The slippage occurs in Leso's discussion of Mussolini's general preference for parataxis. One of the functions of Mussolini's insistent employment of parataxis is, Leso argues, to draw attention away from the semantic content of the discourse toward the person of the orator:

> The attention of the listener is displaced from facts and relations between facts, from the argumentative content of the message, onto the person of the orator. This displacement is all the more inevitable the more the content of the message is lacking from a referential point of view and the person of the orator is accepted, obviously also for extralinguistic reasons, as a charismatic personality. Mussolini uses parataxis, on the one hand, to accentuate in public the impression of a communion between orator and listeners and, on the other, to present his own speech as essential, voluntaristically free of intellectualistic complications and yet intelligently organized.[12]

I want to return later to Leso's evaluation of parataxis; for the moment what is important is the way in which, over and over again, the linguistic analyses discover a void, a lexical "usury," a desemanticization in Mussolini's speeches such that language becomes a "mere instrument of magico-irrational aggregation."[13] The passage cited above presents language as at once nonreferential, having no argumentative content, and referential, referring the listener to the person of the orator; the oration itself is at once "irrational" in its appeal to the emotions and yet "rational," for, as Leso notes in the subsequent sentence, "The organization of any matter, even if only expressive, is always the sign of a rationality." A rationalized irrationality, a referential nonreferentiality: these oxymoronic formulations might stand as definitions of fascism's linguistic practice and recall and explain Kristeva's definition of fascism as the institutionalized unconscious.

But one must, I think, be careful not to separate the terms of these oxymorons, not, that is, to forget that the irrationality of which one speaks is rationally organized, that the language that tends to become "pure sound" is rhetorically organized and "argued," that the "magic" of fascism's appeal to the emotions may be "rationally" accessible to us through language. This tendency remains slight in Leso's work, its trace being his recourse to the "obviously extralinguistic" reasons for Mussolini's "charismatic personality," a reference presumably to the various forms of nonverbal (but still semiotic) behavior that contributed to the formation of the image of the Duce. I want not to dispute the importance of semiotic transformations to the creation of fascist ideology; quite the contrary, such transformations are precisely one of the ways in which fascism defines itself. What I want to emphasize here is the way in which the emptying out of content of Mussolini's rhetoric has the inevitable effect of participating once again in the commonplace according to which fascism has no "ideas." This notion gathers force already in Luigi Rosiello's introduction to the volume containing Leso's essay; summarizing the findings of a number of scholars, Rosiello defines fascist language as:

> The systematic refusal of the use of rational language that aims in its semantic quality toward knowledge of referential reality, to the advantage of the choice of communicative instruments of an emotional kind tending to determine in the mass of listeners immediate and unreflected behavior, to move irrational sentiments, to influence passions without convincing reason; the extensive use of rhetorical figures (metaphor, metonymy, anaphora, hyperbole, etc.); the use of words emptied of meaning and used only as pure phonic and evocatory calls; the use of paratactic syntax . . . these are the characteristics of the oratorical language of Mussolini.[14]

Rosiello's summary manages to sweep up metaphor and metonymy, as well as what could stand as a definition of poetic language, along with his condemnation of fascism's "irrationality." Any cognitive function of "literary" language is swept away in this movement, and the "rational language" that presumably serves as Rosiello's point of comparison begins to take ghostly shape as something like the "bare, hard facts" that Mussolini claimed were his alone. Indeed, the more one reads that fascist discourse bypasses reason and rational faculties, the more one suspects that the "irrational" functions as a "dumping ground for anything one wishes to exclude," to borrow a phrase from Fredric Jameson's not entirely unrelated discussion of Jürgen Habermas's critique of the *Dialectic of Enlightenment*. Reason, Jameson points out, seems to mean "the receiver's point of view — always understanding what the actor's reasons were, why the thing was done in the first place (or why this or that value is defended)."[15] "Irrationality" thus labels values that are unacceptable and functions as a term of judgment rather more than a "rationally" conceived category of understanding. Given this qualification, to argue that fascist discourse is not "irrational" should be taken not as a defense of fascism, but rather as an attempt to emerge from the (historically necessary) battle against fascism, a battle that required harsh judgments, into a struggle for intellectual understanding that takes the necessary risk of "sympathy."[16] Nor is this to say that "oceanic feelings," "emotions," the lure of "voice," sexual fantasies, and so on, were not at play in fascist rhetoric: Klaus Theweleit and Alice Y. Kaplan, among others, have beautifully and disturbingly demonstrated their presence and function and explained "rationally" the role these crucial "irrational" components play in interpellating the fascist subject. But if we may "rationalize" emotions and sexual fantasies, we may also allow that fascist discourse does have an ideological content, however impoverished we might judge it to be, and that, as with the literary texts discussed in previous chapters, a reading that aims to uncover articulations among elements may be able to produce knowledge about that ideology. The literary critic may be particularly well equipped for this task if indeed as Rosiello implicitly claims the desemanticization of fascist discourse is due to its "literarization" and if, as I argue, such articulations are legible as rhetoric.

The Elements of Fascist Style

The work of Italian linguists and historians has given us material sufficient to write up something like a guide to the construction of a Mussolini speech; we have lists of disarticulated elements including everything from verbal tics, characteristic couplings of nouns and adjectives, syntactical and lexical preferences, to topoi and ideologemes. Before proceeding to the analysis of one of Mussolini's most "eventful" speeches, in the sense that Jean Pierre Faye has given to "totalitarian language," it may be useful to attempt to summarize the results of their work, writing as I am for an audience that does not necessarily have access to their work in Italian.[17] I have been sparing in the listing of examples, my purpose being not to redo what has already been done so meticulously but to offer the reader the conclusions to be drawn from that work and pose some questions about both their assumptions and their conclusions.

Generally speaking, the studies in question take Mussolini as their principal object of study for two main reasons. On the one hand, they resort to a kind of *reductio ad ducem* (as Norberto Bobbio puts it) according to which the only thing we can, with certainty, say is fascist discourse is what we find in speeches and writings of the Duce.[18] On the other, this move is not as reductive as it might at first appear, at least historically speaking, since Mussolini's style is imposed as linguistic model throughout the regime; his grammatical, syntactical, and rhetorical practice is imposed through the schools and through the media as correct, "fascist" Italian, and thus itself becomes generalized and codified.

If, then, we were to offer hints for counterfeiting Mussolini, we could start with what is perhaps the most general characteristic, noted by Leso and others: Mussolini's consistent employment of parataxis, the arrangement of phrases or clauses with no subordination and often with no coordinate conjunctions; sheer juxtaposition is his preferred form of syntax. Both Mussolini's contemporaries and the linguists tend to attribute to this syntactical practice an essential ideological content, a meaning immune to linguistic and historical context alike. Mussolini's contemporaries read this lack of syntactic complication as the sign of clarity and masculinity; the editors of the journal *Il selvaggio,* for example, praised Mussolini's style (in what is itself an example of Mussolinian prose!) as "simple, clear, masculine," and Hermann Ellwanger, author of a 1939 study of Mussolini's rhetoric, found in his use of parataxis the source of "concise clarity and monumental relief."[19] Leso, on the other hand, cites Chaim Perelman and L. Olbrechts-Tyteca in support of his claim that parataxis is in collusion with the "irrationality" of fascism: "The hearer is left free to imagine between the events a relationship that by its very lack of precision, assumes a mysterious, magical character."[20] Leso elaborates on this observation, adding that this may mean that while the orator leaves the listener "syntactically" free, the orator has other, nonsyntactic ways of directing the listener to make connections (hence the listener is not free at all), or that though the listener is free to interpret, his interpretation is irrelevant to the aims of the speech (hence though the listener is free, his freedom counts for nought). In either case, argues Leso, the attention of the unfree listener is displaced from the rational content of the message to the charismatic person of the orator.

In reading Leso, one is struck by the pains he takes to qualify the "freedom" that he nevertheless attributes to parataxis. Retracing his steps in developing the argument to Perelman and Olbrechts-Tyteca, one discovers that these authors attribute two rather different ideological colorings to parataxis. While the first, associated with the Bible, is magical, the second is at odds with Leso's conclusions: Perelman and Olbrechts-Tyteca oppose the "greater freedom" of parataxis to the way in which hypotaxis "controls the reader, forces... and constricts interpretations," and attribute to parataxis the "philosophical" impression given by the "carefully composed and balanced sentence of eighteenth century English authors."[21] Why should "freedom" lead to "magic," on the one hand, and "philosophy," on the other? The road from parataxis to irrationality is to be found by retracing Perelman and Olbrechts-Tyteca's steps to Erich Auerbach's discussion of parataxis and epic in *Mimesis*. Auerbach also gives an ideological tint to hypotaxis and parataxis. For Auerbach, the "copious and connected argumentation" that is hypotaxis belongs to the Homeric epic; parataxis, which in classical languages belongs to the low style, characterizes both biblical narrative and French romance and is associated with "narrowness" and "indisputability."[22] Classical culture, with all its refinements and achievements, is associated with hypotaxis, while Christian culture, at its most rigidly formulaic, is said to be paratactic. The magical irrationality that Perelman and Olbrechts-Tyteca (and Leso in their wake) attach to parataxis appears in Auerbach's discussion of the biblical sentence "Dixit que Deus; fiat lux, et facta est lux" [And God said, "Let there be light"; and there was light], a sublime sentence, writes Auerbach, that fills the hearer with awe not simply because of its syntax but because of the contrast within it between "impressive brevity" and "immense content."[23] There can be no doubt that God's creation of light by means of the positional power of language qualifies as "immense content," and the sentence is indeed admirably brief. Such cannot be the magical irrationality that Leso finds in fascist discourse, however, for it is precisely the absence of content that promotes it. But around the opposition classical hypotaxis/Christian parataxis, Auerbach constructs a historical narrative that is secretly echoed in Leso's evaluation. Auerbach explains that the narrowness, rigidity, and immutability of parataxis in, for example, the *Chanson de Roland* is due not to a narrowness of Christianity itself but rather to "the simplified form which Christianity assumed in its clash with exhausted or barbaric peoples."[24] The "irrationality" of the syntactic form would thus seem to have to do not only with its relation to a particular semantic content (as in the case of the Bible) but also with the nature of the audience, the assumption being that "exhausted or barbaric peoples" were not culturally equipped to process the complexity and "rationality" of hypotactic antiquity.

This is the piece of the argument that brings us back to the problematic of fascism, for it interlocks nicely with one of the assumptions that grounds what has been called the "totalitarian" interpretation of fascism.[25] That interpretation emphasizes the analysis of mass society and argues that the influx into the political arena of masses of people who had never before participated in political life, who were not accustomed to political discussion, and who did not have the intellectual tools for rational discussion changed the nature of politics. This uneducated public is, the argument goes, susceptible to strategies that link differences of opinion to differences of race, nationality, and social class, as well as to strategies that appeal to emotion and prejudice rather than rational argument. It thus appears to be the nature of the masses that opens the way to irrationalism and violence and bypasses rational discussion, the "old" way of doing politics. The argument is marked, I think, by a certain nostalgia for the era before the advent of mass society, and the fact that the totalitarian interpretation links fascism and communism leads one to suspect it, at worst, of simply disliking the introduction of the masses into politics. In any case, these "totalitarian" masses neatly fit into the role of the "barbarians" in Auerbach's schema, and their "irrationality" comes to be inserted into the linguistic analysis as the ideological content of a syntactic form. But to accept the attribution of irrationality to parataxis is to accept that the masses are inherently irrational, a notion that the fascists themselves were eager to embrace: as Mussolini put it, "Il numero è contrario alla ragione" [Number is contrary to reason].[26] Yet surely one can imagine that the introduction of the masses into political life does not necessarily lead to totalitarianism. And one can also imagine other ways to interpret the political nuances of parataxis, as do Perelman and Olbrechts-Tyteca in noting its use by eighteenth-century English authors, or as Adorno does in his essay on Friedrich Hölderlin's use of the form.[27] In the case of fascism, in which the populist interpellation is so important, one might argue that parataxis appears to be the syntactic form most suited to the anti-intellectual, antirhetorical populist stance assumed by Mussolini, without however characterizing that populism as "irrational."[28] This would mean taking seriously the reaction of the editors of Il selvaggio not for their acumen as stylists but for their testimony to the interpellative function of the style itself. A similar "populist" interpellative function can be noted in the Anglo-American preference for parataxis, enforced by teachers of composition and copyeditors alike: the "Hemingwayesque" sentence is taken to be the sign of clarity and sincerity (and virility) as opposed to the supposed obscurantism (and femininity) of overwrought Latinate hypotaxis.

Two other characteristics often listed under the rubric of parataxis as corollaries are likewise given ideological content, however unlikely they might seem as candidates for such an attribution; these are binary and ternary sentence structure, and synonymic dittology. The first, noted by Michele Cortelazzo and Augusto Simonini, as well as by Hermann Ell-wanger, refers to the presence of two or three clauses in a single sentence and is an effect of parataxis insofar as the clauses are related through jux-taposition or coordination rather than subordination. The binary structure frequently takes on the form of a dilemma in which of two alternatives presented, only one is acceptable. Cortelazzo takes the dilemmatic structure, combined with "false interrogatives," to have a largely phatic function, re-peatedly testing the channels of communication between orator and crowd. Thus in the dialogue with the orator, the crowd may respond to the false interrogatives with the only possible, and hence semantically empty, answer. (This would be an example of the "reflex action" that Eco locates in the employment of degenerated rhetoric.) It is of interest that Cortelazzo traces the source of this technique of the "rigged dialogue" to the oratory of the pre-1914 socialist Mussolini; D'Annunzio's dialogues with the crowd at Fi-ume are not, he suggests, so much a source as a facilitating stage in the evolution of a rhetorical habit already in place.[29] Luisa Passerini adds that this habit has even older roots in popular language, in which narrative takes the form of dramatic dialogue.[30] One might also suggest that the dilem-matic structure colludes in creating what Jacques Derrida has called a "crisis economy."[31] A "crisis" situation is staged as the moment in which a choice must be made between only two alternatives; part of its function is to limit and give form to an unformed threat, thereby domesticating and neutral-izing it. The fascist rhetoric of crisis functions in particular to present the state of things as beyond the time of discussion; whatever the particulars of the situation, the choice boils down to one between talk and action, the action itself being determined in advance. Again and again, fascist discourse presents itself not as word but as action — it is no longer the time to rea-son, it says, but the time to act — and is thus not so much irrational (or prelogical, as Leso argues) as postrational.

The ternary structure may join its members in various ways, from the simple relative pronoun *che* [that] (whose frequency prompted Piero Bargellini to comment, in his 1939 *Ritratto virile* (Virile portrait), that Mus-solini's "periodo è fissato con tanti *che* come una tenda da campo fissata con tanti picchetti" [sentence is anchored with lots of *that*s like a field tent anchored with lots of stakes]), to the juxtaposition of redundantly synonymous clauses.[32] This reiteration may take the form of synonymic dittology (or "triptology"), that is, couples (or triplets) of terms that are loosely synonymous, especially adjectives that begin with a negative *in-* and contain the same number of syllables. Leso offers the examples "inevitabile e insopprimibile" [inevitable and irrepressible] and "indistruttibile e inseparabile" [indestructible and inseparable] and argues that they are motivated not so much by their semantic content as by their phonic effect. Binary and ternary structures are often filled by a sort of grammatical topos, in which a single root is declined or conjugated. The topos varies in effectiveness; Leso once again invokes phonic motivations and effects. At its worst, the topos gives the impression that the orator can't quite find the right word. Simonini, for example, cites from a 1921 speech (the "Discorso a Bologna," April 3, 1921) a definition of then prime minister Francesco Nitti that seems to find Mussolini groping grammatically: "Nitti, un ministro infame, infamabile, da infamarsi" [Nitti, a minister infamous, defamable, to be defamed]. (This same phrase, we might note, is cited by Ellwanger as an example of the particularly efficacious stylistic means by which Mussolini managed to be one with the soul of the people.)[33] At its best, however, it contributes to an impression of omniscience and universality. Leso notes in particular the use of the same verb in more than one tense (though almost always in the indicative mood), especially in pairs or triplets. Thus, one of Leso's examples glorifies the continuity of the empire: "Salve, Dea Roma! Salve per quei che furono, sono e saranno i tuoi figli pronti a soffrire e a morire, per la tua potenza e per la tua gloria!" [Greetings, Goddess Rome! Greetings for those who were, are, and will be your sons ready to suffer and to die for your power and your glory!]. Another example appears in the "Discorso del 3 gennaio," which we will analyze later: "La soluzione è la forza. Non c'è stata altra soluzione nella storia e non ce ne sarà mai" (140) [The solution is force. There has never been another solution in history, and there never will be].[34] Leso describes this aspect of Mussolini's language as a manifestation of a kind of linguistic "voluntarism," communicating as it does coherence in relation to the past, and resolution and certainty in relation to the future, all dependent upon the will of the speaker. The historical continuity implicit in such voluntarism also underlines the "omniscience" of the speaker, to whom all moments, including the future, are present.

"Omniscience" may be too generous a term, however. Perhaps we should follow Mussolini's lead, in his "Discorso dell'ascensione," and tone down the claim to one of partial and mildly retarded omniscience. In that speech, Mussolini presents himself as a sort of slow and malevolent Santa Claus: "Nessuno si illuda di pensare che io non sappia quello che succede nel Paese fino nell'ultimo villaggio d'Italia. Lo saprò un po' tardi, ma alla fine lo so" [Let no one deceive themselves into thinking that I don't know what happens in this country down to the last village in Italy. I may know it a little late, but in the end I know].[35] Mussolini's aspiration to belated omniscience manifests itself stylistically in a fondness for including numerical data to give an impression of precision and scientificity, particularly during the demographic campaign, and in the use of antithesis. Leso suggests that antithesis works to produce an omniscient effect by suggesting that the orator has total access to the topic and to its contrary, and thus he, the orator, represents an Archimedean point of synthesis. Cortelazzo ideologizes the use of antithesis even more by suggesting that it obfuscates the semantic value of individual terms to the benefit of a global impression and thus that its effect can be called "totalitarian."[36] Mussolini's 1919 definition of fascists provides a metalinguistic example of such a strategic use of antithesis: "E' un po' difficile definire i fascisti. Essi non sono repubblicani, socialisti, democratici, conservatori, nazionalisti. Essi rappresentano una sintesi di tutte le negazioni e di tutte le affermazioni" [It is a little difficult to define the fascists. They are not republicans, socialists, democrats, conservatives, or nationalists. They represent a synthesis of all negations and all affirmations].[37] Stripped of its Hegelian aspirations, Mussolini's definition is in fact not all that inaccurate, as both Kaplan's discussion of fascism as a machine that binds polarities and Zunino's examination of the "overabundance of ideal inspirations" and multiplicity of "ideological rivulets" that flowed into fascism would seem to confirm.[38]

As for rhetorical figures properly speaking, Leso and others find that Mussolinian rhetoric favors metonymy and synecdoche over metaphor: fascists are blackshirts, nationalists blue shirts, the *bersaglieri* plumed hats; the Italian air force is the "Italian wing," the military, "Italy in grey-green." During the most delirious years of the demographic battle, the landscape is littered with "coffins" and "cradles," and Mussolini accuses the unborn of a "cradle strike." Once again, there is a tendency in linguistic studies to give an essential ideological content to a rhetorical element; in keeping with his overall thesis of the desemanticization of fascist language, Leso suggests that metonymy is the figure of promise, in which a diminished and empty part evokes an ungraspable and future whole; that is to say, a promised whole replaces a semantically empty present.[39] The examples cited, however, seem to serve a more concrete and banal interpellative purpose by naming individuals only insofar as they are the part of a unit organized by a larger political body and, most frequently, by the state. If there is a promised whole it is the body politic of the nation; metonymy serves to reattach the "parts" that are individuals by figuring them only in their relation to that body. In the examples cited above, they are the "dressing" of the state, its shirts, its hats, its khakis. Metonymy thus has a role to play in the ideological fantasy of the unity of the social body. We return to the question of this social body in the last section of this chapter.

A more general strategy in Mussolini's rhetoric concerns what Kenneth Burke, in his discussion of Hilter's *Battle,* calls the spiritualization of material issues.[40] In Mussolini's case this accounts for one of the strategic functions of religious terminology and contributes to the antieconomism of fascist discourse in general. Religious terminology functions as euphemism for economic realities.[41] Mussolini typically responds to economic arguments with spiritualistic ones: one of the most dramatic examples appears in the 1935 "Discorso della mobilitazione" (Declaration of war on Ethiopia). In response to the sanctions imposed as a result of Italy's military action in Ethiopia, Mussolini writes: "Alle sanzioni militari risponderemo con misure militari. Ad atti di guerra risponderemo con atti di guerre," but "Alle sanzioni economiche opporremo la nostra disciplina, la nostra sobrietà, il nostro spirito di sacrificio" [To military sanctions we will respond with military measures. To acts of war we will respond with acts of war. (But) to economic sanctions we will oppose our discipline, our sobriety, our spirit of sacrifice]. Fascism distinguishes itself from its enemies not through its military force but through its transcendence of the economic, for "discipline," "sobriety," and "spirit of sacrifice" are the spiritualized code words that refer to the policy of economic autarky.

This is, to be sure, not the only function of religious language in fascist rhetoric. The role of religious terminology in fascist rhetoric is an area that, though often noted, remains to be studied in all its complexity and particularity; too often its function is assumed to be self-evident, either assigned to the "irrationality" of fascism (insofar as it appeals to faith rather than reason) or identified with the fascist rhetoric of sacrifice and martyrdom, a rhetoric whose ideological implications are assumed to be immutable. That rhetoric can be traced to D'Annunzio's occupation of Fiume, during which the elements of what Michael Ledeen has called a "political passion play" were brought together in choreographed form: soldiers fallen in World War I became martyrs to the cause of annexing Fiume to Italy (or, as D'Annunzio put it, annexing Italy to Fiume); their deaths were sacrifices to the *patria,* and their blood was consecrated and became the ink with which to write the history of the Italian people; the banner of Fiume was a *sudario,* a

Veronica's veil upon which was impressed the face of a fallen soldier; Fiume itself becomes the "holocaust," the burnt offering meant to purify the violent; Italy, in the person of D'Annunzio, "Il comandante," was figured as the *Christus patiens,* betrayed by the Allies at Versailles.[42] D'Annunzio's rhetoric may, in turn, be traced to Georges Sorel's *Reflections on Violence,* in which Sorel used the early Christians as an analogy to the modern proletariat in its fight against a new "Rome," the capitalist bourgeoisie. Scenes of martyrdom, Sorel argued, functioned to infuse an epic quality into an ideological struggle and could be put to good use in modern-day struggles.[43] The difficulties posed by this very quickly sketched genealogy seem to me to consist in asking to what extent these rhetorics can be said to be "the same," to what extent they are specific to fascism, and to what extent they are indistinguishable from the "sacrificial culture" of Western civilization in general. The task is too vast an undertaking for my project here, but I would like to open a parenthesis to consider some possible answers to these questions.

Fascism adopts religious metaphors in order to create a ritualistic political culture. About this, all agree. But disagreement begins when the question of how to read these metaphors crops up. Emilio Gentile's essay, "Fascism as Political Religion," provides an example of one way to read them. Gentile takes fascism's employment of religious, and specifically Christian, metaphors literally. He documents the regime's elaborate rituals commemorating the sacrifices of fascist martyrs, and reports statements by Mussolini, Giovanni Gentile, and other fascist intellectuals to the effect that fascism "is a religion," in order to argue that fascism constructs itself as a secular religion for four reasons. First, to elicit support among the masses, assumed to respond more passionately to appeals to faith than to reason; second, to legitimize itself through the illustrious precedent of the Catholic Church; third, to rival and replace traditional religion; and, finally, to create a sense of community that would transcend divisions, principally those of class and generation, but also, and interestingly, those between the living and the dead. (The fascist ritual of martyrdom, in which martyrs' names were called and those present were to respond "Presente!" to the names of the dead, is an eerie example of this.)[44]

This is, on the one hand, unimpeachable; the historical evidence is there: fascism said it was a religion, and it set out to make sure it had all the right accessories. But to say that fascism is a religion (as Giovanni Gentile indeed does, in the "Manifesto degli intellettuali fascisti") is to employ a metaphor; to employ the rituals of the Catholic Church in a secular context is to cite, to put those rituals between quotation marks, as it were. These are rhetorical operations, and while they can be taken literally, they need also to be read figurally. "Fascism is a religion" is a metaphor, just as "Achilles is a lion" is a metaphor. As metaphor, it is based on the transfer of a property that each member of the metaphor (fascism and religion in the one case, Achilles and lion in the other) is presumed to share; this property, the basis for the transfer, constitutes the "proper" meaning of the metaphor. In the case of Achilles and the lion, we conventionally assume that that property is courage: the lion is courageous, Achilles is courageous, therefore Achilles is a lion (the lion, as a result of this tropological exchange, can equally well be an Achilles). In the case of fascism and religion, Emilio Gentile's reading assumes that a number of properties facilitate the exchange: like religion, fascism is a faith, it requires sacrifice and devotion, it creates continuity between the living and the dead. Of course, once exchanges begin, they cannot easily be stopped, so that to accept the legitimacy of the metaphor "fascism is a religion" is also implicitly to sanction the metaphor "religion is a fascism" (as indeed it may be for a certain element of the left [religion is the "opiate of the people," and so on]). But the assumption is that both terms of the metaphor, the literal "religion" and the figural "fascism," have a property, a "proper meaning," that allows the exchange to take place. If this elementary lesson in metaphor seems far afield of the point, let us take a look at Croce's response to Giovanni Gentile's "Manifesto" and its claim that fascism is a religion. In his "countermanifesto," Croce writes that "Ma il maltrattamento delle dottrine e della storia è cosa di poco conto, in quella scrittura, a paragone dell'abuso che vi si fa della parola 'religione'" [The mistreatment of doctrines and history is of small account, in this writing, compared to the abuse done there to the word "religion"].[45] In calling the fascist employment of "religion" an "abuse ... of the word," Croce implicitly renames Gentile's rhetorical strategy, for an abuse of metaphor constitutes a different figure: catachresis.

Catachresis is the figure in which a "substitution" is made not on the basis of a preexisting similarity between two terms; there is no literal term for which "the arm of the chair" or "the eye of the storm" substitutes. A catachresis, one might say, puts something in the place of nothing. Croce's strategy in the countermanifesto, in fact, is to argue that fascism puts "religion" in the place of its ideological void: fascism is *not* a religion, but precisely because it isn't, it pretends to be one in order to cover over its intellectual debilities, to give itself a coherence and unity that it lacks. Croce objects *not* because he finds "faith" and "politics" to be antithetical; while refusing to adopt the term "religion" in relation to fascism, disowning it between quotation marks, he announces: "Per questa caotica e inafferrabile 'religione,' noi non ci sentiamo, dunque, di abbandonare la nostra vecchia fede: la fede che da due secoli e mezzo è stata l'anima dell'Italia che risorgeva, dell'Italia moderna" [For this chaotic and ungraspable "religion," we do not feel like abandoning our old faith, the faith that has for two centuries been the soul of resurgent Italy, of modern Italy], the faith, that is, of the Risorgimento.[46] In other words, Croce's strategy allows him to refuse the contamination of exchange that acceptance of the metaphor entails; if "fascism is a religion" is a catachresis, it cannot be said that "religion is a fascism," and the employment of religious language in a political context is not assumed to be essentially fascist. This seems to me an important step not so much because one might want to protect religion but rather for two related reasons: first, because it refuses fascism's appropriation of a name for its unnamed essence, refuses to give a "proper" name to fascism's impropriety, to its appropriations of other ideologies as its own. In so doing, what we have been calling the "binding mechanism" of fascism remains legible and is not sutured to an essential content; its heterogeneity is not domesticated by a familiar homogeneity. Second, Croce's approach leaves room in which to recognize the differential meanings of rhetorical strategies. By this I mean that while the "property" that Giovanni Gentile has in mind as the one that fascism and religion share is sacrifice — or as Gentile puts it, fascism "felt and promoted politics as a training gym for the sacrifice and abnegation of the individual to an idea in which the individual can find his reason for living, . . . an idea that is the fatherland" — sacrificial cultures and rhetorics may not all function in the same way (at the same time as they share a basic structure).

An example of the differential meanings of this rhetoric might be found in a brief comparison of the regime's use of the choreography of martyrdom and that of D'Annunzio at Fiume. Both make elaborate use of the culture of sacrifice, as it is played out in the logics of redemption and sacrifice. The martyr, etymologically a "witness," is one who sacrifices himself so that a cultural order may be created, saved, reconciled with the gods. D'Annunzio's martyrs were the Arditi fallen in World War I, who bore witness to and emblematized Italy's sacrifice; the martyrs of the fascist regime were those who fell in the "revolution" that brought fascism to power and who would continue to fall as long as fascism was in the making (which, by fascist definition, would be forever). Both share in the paradoxical structure of martyrdom (and testimony); as an event, martyrdom is at once necessarily singular and necessarily iterable.[47] That is to say, the martyr must make a sacrifice that is absolutely unique — losing an eye, a breast, a life — and yet must be ready to undergo that sacrifice over and over again (just as the witness must be able to repeat her testimony). But D'Annunzio at Fiume and the fascist regime inflect this structure differently because of a difference in their relation to the future. In D'Annunzio, there is a knowledge of the impossibility of the future (a version of which we have seen in *Le vergini*), coupled with a disavowal of that knowledge. Every attempt to look forward ends up in looking backward. Thus Fiume becomes for him an attempt to make the sacrifice of the Great War absolutely singular, an attempt whose impossibility is its characteristic stamp. The fascist regime, on the other hand, attempts to exploit the necessary iterability of martyrdom, showcasing its martyrs in exhibitions such as the 1932 Exhibition of the Fascist Revolution and recommending an *imitatio fascisti*.[48] Its purpose is to commemorate in order to perpetuate, always in preparation for the "war" that awaits in the future.[49]

No list of disarticulated elements of Mussolini's rhetoric would be complete without sampling the realm of invective, particularly rich in the production of neologism. The early Mussolini is fond of a sort of positivistic insult that equates physiology with intelligence; especially favored are references to the size of the brain ("microcephalic," "microcerebral") or to stages of evolution (the anticlerical Mussolini referred to priests as the "zoological species of black anthropoids").[50] World War I spawned its own jargon, which persisted in fascist discourse as part of Mussolini's self-presentation as the man from the trenches. Terms like *pacifondaismo, panciafichismo,* and *pantofolaio* [peace mongering, save-your-tummy-for-the-figs-ism, bedroom-slipper-ism] owe their coinage to the interventionists' scorn for those against entry into World War I. And the regime produced new institutions and practices that had to be named: a newspaper column devoted to ridiculing the enemies' propaganda came to be known as the *stupidario* or "stupidary"; the leaders of the staunchly agrarian squads were called *ras,* a word originally referring to semi-independent Abyssinian chieftains; the term *viricultura* [viri-culture] was coined to refer to the improvement of the race through the selection of eugenically desirable males. As "autarchic" measures were imposed, new fabrics appeared and with them new names. The most important of these was *lanital,* a fabric made from casein, a phosphoprotein of milk and chief constituent of cheese (in its earliest versions it stank and grew larger when wet).[51] The most important of such neologisms was of course the term *fascism* itself, and all its derivatives, *fascista, fascistizzazione, afascista,* and *antifascista.*[52]

Related to the production of neologism is what one might loosely call "resemanticization" (as opposed to the desemanticization that the linguistic studies in general emphasize). I use "resemanticization" to refer to the process by which terms are differently polarized in fascist language: as Mario Isnenghi has noted, what were, in prefascist parlance, positively charged terms now become negatively charged ones. As the examples that follow will demonstrate, this resemanticization is part of the popular-democratic interpellation in fascist discourse, as theorized by Ernesto Laclau. Fascist discourse succeeds in presenting itself as the voice of "the people," apart from any specific class belonging, and at once retains the Jacobin radicalism of a revolutionary confrontation with the system in power and obstructs any channeling of this revolution in a socialist direction.[53] Resemanticization thus largely concerns the erasure or redeployment of socialist terminology. *Socialista* [socialist] becomes the insulting *sozzalista* ["soilist" might be the closest translation]; previously positively charged terms, like "Bolshevik," "subversive," and "anarchy," become negative or, as in the case of *padrone* and *capitalista* [boss, capitalist], are replaced by fascist terms that recode and displace the notion of class struggle: the boss becomes a *datore di lavoro* [giver of work], and capitalism is superseded by *plutocrazia* [plutocracy]. The same recoding tendency underlies Mussolini's scorn for, and elimination of, the term "the masses," a term for him inseparable from socialist taint, and its replacement by the positively valorized *popolo,* as well as the phasing out and recoding of the word "class" and its replacement by the term "nation." The way in which, as Laclau writes, "class interpellations were retained but their meaning at the political level was denied" is illustrated by the way in which terms for class come to be applied to the nation; thus the invocation "Italia proletaria!" is addressed not to the Italian proletariat but to Italy itself as proletarian nation in the world of "plutocracy."

Isnenghi notes that the process works both ways; terms like *autorità* and *gerarchia* [authority, hierarchy], which decades of socialist, anarchist, and broadly speaking democratic propaganda had made negative, are with some difficulty transformed into positive terms. Some terms, however, had to retain their positive charge in order to produce the popular-democratic interpellation and perpetuate the binding of left and right. Thus, while much gleeful energy is devoted to deriding the liberal-democratic tradition scorned by fascism ("demoliberal," "demoplutocratic," "socialmassonic," and "liberaldemosocialmassonic" are translations of some of the terms cited by Simonini), the terms "democracy" and "revolution" are spared ridicule and "fascistized." "Fascistization" here refers to the formation of what, for the liberal-democratic tradition, amount to ideological oxymorons. The revolution becomes a *rivoluzione conservatrice* or *la rivoluzione fascista* [conservative revolution, fascist revolution]; the democracy of the leftist tradition is derided as *canagliocrazia* (a neologism that could be translated "rabbleocracy") and is replaced by a fascistized democracy that appears variously as *democrazia organizzata, democrazia gerarchica, democrazia centralizzata,* and even *democrazia autoritaria* [organized democracy, hierarchical democracy, centralized democracy, authoritarian democracy].[54] Oxy-moronic, indeed.

Fascist Violence, Fascist Rhetoric

Voi sapete che io non faccio grandi parole, ma dei fatti. Del resto, i miei discorsi sono dei fatti: o li registrano o li annunziano [You know that I am not a man of big words but of deeds. Besides, my speeches are deeds: either they report them or they announce them].

> — *Benito Mussolini,* "Sintesi della politica fascista,"
> November 18, 1925

Car tout, dans le discours de Gentile ou de Rocco, de Mussolini et de Farinacci, n'est, si l'on veut, que langage. Mais ce langage est à chaque moment l'action même, et sa performance: sans avoir besoin de revêtir les formes grammaticales particulières de ce qui a été appelé le "performatif" [For everything in the speeches of Gentile or Rocco, of Mussolini and Farinacci, is, if you will, only language. But this language is at every moment the action itself and its performance, without even needing to dress its particular grammatical forms in what has been called the "performative"].

> — *Jean Pierre Faye,* Langages totalitaires

When the historian Franco Venturi called fascism a "reign of the word," he did so with the sarcastic assurance of the materialist who knows that changing words won't change the world: if fascism thought that "words rule the world, that it sufficed to change calendars, names, terms, designations, in order to change years, men, concepts, tools," it was because it was caught in an idealist illusion.[55] For antifascist, materialist (or at least leftist) historiography, it has long been considered ideologically suspect to take seriously Mussolini's assertion that his words could indeed act upon the world; only someone woefully unaware of the relations between base and superstructure could make such a mistake. Jean Pierre Faye's remarks, cited above, on the performativity of fascist language represent a departure from this attitude, a departure that is more than a simple inversion of the relation between "language" and "action," and other than an idealist (or rightist) reevaluation of the superstructure. The so-called "linguistic turn" in literary studies, of which Faye's study was part, has led not simply to a reevaluation of language and rhetoric, such that, as Mario Isnenghi has written, rhetoric has "lost its pejorative connotation"; it has led to new theorizations of "discourse" as a totality that comprises and precedes the opposition between "word" and "thing," and of the "performative" as well as "positional" function of languages, in which language constitutes itself as act and as event.[56] These theorizations, along with reevaluations of the importance of ideology in the emergence of fascism, allow us to think of fascism as a discursive regime in which the relation between language and event is to be thought of no longer as one in which language functions to mystify a reality of pure force but rather as one in which language itself may function as one of the realities of force and violence.

To take seriously Mussolini's claim should not, however, be understood as endorsing the claim, its assumptions and presuppositions. When the apologists for the regime followed Mussolini's lead in asserting that his words were action, they did so by taking up his antirhetorical and antithetical stance: it was because they assumed that rhetoric was *not* action that they had to assert that Mussolini's *was*. In Ellwanger's words: "Mussolini had to break not only with old political principles but also with political forms and methods. For him especially political discourse had undergone a complete devaluation as a result of parliamentary abuse; the word was often an end in itself, and political discourse had become a parliamentary jargon, weak and worn away."[57] The new style he invents must therefore be one in which, as Ellwanger writes, echoing Mussolini, words should submit to the law of action and tend toward praxis. The claim is thus produced by what we have called the fascist rhetoric of crisis; "now is no longer the time for words, but for action." The theorizations of discourse and of speech acts that underlie a claim like Faye's, however, spring not from an opposition between language and action (in which we have language on one side and action on the other) but from an interrogation and rewriting of that opposition such that actions are understood not as prediscursive but as part of the discursive formation itself.

I am interested here in attempting to understand how one particular speech performed itself as an event, how, to put it in Faye's terms, the speech rhetorically performs an action. This speech occupies a privileged position in the history of the fascist regime and has, I think, synecdochic implications for fascism as a whole.

Of all the thousands of speeches that Mussolini delivered during the two decades of his rule, one stands out as the privileged place in which language becomes event: the "Discorso del 3 gennaio," as it is known in histories of fascism, decisively put an end to the liberal, constitutional state and began what we now call the fascist regime. On this point both Mussolini and historians of fascism concur. Denis Mack Smith reports that Mussolini regarded this speech "as one of the two or three most decisive events in the fascist revolution," and Renzo De Felice considers it the true break that, while not yet constituting the abrogation of the constitution that will be accomplished throughout 1926, politically completes what had begun with the March on Rome and founds the new regime.[58]

The actions the speech is said to have accomplished are several. January 3, 1925, found Mussolini facing a number of threats to his continued rule, all of them aggravated by the assassination of the socialist deputy Giacomo Matteotti.[59] Matteotti, who had spoken against Mussolini's government and against fascism as a whole, disappeared on June 10, 1924, kidnapped and then murdered by a fascist squad. While the details of Mussolini's involvement have not to this day been clarified fully, it was widely and immediately thought that he was personally in some way involved. This event provoked what is known as the "Aventine Secession" (which Mussolini snidely refers to in his "Discorso del 3 gennaio" as the "Aventine Sedition"): deputies of the Socialist, Republican, Constitutional, Popular, Social Democratic, and Communist parties vacated the parliament in protest and declared themselves the true representatives of the Italian people. De Felice describes the period following the assassination of Matteotti as one of extreme tension, in which both antifascist and anti-Mussolini sentiment were high, the stability of Mussolini's government precarious at best, and the possibilities for antifascist action ripe. That no such effective action took place was, De Felice argues, largely the fault of the Aventine Secession itself. Content to attack the fascists and Mussolini from a moral point of view, pointing to the illegal violence of the fascist squads as well as the shadiness of fascist finances, the deputies who made up the secession (with the exception of the communists) hoped to remove Mussolini through legal, parliamentary channels and hoped in addition for the help of the king. Verbal attacks increased in November, and by December the situation was critical for Mussolini: the militia threatened to turn against him; the opposition, both within and without the Fascist party, threatened to make further revelations of criminal activity; the king seemed on the brink of dismissing him; the conservative liberals headed by Antonio Salandra threatened to leave the government's coalition. What happened next is the same in all accounts: one speech turned the tide, and the opposition to fascism lost its battle.

How could a single speech match up to the difficulties facing Mussolini's government so effectively as to constitute the turn to dictatorship? Precisely how does the speech perform an action? The most obvious way in which the speech constitutes itself as event is through Mussolini's assumption of responsibility for all that fascism had done up to that point, whether violent or not, whether illegal or not:

> Dichiaro qui, al cospetto di questa Assemblea e al cospetto di tutto il popolo italiano, che io assumo, io solo, la responsabilità politica, morale, storica di tutto quanto è avvenuto.[60]

> [I declare here, in the presence of this assembly and in the presence of the entire Italian people, that I assume, I alone, the political, moral, historical responsibility for everything that has happened.]

This declaration qualifies as what J. L. Austin has theorized as a speech act. Indeed, Mussolini takes care to include in his speech even what Austin calls the conditions of "felicity" pertaining to this particular performative utterance: in the presence of the parliament, representative of the Italian people, such a declaration by the head of the government becomes valid. It is an act, then, as a performative utterance is an act, but not, at first glance, a tide-turning one, for one would expect that the assumption of responsibility would imply an admission of guilt, the suspicion of which had led to the crisis of Mussolini's government in the first place. This responsibility, after all, responds to the accusation that Mussolini raises against himself at the very beginning of the speech: "Sono io, o signori, che levo in quest'Aula l'accusa contro me stesso. Si è detto che io avrei fondato una *Ceka*" [It is I, oh gentlemen, who raise the accusation against myself in this hall. It has been alleged that I founded a Cheka].[61] An allegation calls for an answer on the order of cognition; it is either true or false, according to verifiable criteria. A response to such an allegation, and responsibility is a form of response, should belong to that order; if I say, "Yes, I am responsible," then I am saying, "Yes, it is true; I am guilty." But we have here a structure similar to that noted by Paul de Man in his essay on "excuses" in Rousseau's *Confessions:* the speech inverts the Italian saying "Chi si scusa si accusa" [He who excuses himself, accuses himself] so that it becomes "He who accuses himself, excuses himself."[62] The place of confession is blotted out by excuse. And indeed, Mussolini moves to eliminate the order of cognition early on in his speech; immediately after the self-accusation quoted above, Mussolini writes: "Dove? Quando? In qual modo? Nessuno potrebbe dirlo!" [Where? When? How? No one could say!]. This tactic, formulated in a kind of *argumentum ad ignorantiam* (Who could say? What does anyone know about it? The proposition is true if it can't be proven false!), eliminates the possibility of verifiable evidence, and with it the cognitive dimension. The effect is to sever guilt from responsibility. The responsibility that is left is the sort of responsibility a parent might assume for a window broken by a delinquent, or merely clumsy, child; not guilty of the act itself, the parent is answerable for the general conditions that allowed the act to take place. Just so, Mussolini is "not guilty" of the acts themselves but answerable for the general historical conditions that produced the violence of the fascist squads:

> Se tutte le violenze sono state il risultato di un determinato clima storico, politico e morale, ebbene a me la responsabilità di questo, perché questo clima storico, politico e morale io l'ho creato con una propaganda che va dall'intervento ad oggi.

> [If all acts of violence were the result of a particular historical, political, and moral climate, well then the responsibility for this is mine, because I created this historical, political, and moral climate with propaganda that began with the intervention into the war and continues today.] (239)

Fascism's my baby, my responsibility, says Mussolini, but that's not a responsibility that can be tied to anything resembling a specific act on my part. Those acts are in any case not open to verification (Where? When? How?) but rather should be judged according to different criteria. Thus Mussolini's "proof" that he did not found a *Ceka* goes like this:

> Se io avessi fondato una *Ceka,* l'avrei fondata sequendo i criteri che ho sempre posto a presidio di quella violenza che non può essere espulsa dalla storia. Ho sempre detto, e qui lo ricordano quelli che mi hanno seguito in questi cinque anni di dura battaglia, che la violenza, per essere risolutiva, deve essere chirurgica, intelligente, cavalleresca. Ora i gesti di questa sedicente *Ceka* sono stati sempre inintelligenti, incomposti, stupidi. (236)

> [If I had founded a Cheka, I would have founded it following the criteria that I have always placed in command of that violence that cannot be expelled from history. I have always said, and here those who have followed me in these five years of battle will remember, that violence, to be resolute, must be surgical, intelligent, chivalric. But the acts of this so-called Cheka have always been unintelligent, disorderly, stupid.]

The passage responds grammatically to the question of guilt in its contrary-to-fact form: "If I had... then it would" always implies "But I didn't, so it wasn't." But as an answer to the allegation, the hypothetical mode responds rhetorically not to criteria of truth or falsehood but to criteria of *verisimilitude.* The question of guilt, severed from that of responsibility, is thus displaced from the order of truth to the order of fiction.

The fiction generated by this displacement is made up of a series of hypothetical statements that feature a Mussolini too intelligent to have botched anything more than a few sentences. At no point does he deny having committed any of the criminal acts to which he refers, but he repeatedly appeals to the rules of verisimilitude that govern the behavior of the fictional Mussolini:

> Ma potete proprio pensare che nel giorno successivo a quello del Santo Natale, giorno nel quale tutti gli spiriti sono portati alle immagini pietose e buone, io potessi ordinare un'aggressione alle 10 del mattino in via Francesco Crispi, a Roma, dopo il mio discorso di Monterotondo, che è stato forse il più pacificatore che io abbia pronunziato in due anni di Governo? Risparmiatemi di pensarmi così cretino. (236)

> [But can you truly think that, on the day following that of Holy Christmas, a day in which all spirits are given to pious and good images, I could order an attack at ten in the morning in Via Francesco Crispi in Rome, after my speech at Monterotondo, which was perhaps the most pacificatory of the speeches that I have given in two years of Rule? Spare me from thinking me so idiotic.]

Adding piety to his personality profile, Mussolini may seem to us less than convincing; after all, according to the rules of verisimilitude of the detective novel (the genre we seem to be inhabiting at the moment), the most successful crime is one that is least expected, least verisimilitudinous, and therefore the best day to commit one is a day that no good Christian would suspect. Even the precision of the allusion to the place and time of the crime (ten in the morning in Via Francesco Crispi), while clearly meant to communicate the absurdity of such an action, reads instead as though it were an unconscious echo of the giving of the order itself. But what is important here is not what we might judge to be the success of the strategy according to our own fictional rules of what is verisimilitudinous and what is not; too often, consensus studies have fallen victim to such judgments and ended up producing a picture of fascism as what Zunino calls "collective nicodemism," a "fascism without fascists" in which no one believed (a judgment we can make now because fascism seems to be beyond belief) and hence in which — because the fascist regime did after all exist for twenty years — everyone must have merely pretended to believe.[63] The question I am asking is not whether one finds the speech believable, but rather how it is that the speech establishes its own criteria of believability and validation. In this case, by switching the criteria from those of verifiable evidence to those of verisimilitude, Mussolini recasts the question of violence; it is now not an ethical question (Was it moral or immoral?) but a question of quality (Was it stupid or intelligent?). Idiotic actions do not fit into the fiction of the peaceful, pious, intelligent man being constructed in the speech. Even less verisimilitudinous would be the assassination of a socialist deputy:

> E come potevo, dopo un successo, e lasciatemelo dire senza falsi pudori e ridicole modestie, dopo un successo così clamoroso, che tutta la Camera ha ammesso, comprese le opposizioni, per cui la Camera si aperse il mercoledì successivo in un'atmosfera idilliaca, da salotto quasi, come potevo pensare, senza essere colpito da morbosa follìa, non dico solo di far commettere un delitto, ma nemmeno il più tenue, il più ridicolo sfregio a quell'avversario che io stimavo perché aveva una certa *crânerie,* un certo coraggio, che rassomigliavano qualche volta al mio coraggio e alla mia ostinatezza nel sostenere le tesi? (237)

> [And how could I, after a success, and let me say this without false shame and ridiculous modesty, after such a clamorous success, that the entire House admitted, including the oppositions, for which [reason] the House opened the following Wednesday in an idyllic atmosphere, almost like a drawing room, how could I think, without having been stricken by morbid madness, not only of having a crime committed, but of the meekest, most ridiculous scratch on that adversary who I held in esteem because he had a certain *crânerie,* a certain courage, that sometimes resembled my courage and my obstinacy in defending my positions?]

What sense would it make to stir up the waters just when things were becoming comfortable, the House as idyllic as your living room, your enemy as admirably stubborn as yourself? This is not an appeal to irrational emotions but rather to reason and common sense: you'd have to be crazy to do such a thing, and the Mussolini of this fiction is a man whose rational faculties are as intact as his listener's. Here the fictional persona constructed in the speech begins to clash with the fascist fiction of the *uomo nuovo,* however, for the new man's virility is in part dependent upon a scorn for the *vita comoda,* and for peacefulness in general.[64] It thus has to be modified a few lines later when, in justification of his lack of forceful action immediately following the assassination, Mussolini reassures his audience that it's not as though he isn't capable of *gesti di energia* [acts of energy] — take the bombing of civilians in Corfu, for example! — he simply didn't find it intelligent under the circumstances.

As Mussolini spins them out, the hypothetical statements to be measured against criteria of verisimilitude come closer and closer to the "truth" as the opposition sees it. At the same time, they slide from contrary-to-fact constructions into what in Italian is known as the "hypothetical of reality" ("if" clauses in the indicative rather than in the imperfect subjunctive). He continues:

> Se le frasi più o meno storpiate bastano per impiccare un uomo, fuori il palo e fuori la corda! Se il fascismo non è stato che olio di ricino e manganello, e non invece una passione superba della migliore gioventù italiana, a me la colpa! Se il fascismo è stato un'associazione a delinquere, io sono il capo di questa associazione a delinquere. (238–39)

> [If more or less mangled sentences are enough to hang a man, out with the post and out with the rope! If fascism was nothing other than castor oil and bludgeon, and not instead a proud passion of the best Italian youth, then the fault is mine! If fascism was a gang of hoodlums, I am the head of this gang of hoodlums!]

These three sentences differ in their relation to hypothetical reality, the first two maintaining a contrary-to-fact meaning even while no longer assuming the grammatical form. Thus, the enthymeme underlying the first sentence goes like this: "If rhetoric is a cause for hanging, then hang me! But clearly it's not, one doesn't hang a man for a few mispronounced sentences, so don't convict me!" (It is unclear, by the way, whether Mussolini had any particular mangled sentences in mind or is merely adopting an antirhetorical stance. One could think of some "mangled sentences" in the context of the Matteotti affair. Particularly "mispronounced" were the words he was heard to have said after Matteotti's last speech: "Cosa fa questa *ceka*? Cosa fa Dumini? Quell'uomo [Matteotti] dopo quel discorso non dovrebbe più circolare" [What is this Cheka doing? What is Dumini doing? That man (Matteotti) shouldn't be allowed to circulate after that speech].)[65] The enthymeme underlying the second sentence goes like this: "If fascism was only violence, then it's my fault! But it wasn't, it was rather a superb passion, so don't hold me responsible for violence!" In the third sentence, however, something isn't quite right. The logic loops back upon itself, in almost stand-up comedian fashion: "I am the head of fascism; if fascism was a criminal organization, then I am the head of a bunch of hoodlums; but it wasn't a criminal organization, so I'm not the head of fascism. . . . But I am! So it was?" The "stupid violence" from which he had separated himself and for which he had assumed responsibility without however being guilty of it is once again laid at his feet. Whether or not Mussolini "meant" for the sentence to boomerang in this way (perhaps this is one of the *frasi storpiate* to which he refers in the same paragraph!), it is in keeping with the logic of the speech that the violence should be returned to him. That "logic" at this point is more akin to Freud's kettle logic than anything else, since it allows Mussolini both to deny and to admit guilt by claiming responsibility for violence for which he is not responsible. Kettle logic owes its name to a joke recounted in *Jokes and Their Relation to the Unconscious* in which a man returned a borrowed kettle with a large hole in it. His excuse ran like this: "First I never borrowed a kettle from B. at all; secondly, the kettle had a hole in it already when I got it from him; and thirdly, I gave him back the kettle undamaged."[66] Unlike the kettle example, however, in which one excuse denies ever having borrowed the kettle at all, Mussolini's speech never denies that the violence itself took place and never eliminates it from the discussion. It took place; what is at stake in the speech is the excusing and then reutilization of the violence. The guilt that is never directly denied floats at the edges of the speech until, at the very end, it loops back, as though Mussolini's kettle logic went like this: "I didn't do it, but I am responsible; I'm responsible, so I must have done it."

The next move of the speech transforms the violence perpetrated into violence undergone. This takes place in what seems at first a return to the order of cognition, truth, and verifiable evidence, and is signaled in the earlier outburst: "Non è menzogna!" [It's not a lie!]. The first "fact," the first piece of verifiable evidence that Mussolini cites, is the presence of hundreds of fascists in prisons; after his historic assumption of responsibility, he then continues with a whole series of "facts" concerning innocent fascists who fell victim to "subversive" violence, defenseless *carabinieri* attacked by overheated women, and the like (the unruly women will, as we shall see, be disciplined at the end of the speech). I say that this turn only seems to be a return to the order of cognition because it functions rhetorically as excuse (fascist violence was really only self-defense: Look at how persecuted we are!) and therefore remains within the performative dimension.

By the conclusion of the speech, then, the peaceful, intelligent, pious Mussolini has been forced by the facts of history into a defensive position from which there is only one route of escape (this at least is the fiction performed by the speech): force, the use of that violence of which he is not guilty yet for which he is responsible. What began as an *argumentum ad ignorantiam* ends as an *argumentum ad baculum,* or appeal to force:

Quando due elementi sono in lotta e sono irriducibili, la soluzione è la forza. Non c'è stata altra soluzione nella storia e non ce ne sarà mai....

Vi siete fatte delle illusioni! Voi avete creduto che il fascismo fosse finito perché io lo comprimevo, che fosse morto perché io lo castigavo e poi avevo la crudeltà di dirlo. Ma se io mettessi la centesima parte dell'energia che ho messo a comprimerlo, a scatenarlo, voi vedreste allora.

Non ci sarà bisogno di questo, perché il Governo è abbastanza forte per stroncare in pieno definitivamente la sedizione dell'Aventino.

L'Italia, o signori, vuole la pace, vuole la tranquillità, vuole la calma laboriosa. Noi, questa tranquillità, questa calma laboriosa gliela daremo con l'amore, se è possibile, e con la forza, se sarà necessario. (240)

[When two elements are in struggle and are irreducible, the solution is force. There has never been another solution in history and there never will be....

Gentlemen! You have deluded yourselves! You believed that fascism was finished because I restrained it, that it was dead because I castigated it and then had the cruelty to say so. But if I were to put into unleashing it a hundredth of the energy that I put into restraining it, then you would see.

There will be no need of this because the government is strong enough to crush fully and definitively the Aventine sedition.

Italy, gentlemen, wants peace, wants tranquility, wants industrious calm. This tranquility, this industrious calm, we'll give it to her with love, if possible, and with force, if necessary.]

The speech, we now see, amounts to a kind of stockpiling of force on Mussolini's part, for the recourse to threat depends for its efficacy upon the violence that it has been the aim of the speech to excuse. And that excusing of violence has increased the violence; as de Man writes, "Excuses generate the very guilt they exonerate, though always in excess or by default."[67] By assuming responsibility, a posteriori, for the illegal violence of the fascist squads, Mussolini has put himself in a position to claim control, a priori, of both the violence perpetrated and that which was "held in check." The violence that existed "out there" has been fully rhetoricized, recycled as performative language — as promise and threat. Rhetoric and violence are interdependent; the positing of nonverbal violence gives meaning to the rhetoric, while rhetoric gives renewed meaning, as performative threat, to violence already committed.

This rhetoricization of violence accounts for the irrelevance of the question of belief to an understanding of the efficacy of the speech. Belief is no more relevant to the speech than it is to the success of any performative. When, for example, Mussolini exhorts the listener "not to think him so stupid" he is already wielding the threat that takes on full force at the end of the speech. After all, we know that Mussolini's "intelligence" is one with violence, surgical and intelligent; thinking him stupid might just provoke an "act of energy."

The rhetoricization of violence also accounts for the turn to rape at the end of the speech. Here we have a knot of fascist articulation in which the "elements" of violence, nationalism, and sexuality are bound together to produce what Teresa de Lauretis has called a "violence of rhetoric," the violence resulting from the implication of all representations of violence in a particular model of sexual difference.[68] De Lauretis posits two main kinds of violence, one whose object is "female," in the sense that it is represented as feminine, and one whose object is "male," in the corresponding sense. An example of the first is the "rape of nature," a metaphor that invokes a scenario of a male subject doing violence to a feminine other; an example of the second is the "violent reciprocity" and rivalry between men, as theorized by René Girard. I cite these examples because it seems to me that the introduction of gender into Mussolini's speech accomplishes a rerouting of violence from "male" to "female." That is to say, the introduction of a feminized "Italia" here is not merely a clichéd flourish but rather plays a crucial interpellative role in redirecting the violence that threatened to erupt among men (the threat to which the speech responds) toward a "woman" to be loved or raped. Nationalism is the channel that accomplishes the redirection, for here as elsewhere the model for nationalism is a heterosexuality of which, as Catherine MacKinnon has written, force is a normal part.[69] The Machiavellian terms "force" and "consent" invoked in the speech, and recurrent both in Mussolini's rhetoric and in studies on fascism, are inseparable from such a gendered representation of violence.

If the speech ends with a gang bang, it is because the homosocial bond is enlisted in the aid, and in the absence, of political unity. But the gang bang is, Mussolini hastens to add, done out of love:

> Tutti sappiamo che ciò che ho in animo non è capriccio di persona, non è libidine di Governo, non è passione ignobile, ma è soltanto amore sconfinato e possente per la patria. (240)

> [We all know that what I harbor in my soul is not personal caprice, it is not lust for rule, it is not ignoble passion, but only boundless and potent love for my country.]

What's love got to do with it? Tina Turner might say. And she'd be right to ask. Macciocchi has already described this move for us as that of the pimp who tells his whore that love will come after the blows. It was, she argued, the principal strategy of Mussolini's speeches addressed to women. Here, however, the addressee is interpellated as the virile man who will join in the nationalist beating, and call it potent love.

All this may suffice to explain the way in which Mussolini's "Discorso del 3 gennaio" can be considered an act; but how may it be considered an event, and a tide-turning one at that? Here we may turn for a final moment to Austin's theorization of the performative and remind ourselves that the conditions of felicity for any performative utterance are anchored in a juridico-political system or context that is already in place. A performative does not bring into existence the circumstances according to which it "comes off." To marry someone is, to use one of Austin's favorite examples, a case not merely of saying a few words but of saying a few words within the context of prescribed circumstances. In the case of Mussolini's speech, we have noted his opening invocation of the juridico-political context that rendered felicitous his initial assumption of responsibility. But what context validates his threat? I would argue that the context is, by the end of the speech, no longer the same as the initial one, that Mussolini has, through the process we have described above, brought into existence a different juridico-political context. The speech moves steadily from a context in which laws still hold (Mussolini even cites an article of the Statute, reminding the House of its right to accuse the king's minsters of a crime), to one of lawlessness. Mussolini's assumption of responsibility for all prior violence is an assumption of responsibility for lawlessness as well, and the claim that he created the conditions that led to such acts at once establishes him as the context that created the lawlessness and as the bringer of a new law. The speech thus brings into existence, through its speech acts, the juridico-political conditions that grant the performative its felicity. The speech consequently *validates itself.* In this sense it is no longer a performative act but is an event made possible by the positional power of language (its power to posit: *Fiat Dux!*) as well as by the violence — both "linguistic" and "extralinguistic" — that the speech has yoked together.

Demographic Delirium in the Prophylactic State

"Se si diminuisce, signori, non si fa l'Impero, si diventa una colonia!"[70] [If our numbers decrease, gentlemen, we won't create the empire; we'll become a colony!]. Nothing could better capture the knot that binds together the fascist regime's reproductive policies and the colonial aspirations of Mussolini's Italy than these words, spoken on May 26, 1927, as part of the "Discorso dell'ascensione." Since the nineteenth century, Italy's colonialism had been justified as "demographic," as a "need" caused by the large numbers of Italians who had been forced to emigrate abroad in order to find work and sustenance. There were, from this point of view, too many Italians, and colonialism was seen as the solution to the loss of citizenry; it turned "abroad" into "home" and, to use the parlance of the period, gave the emigrants-turned-colonizers "a place in the sun." But as Pier Giorgio Zunino notes, fascism's demographic calculations produced an "impossible equation" according to which there were at once too many *and* too few Italians. Indeed, a continued increase in population was deemed necessary in order to provide the nation with this pressing "need" to expand its borders; a demographic boom was intended to supply Italy with both the motivation and the means (soldiers, cannon fodder, martyrs) to acquire colonies and satisfy the increasing imperial ambitions of the fascist regime. Too many, or too few? Resorting once again to the criterion of intelligence, Mussolini rationalizes the contradiction by attributing to "qualche inintelligente" the former view:

> Qualche inintelligente dice: "Siamo in troppi." Gli intelligenti rispondono: "Siamo in pochi." Affermo che, dato non fondamentale, ma pregiudiziale della potenza politica, e quindi economica e morale delle nazioni, è la loro potenza demografica. (364)

> [Some unintelligent people say: "There are too many of us." The intelligent ones respond: "There are too few of us." I affirm that demographic power is a not a fundamental but a prejudicial given of the political, and hence economic and moral, power of nations.][71]

One doesn't have to be a genius, however, to understand what "intelligence" stands for here: later in the speech Mussolini will take up the criterion of intelligence once again, this time in order to argue that an opposition is *stolta* [stupid] in a fascist regime. Fascists and antifascists line up along the line of intelligence, a line that, as we shall see, retains the link with violence established in the "Discorso del 3 gennaio." What interests me here, however, is the link that Mussolini establishes between demographic and political power. Mussolini's formulation makes clear the degree to which the regime's policing of gender and sexuality, its codification of that policing in pronatalist policies and reproductive incentives and controls, was no afterthought but a part of the very formation of fascist ideology. As the Duce puts it, "L'Italia, per contare qualche cosa, deve affacciarsi sulla soglia della seconda metà di questo secolo con una popolazione non inferiore ai sessanta milioni di abitanti" (364) [If Italy is to count for something, it must appear on the threshold of the second half of the century with a population of not fewer than sixty million inhabitants]. Or, to put it more succinctly, in order to count for something, Italy has to start...counting. The fascist regime's aspirations to be a world power and its demand for an increase in population are strictly linked, the latter the means to the former. Yet this particular strand of fascist ideology does not appear in lists of "protofascist elements" or "ideas" that might be recognized as "intellectual sources" of fascism.[72] Rather, it tends to be shunted off to the rubric of "women and family" and only recently has been given serious attention by historians who have begun work on women under fascism.[73] That work has begun to make visible the degree to which fascism's principal fantasy was a reproductive one.

Though not as tide-turning as the "Discorso del 3 gennaio," the "Discorso dell'ascensione" established as policy some of the elements of the reproductive fantasy and gave an official form to the demographic delirium that would lead Mussolini, in a 1934 article, to blame World War I on "i dieci milioni di francesi non nati" [ten million unborn French] — his theory being that had those ten million French been born, Germany would not have perceived France as weak and vulnerable, and the war might have been avoided.[74] "Il numero è forza" [There is strength in numbers], Mussolini was wont to say, and if the unborn could be the cause of a world war, surely an increased birthrate should lead down the royal road to empire. The speech also sets out the principal measures of repression put into effect by the fascist regime — suppression of freedom of the press, suppression of parties of opposition, creation of a special police force and of the practice of the *confino*, or internment of political prisoners — and outlines the future of the fascist state. What is the relation between these aspects, or is their inclusion in a single speech due to a stepping up of policy-making activity, mere chronological coincidence? In this section I would like to propose, through a reading of the "Discorso dell'ascensione," that this reproductive fantasy was, as Mussolini himself says, "pre-judicial," that is, that it logically preceded and in fact determined other questions and aspects that make up fascist ideology.

State intervention into private matters is the explicit topic of the speech. Before issuing the command to multiply, which implicitly places sexual reproduction at the center of the speech, Mussolini broaches the less troublesome topic of the control of disease. Thus in the opening paragraphs he clearly marks the difference of the fascist state from the "liberal" states that preceded it: "Qualcuno, in altri tempi, ha affermato che lo Stato non doveva preoccuparsi della salute fisica del popolo" (361) [Someone, in other times, claimed that the state shouldn't intervene in the physical health of the people]. It is the "social" nature of disease that appears to justify intervention into the private sphere on the part of fascism; there are, says Mussolini, "malattie sociali" on the rise: named are tuberculosis, pellagra, and yellow fever. (Venereal diseases are conspicuously absent from the discussion.) Caused by external agents that invade the body, these contagious diseases can be eliminated through the elimination of the agents that carry them. Mussolini, however, recommends not immunization but rather "la difesa sanitaria alle frontiere marittime e terrestri della Nazione" (362) [the sanitary defense of the maritime and land borders of the nation]. The languages of hygiene and those of vigilance and defense intersect: the "battle" against pellagra has been won; the "struggle" against tumors continues; "vigilance" over foodstuffs must be maintained; the "borders" to be defended turn out to be not those of the body but those of the state. This intersection is manifest in the description of the principal agents of infection as rats, those rodents who "portano dall'Oriente malattie contagiose: quell'Oriente donde ci vengono molte cose gentili, febbre gialla e bolscevismo" (362) [bring from the Orient contagious diseases: that Orient whence come so many nice things, yellow fever and Bolshevism]. The reference to Bolshevism is, on the one hand, just a little fascist witticism — those rats ought to be eliminated, like little communists! — but it is, on the other hand, also the subject of the second part of the speech: those communists ought to be eliminated, like big rats! The campaign to *derattizzare* [to rid of rats], an indisputably valuable hygienic measure (any traveler to Italy will have noted still today signs announcing *zona derattizzata,* an expression to which the "Discorso dell'ascensione" gives renewed meaning), provides the model for and becomes inseparable from a rather more controversial measure taken against "foreign agents" within the body politic. The *confino,* the geographical confinement of the political opposition to small villages and islands, is addressed later in the speech and justified with reference to medical practice: "Si levano questi individui dalla circolazione come un medico toglie dalla circolazione un infetto" (378) [These individuals are to be taken out of circulation just as a doctor takes an infected individual out of circulation]. Both of these cures — quarantine of the political opposition, policing of the national borders as defense against social diseases — assume an externalization of the source of "infection." If the agent is internal, the solution is to expel it, make it external by "taking it out of circulation"; if it is already external, the solution is simply to keep it so. Externalization allows for easy isolation of the offending agent through the enforcement and creation of boundaries.

The speech thus accomplishes a reconfiguring of the relation of the public and the private in the fascist state, such that the two exist along a continuum in which the private is overtaken by the public, and the public by the private. To this interpenetration of public and private corresponds an exchange of literal and figurative meanings. The principal metaphor along which public and private slide is that of hygiene, a "private" operation that here becomes social. This transfer is built upon another metaphor, assumed to be already in place, for the property that public and private presumably share is a "body." Presiding over the operation is, of course, Mussolini, who portrays himself as master hygienist: "Io sono il clinico che non trascura i sintomi" (367) [I am the doctor who doesn't overlook symptoms]. The metaphorical doctor who looks after the body politic recalls Machiavelli's *Prince* and is hardly new in the history of political thought. Slavoj Žižek, in fact, remarks that the notion of society as a social body is the fundamental ideological fantasy, that is to say, a fantasy of a society that is not riven by antagonism.[75] It is, to be sure, a fundamental ideological fantasy of fascism, one that will be replicated and "reproduced" throughout the speech. The externalization of the infecting agent, for example, serves to perpetuate the fantasy of an organic unity of the people. What is perhaps new with fascism, however, is the way in which the metaphor is employed in order to establish and legitimate state intervention into "private" matters, on the one hand, and "personal" intervention into matters of state, on the other.

It would be a mistake to think of one of these terms as more "literal" than the other. Though it is tempting to attribute priority to the no less phantasmatic notion of the integrity of the body, in the speech they appear to be equally phantasmatic, one fantasy reinforcing and structuring the other. That is to say that if the fantasy of the whole body provides a foundation for a notion of the state as a unified "body" that can be diseased, infected, but also cured and purified, the fantasy of the unified state in turn provides a foundation for the notion of the integrity of the human body, a body that, like the state, comes to have "borders" that must be "policed."

Border patrol seems, in fact, to be the organizing principle of the speech, and leads from the defense of various sorts of *confini* [borders] to the creation of the fascist *confino* [internment]. Mussolini insists, for example, that Bolzano, or fascistically speaking, Bolgiano, is *italianissima*. Its *intedescamento*

[Germanification] is to be resisted, and the *confine del Brennero* that marks Italy's northern border is to be held sacred and inviolable. A deleterious example of crossing borders is offered in Mussolini's version of the topos of the *contadino che s'inurba* [country cousin in the city]. In a typical fascist marriage of a mode of production to a question of biological reproduction, Mussolini adds to the traditional image of the big city as lure to the foolish peasant ("le grandi città, dove ci sono tutte quelle cose piacevoli e stupide che incantano coloro che appaiano nuovi alla vita" [367] [the big cities, where there are all those nice and stupid things that enchant those who appear to be new to city life]) the sterilizing effect of the modern city upon those who enter within its borders: "L'urbanesimo industriale porta alla sterilità le popolazioni" (367) [Industrial urbanism leads populations to sterility].[76] Yet again, the discussion of the organization of local governments is framed in terms of mapping borders: "Dovremo finalmente delineare i confini giuridici, amministrativi e morali della provincia" (371) [We must finally delineate the juridical, administrative, and moral boundaries of the provinces]. And the efficiency of the fascist Special Tribunal is presented as dependent upon the expulsion of an agent of infection:

Il Tribunale speciale...funziona egregiamente e non ha dato luogo ad inconvenienti, e meno ne darà, specialmente se si adotterà la misura di escludere dalle sue mura l'elemento femminile, il quale spesso porta nelle cose serie il segno incorreggibile della sua frivolezza. (376)

[The Special Tribunal functions excellently and has not created difficulties, and will create even less, especially if it adopts the measure of excluding from its walls the feminine element, which often brings the indelible sign of frivolity to serious things.]

The exclusion of women from the body politic follows a "body politics" familiar to feminist psychoanalysis; women are castrated, cut off and cut out by the law. Immediately following this entreaty to exclude women from the "walls" of the law, Mussolini announces, as the culmination of the series, the new fascist approach to dealing with its political opposition: "E' stata applicata la pena del confino" [The punishment of internment has been applied].

The threat of infection, both physiological and political, and the borders erected in response to this imagined threat are presented as the causes of the state itself:

Non so nemmeno pensare nel secolo XX uno che possa vivere fuori dello Stato, se non allo stato di barbarie, allo stato selvaggio. E' solo lo Stato che dà la coscienza di se stessi ai popoli. Se il popolo è organizzato, il popolo è uno Stato, altrimenti è una popolazione che sarà alla mercè del primo gruppo di avventurieri interni o di qualsiasi orda di invasori che venga dall'esterno. Perchè, o signori, solo lo Stato con la sua organizzazione giuridica, con la sua forza militare, preparata in tempo utile, può difendere la collettività nazionale: se la collettività umana si è frazionata e ridotta al nucleo familiare, basteranno cento normanni per conquistare le Puglie. (389)

[I can't even imagine someone living outside of the State in the twentieth century, unless it be in the state of barbarianism, in a savage state. Only the State gives self-consciousness to peoples. If the people are organized, the people are a State; otherwise, they are a population that will be at the mercy of the first group of internal adventurers or of any horde of invaders that comes from abroad. Because, gentlemen, only the State with its juridical organization, with its military strength, ready at hand, can defend the national collectivity: if the human collectivity is divided and reduced to the familial nucleus, a hundred Normans could conquer Puglia.]

Peoples who exist outside of the State not only lack form and order, but, living as they do in a primitive, "savage" state, are also throwbacks to an evolutionarily prior state: indeed, in a version of this speech published in 1934, the second sentence reads, "Solo lo Stato da l'ossatura ai popoli" [Only the State gives a backbone to peoples], rendering them not only barbarian but invertebrate.[77] Outside of the State, they are not "people," both in the sense that they then belong to a lower order and are consequently subhuman and in the sense, elucidated by Žižek, that belonging to the State is "rigidly designated" by the political term "the people"; that is to say, belonging to the State is the only feature that belongs to "the people" in all possible worlds (according, that is, to the totalitarian world).[78] There is consequently no *popolo* outside of the State, but only a *popolazione,* a population of huddled nuclear families that make easy prey for those fierce Normans. Mussolini is right to say that he cannot even imagine an alternative to his own regime, for the fantasy of an organic whole, threatened with external antagonism, functions to cover over any internal antagonism that might tear at the social fabric from within, even when that social fabric (the "population") is the one that is abjected. Thus the "population" Mussolini imagines is not riven by *internal* dissent but, like the "national collectivity," threatened from without; even the supposed internal threat, the *avventurieri interni,* turns out to be an external one, for adventurers are by definition crossers of borders; Zingarelli's dictionary defines the adventurer as "he who goes about the world in search of fortune," oblivious to national borders.

It is interesting, then, that Mussolini argues against the necessity of a political opposition on the grounds that the only opposition that fascism needs is *internal*. An opposition was useful, he claims, only in "easy times" when all there was to do was to discuss when, how, and where socialism would be realized, when there was time to be wasted in a parliament. (This is another example of the association of "rhetoric" and parliamentarism that we noted earlier in the chapter.) As always in fascist rhetoric, times have changed:

> L'opposizione non è necessaria al funzionamento di un sano regime politico. L'opposizione è stolta, superflua in un regime totalitario come è il regime fascista.... Ma l'opposizione l'abbiamo in noi, cari signori; noi non siamo dei vecchi ronzini che hanno bisogno di essere pungolati. Noi controlliamo severamente noi stessi. L'opposizione sopra tutto la troviamo nelle cose, nelle difficoltà obiettive, nella vita, la quale ci dà una vasta montagna di opposizioni, che potrebbe esaurire spiriti anche superiori al mio. (379)

> [A healthy political regime does not need an opposition. An opposition is stupid, superfluous in a totalitarian regime like the fascist regime.... But we have the opposition within us, dear gentlemen. We are not old nags who have to be spurred on. We control ourselves severely. We find opposition above all in things, in objective difficulties, in life, which gives us a vast mountain of oppositions that could exhaust even spirits superior to my own.]

A political regime may be called "healthy" only on the basis of a property shared with bodies: here that property is explicitly fantasized as "unity." Indeed, the passage nicely documents the workings of the logic of totalitarianism, as Claude Lefort has defined it. According to Lefort, totalitarianism denies the social division made visible by democracy and aims to restore the unity of power, law, and knowledge (a unity shattered by democracy) by reasserting the existence of a unitary people. The totalitarian denial takes place as a double movement: "the annulment of the signs of the division of the state and society, and of those of the internal division of society."[79] In the "Discorso dell'ascensione," both of these annulments are facilitated by the metaphor of the social body, which allows for exchanges to shuttle back and forth between state and society, public and private, social and personal hygiene, and so on. In the passage above, the shuttling movement takes us from a social body to a private one whose function it is to contain and transcend political antagonism by constituting a new, apparently apolitical, spiritual unity. That is to say, no political or social division is necessary to fascism because another division precedes and displaces it — a division that is neither political nor social but rather one created by the opposition between matter and spirit. The internal division renders the external one superfluous and is itself resolved by its containment within a singularity: "my spirit." Spirit conquers matter, conquers the division. Yet the personalization of the spirit attaches it to a person, to a body, that works at once to depoliticize antagonism — it is only a question of spirit and matter — and to repoliticize it. By attaching the question of spirit to the personal body of the Duce (and the virile Duce is of course known for controlling himself severely), the speech links it to a political embodiment whose "personal" unity stands in the place of the political and social antagonism that it works to deny. To the internalization and personalization of antagonism corresponds an externalization of explicitly political antagonism: the metaphor of "mountains of opposition," in fact, works to repoliticize the scenario, for, in the context of border patrol, it evokes the mountains that serve as Italy's "natural" geographical boundary, a boundary that separates a spiritual, fascist Italy from the materialist opposition that lies beyond. Spirit conquers matter, just as fascist Italy conquers materialism.

Antagonism is simultaneously denied and recognized: here lies the disavowal that structures the ideological fantasy of the people as organic whole. Traces of recognition and denial litter the speech, producing the floundering, self-contradictory effect common to Mussolini's speeches. This effect of "self-contradiction" is the result not so much of feeble intellectual powers as of the surfacing of the contradictory logic that underlies all ideological fantasy. Mussolini knows very well that there are antifascists, and yet all the same his goal in this speech is to deny their very existence, even as he announces the measures taken to *end* their all-too-irritating and real existence. Thus the *confinati,* or interned prisoners, are represented first as, in the majority, common criminals of the most sensationalist sort ("autentiche canaglie, ladri, sfruttatori di donne, venditori di stupefacenti" [376] [genuine rabble, thieves, exploiters of women, drug dealers]); of these there are, notes the arithmetically gifted Duce, 1527. Of political *confinati,* a mere 698 have been sent to the islands, Mussolini claims: "Ma nessuno di questi confinati vuol essere antifascista e qualcuno ha l'aria di essere fascista" (377) [But none of these prisoners wants to be antifascist, and some seem to be fascist]. This last statement shows us fascist wit at work again, for it suggests that the *confinati* themselves deny their antifascist associations and claim to be fascist to save their own skins. Nothing could play better into Mussolini's hands, since it allows him to accept the imputed protest as figurative when meting out punishment (thereby vilifying the antifascists as cowards) and yet to utilize it as literal when claiming not to need to resort to such measures: they are antifascists, and liars, in the former moment, and fascists, and truth tellers, in the latter.

So vehement is the denial of the existence of an opposition that the only trace of its existence is in fact the series of harsh measures taken to suppress it. If postwar historiography has sometimes produced a "fascism without fascists," Mussolini might here be said to produce an "antifascism without antifascists." Their existence fades in and out, like a weak radio signal; thus the opposition can be recognized only as dying ("La generazione degli irriducibili, di quelli che non hanno capito la guerra e non hanno capito il fascismo, ad un certo momento si eliminerà per legge naturale" [384] [The generation of irreducibles of those who did not understand the war and did not understand fascism, will naturally eliminate itself at a certain moment]) or as phantasmatic ("Il consenso del popolo c'è. Difatti l'opposizione si riduce a qualche conato vociferatorio, ma così fantastico e pacchiano, che lo stesso popolo ne fa giustizia" [385] [The consent of the people is there. In fact the opposition is limited to some rumored attempts, so boorish and fantastic that the people themselves mete out justice]. Why then should the principal political action of the fascist state be to target the phantasmatic *antirivoluzione* (and I list in order of presentation the measures announced by Mussolini): to withdraw and review all passports; to order that whoever is caught in the act of clandestinely crossing the border should be shot without warning; to dissolve all antifascist (or suspected to be such) associations, organizations, and groups; to deport all those suspected of antifascism or of counterrevolutionary activity, and all those who illegitimately wear the black shirt? Mussolini's answer brings us back to the reproductive considerations with which the speech begins: "Terrore, signori, questo? No, non è terrore, è appena rigore. Terrorismo? Nemmeno, è igiene sociale, profilassi nazionale" (378) [Terror, gentlemen? No, it is not terror, it is barely even rigor. Terrorism? Not even that, it is social hygiene, national prophylaxis].

Prophylaxis, from the Greek "to stand on guard before," may refer both to measures taken to prevent disease and to contraceptive measures taken to prevent conception. Both meanings attach themselves to national prophylaxis: at once prevention of the "disease" of a political opposition and a contraceptive measure taken to ensure that antifascists are not reproduced. In the context of the speech, the institution of a *state* prophylaxis stands in sharp contrast to the prohibition of *personal* prophylaxis — the institution, that is, of a tax on "celibate" men and the threat of a future tax to be imposed on "sterile marriages," both measures taken in the interest of encouraging biological reproduction.[80] If national prophylaxis is to be encouraged, it is in the interest of guarding against the social reproduction of antifascism, as though it were a biological process of the reproduction of political bodies; personal prophylaxis, on the other hand, is to be discouraged in the interests of promoting the biological reproduction of fascists. The fantasy is not only that more and more bodies would be produced but that the offspring would physically embody a political doctrine.[81] Fascist racism is contained in this conflation of social and biological reproduction (rather than in a belief in "racial purity," for example).[82] Fascists are born and not made; in fact, in yet another example of fascist wit, Mussolini announces in this speech that it is too late to "become fascist": "Adesso non si diventa più fascisti. Tanto peggio per i ritardatari. I nostri treni non li aspettano!" (383) [Now one can no longer become fascist. So much the worse for the latecomers. Our trains won't wait for them!]. Fascist eugenics plans for the gradual and "natural" elimination of the generation of antifascists and afascists (it will eliminate itself according to "natural law," says Mussolini) and the birth of new generations of ideologically pure fascists (the *razza italiana* [Italian race] to which he refers at the beginning of the speech) and the touted *giovinezza* [youth] of the fascist anthem. This biopolitical reproduction may eventually produce "another Mussolini," an ideological clone to take his place — but (in a notable reversal of the fascist rhetoric of crisis) the time has not yet come: "Non è ancora nato il mio successore" (385) [My successor has not yet been born], announces Mussolini.

Such a clone would have to be physiologically as well as ideologically exact in order to reproduce the mode in which Mussolini intervenes personally in matters of state in the speech. Like state intervention in private matters, personal intervention into matters of state is facilitated by the metaphor of hygiene as protection against "disease." In perhaps the most violent passage of the speech, Mussolini gives a physiological reason for the elimination of the fascist squads that brought him to power, but whose continued existence was both a threat to his power and a source of embarrassment: "Io non posso soffrire fisicamente coloro che sono ammalati di nostalgia, che ad ogni minuto traggono dai loro petti sospiri e respiri profondi: 'Come erano belli quei tempi!' Tutto ciò è semplicemente idiota!" (381) [I cannot physically tolerate people who are sick with nostalgia, who at every moment draw deep sighs and breaths from their chests: "Those were the good old days!" All that is simply idiotic!]. Within the context of the fantasized social

body, the fate of those nostalgic for the days of illegal, revolutionary violence is clear: these "sick" ones will have to be expelled from the healthy
body that is at once the Duce's and that of the fascist regime. There is
more fascist wit at work in the passage: Mussolini had, at the beginning of
the speech, announced that its topic was the *quadro,* the "big picture" of the
physical health of the people in the regime; following the passage, Mussolini
makes a policy announcement: "Tutti gli elementi di parte sono *inquadrati:*
del resto, quando non lo sono, li colpisco" (382) [All of the partisan elements have been brought into line (into the picture): besides, when they
are not, I strike them down]. *Squadrismo,* notes the sarcastic and linguistically
aware Mussolini, was derived from *squadra;* once on the etymological path,
we can follow the Duce's lead and also note that it derives from *squadrare,*
which in turn derives from the Latin *exquadrare,* to *ridurre in quadro,* reduce
to a square, to a *quadro.* Mussolini plays doubly on the linguistic here; on
the one hand, *squadra* appears to be destined linguistically to be brought
inside the *quadro;* on the other, paronomastically and through its privative
s, a *squadra* remains outside of any *quadro,* fascist or not. Its expulsion is
further dramatized rhetorically by the proliferation of adjectives indicating
stupidity, a figure, we now recognize, for violent acts to be taken against
those branded as such. *Squadrismo* was, Mussolini announces, a great thing
as an instrument of fascist activity, but it is "assurdo, ridicolo, e stupido di
farne qualche cosa a sé" (381) [absurd, ridiculous, and stupid to make of
it a thing in itself]. What's more, "squadrismo fatto in ritardo" is "simply absurd," and those nostalgic for it are "simply idiotic." Fair warning for
measures to come.

Paragraphs later in the speech Mussolini once again treats us to a physio-
political reaction. In response to stockbrokers and analysts who dared to
speculate that the fascist regime was bringing financial catastrophe, Mussolini retorts: "Mi danno la nausea. E non è facile, dato il mio regime
dietetico" (387) [They nauseate me. And that's not easy, given my dietetic
regime]. Dietetic and political regimes are one and the same, contained by
the same sociopolitical and yet personal body that is the Duce's. Public and
private, political and personal, the Duce's body is produced through a condensation of the fantasies of the integrity of the human body and of the
unity of the social body. The product of this condensation is necessarily
virile, for it is the male body that, psychoanalytically speaking, is fantasized as unfragmented, uncastrated, unmutilated, whole. The "totalitarian"
body is thus a virile one not because the Duce, manly man that he was,
happened to be its model; rather, the Duce's body is virile because it is

"totalitarian," because of the function that it serves in relation to the social body that it represents: it is the unriven whole, the sublime body that will survive all deaths. The reproduction of such a body could only be a national undertaking. And indeed it was: during the decade of the 1930s, the Duce's body, his "charisma," became the single most compelling binding mechanism of the fascist regime. Its "unity" stood in the place of all divisions and heterogeneities, ideological, political, sexual, and racial, that fascism sought to deny.

Notes

Preface

1. Klaus Theweleit, *Male Fantasies*, 2 vols. (Minneapolis: University of Minnesota Press, 1987).

2. Zeev Sternhell's work has been controversial precisely because it violates these two positions by proposing that fascism possesses an ideology as coherent as that of liberalism and Marxism. See his *Neither Left nor Right: Fascist Ideology in France*, trans. David Maisel (Berkeley: University of California Press, 1986), and *The Birth of Fascist Ideology*, with Mario Sznajder and Maia Asheri, trans. David Maisel (Princeton, N.J.: Princeton University Press, 1994). For the terms of the controversy, see Antonio Costa Pinto, "Fascist Ideology Revisited: Zeev Sternhell and His Critics," *European History Quarterly* 16, no. 4 (1986): 465–83, and Robert Wohl, "French Fascism, Both Right and Left: Reflections on the Sternhell Controversy," *Journal of Modern History* 63, no. 1 (1991): 91–98.

3. A good example of this appeared just as this book went to press. In an essay entitled "Eternal Fascism" (*New York Review of Books*, June 22, 1995), Umberto Eco writes: "Contrary to common opinion, fascism in Italy had no special philosophy. . . . Mussolini did not have a philosophy; he had only rhetoric" (12).

4. See Ernesto Laclau, "Fascism and Ideology," in *Politics and Ideology in Marxist Theory: Capitalism, Fascism, Populism* (London: Verso, 1977), 102. I allude to Louis Althusser's essay "Ideology and Ideological State Apparatuses: Notes toward an Investigation," in *Lenin and Philosophy*, trans. Ben Brewster (New York: Monthly Review Press, 1971), 127–86.

5. Laclau, "Fascism and Ideology," 102. Laclau's own thesis is that the popular-democratic interpellation "the people" organizes all the other interpellations in fascist discourse. I would argue that the popular-democratic interpellation is, in the case of fascism, always bound up with the rhetoric of virility, understood as a "masculinity"; indeed, in fascist discourse the *popolo* exists precisely in opposition to the "feminine" and socialist "masses."

6. Jean Laplanche and J. B. Pontalis introduce the metaphor of syntax in their essay "Fantasy and the Origins of Sexuality," in *Formations of Fantasy*, ed. Victor Burgin, James Donald, and Cora Kaplan (New York: Routledge, 1986).

7. Alice Y. Kaplan, *Reproductions of Banality: Fascism, Literature, and French Intellectual Life* (Minneapolis: University of Minnesota Press, 1986).

1 / Rhetorics of Virility

1. Carlo Emilio Gadda, *Eros e Priapo* (Milan: Garzanti, 1967), 73.

2. See Zeev Sternhell, "Fascist Ideology," in *Fascism: A Reader's Guide,* ed. Walter Laqueur (Berkeley: University of California Press, 1976), 315–76.

3. See Philip V. Cannistraro, *La fabbrica del consenso: Fascismo e mass media* (Bari: Laterza, 1975), 67–98.

4. For formulations of this commonplace, see Sternhell, "Fascist Ideology," esp. 340–41, and Adrian Lyttelton, introduction to *Italian Fascisms: From Pareto to Gentile* (London: Jonathan Cape, 1973), 28.

5. Giovanni Lazzari, *Le parole del fascismo* (Rome: Argileto, 1975).

6. Furio Jesi, *Cultura di destra* (Milan: Garzanti, 1979), 104.

7. See John M. Hoberman, *Sport and Political Ideology* (Austin: University of Texas Press, 1984).

8. See Wilhelm Reich, *The Mass Psychology of Fascism,* trans. Vincent R. Carfagno (New York: Farrar, Straus and Giroux, 1970), and Jean-Paul Sartre, "Qu'est-ce qu'un collaborateur?" (1945), in *Situations III,* 5th ed. (Paris: Gallimard, 1949), 43–61.

9. On Sartre's essay, see David Carroll's remarks in his *French Literary Fascism: Nationalism, Anti-Semitism, and the Ideology of Culture* (Princeton, N.J.: Princeton University Press, 1995), 149–52.

10. See Klaus Theweleit, *Male Fantasies,* 2 vols. (Minneapolis: University of Minnesota Press, 1987).

11. In both cases the "atypicality" of the Italian collaborator displaces the question of political responsibility; indeed, in *1900,* the perverted Italian fascist, Attila, isn't really Italian at all: Attila, as in Attila the Hun, is figurally a German in disguise.

12. See Neil Hertz, "Medusa's Head: Male Hysteria under Political Pressure," in *The End of the Line: Essays on Psychoanalysis and the Sublime* (New York: Columbia University Press, 1985), 161–93.

13. Banality itself has become a crucial area of investigation in cultural studies and specifically in the study of (Nazi-)fascism. Recent studies of fascism, in particular those of Theweleit and Alice Y. Kaplan, have built upon Hannah Arendt's suggestion that the strength and "evil" of fascism lie precisely in its banality and have turned to a cultural analysis attentive to the "everyday" and the "average." See Alice Y. Kaplan, *Reproductions of Banality: Fascism, Literature, and French Intellectual Life* (Minneapolis: University of Minnesota Press, 1986), in particular the chapter "Fascism and Banality," 41–58.

14. Edward Tannenbaum, *The Fascist Experience: Italian Society and Culture 1922–1945* (New York: Basic Books, 1972), 3. See also Renzo De Felice's discussion in *Intervista sul fascismo,* ed. Michael Ledeen (Bari: Laterza, 1976).

15. For an excellent discussion of this view, see Pier Giorgio Zunino, *L'ideologia del fascismo: Miti, credenze e valori nella stabilizzazione del regime* (Bologna: Il Mulino, 1985), esp. 11–62. Umberto Eco recycles such a view in his essay "Eternal Fascism," when he writes that "fascism had no quintessence. Fascism was a *fuzzy* totalitarianism, a collage of different philosophical and political ideas, a beehive of contradictions" (*New York Review of Books,* June 22, 1995, 13).

16. Kaplan points out that such splitting is a temptation for those who study fascism, a temptation that should be resisted, for "splitting, after all, is really much the same activity

as binding done in reverse" (*Reproductions,* 24). It thus mimes the bindings and splittings worked by fascism itself.

17. Maria-Antonietta Macciocchi, "Les femmes et la traversée du fascisme," in *Eléments pour une analyse du fascisme* (Paris: Union Générale D'éditions, 1976), 1:147.

18. See George Mosse, *Nationalism and Sexuality: Respectability and Abnormal Sexuality in Modern Europe* (New York: Howard Fertig, 1985), and idem, "Futurismo e culture politiche in Europa: Una prospettiva globale," in *Futurismo, cultura e politica,* ed. Renzo De Felice (Turin: Edizioni Della Fondazione Giovanni Agnelli, 1988), 2–31. Mosse links the alliance between nationalism and the ideal of manliness, or respectability, to the bourgeoisie's constitution of itself as a class.

19. F. T. Marinetti, "Contro il matrimonio," from *Democrazia futurista,* in *Teoria e invenzione futurista,* ed. Luciano de Maria (1968; reprint, Milan: Mondadori, 1983), 370.

20. F. T. Marinetti, "Marriage and the Family," in *Marinetti: Selected Writings,* ed. R. W. Flint, trans. R. W. Flint and Arthur A. Coppotelli (New York: Farrar, Straus and Giroux, 1971–72), 78; translation modified.

21. Marinetti, "Contro il matrimonio," 371.

22. Marinetti, "Marriage and the Family," 79; translation modified.

23. F. T. Marinetti, "Orgoglio italiano rivoluzionario e libero amore," from *Democrazia futurista,* in *Teoria e invenzione,* 372.

24. F. T. Marinetti, "Contro il lusso femminile," from *Futurismo e fascismo,* in *Teoria e invenzione,* 547.

25. There will be later, less jocular versions of this recommended cure: Himmler will require male homosexuals to lie with a woman and to be killed or freed according to their reactions. See Mosse, *Nationalism and Sexuality,* 169.

26. Charles Baudelaire, "Un mangeur d'opium," from *Paradis artificiels,* in *Oeuvres complètes,* ed. Y. G. Le Dantec, revised by Claude Pichois (Paris: Gallimard, 1961), 444–45.

27. Marinetti, "Contro il lusso femminile," 548–49.

28. Two endings have been proposed for the "first" futurism: one in 1915–16, marked by the deaths of Umberto Boccioni and Antonio Sant'Elia as well as World War I, taken as fulfillment of the futurists' bellicose desires; and a second in 1920, marked by Marinetti's (temporary) rift with Mussolini. For a polemical discussion of this practice, see Enrico Crispolti, *Storia e critica del futurismo* (Bari: Laterza, 1986), in particular the chapters "Appunti sul futurismo e fascismo: Dal diciannovismo alla difesa contro l'operazione 'arte degenerata'" (183–224), and "Il problema del secondo futurismo nella cultura italiana fra le due guerre" (225–46). See also idem, "La politica culturale del fascismo, le avanguardie e il problema del futurismo," in *Futurismo, cultura e politica,* ed. Renzo De Felice (Turin: Edizioni della Fondazione Giovanni Agnelli, 1988), 247–79.

29. Marinetti does of course repeat that his "disprezzo della donna" is scorn of a certain conception of woman, not of women themselves, and frames his remarks on the intellectual inferiority of women with historical considerations: "Quanto alla pretesa inferiorità della donna, noi pensiamo che se il corpo e lo spirito di questa avessero subito, attraverso una lunga serie di generazioni, una educazione identica a quella ricevuta dallo spirito e del corpo dell'uomo, sarebbe forse possibile parlare di uguaglianza fra i due sessi" [As for the supposed inferiority of woman, we think that if, over a long sequence of generations, her body and spirit had undergone an education identical to that received by the spirit and body of man, it would perhaps be possible to speak of equality between the two sexes] ("Contro l'amore e il parlamentarismo," in *Teoria e invenzione,* 293). This statement is equivocal at best, for equality is postponed until some future, and rather dubious ("sarebbe forse possible"), date.

30. See Eve Kosofsky Sedgwick, *Between Men: English Literature and Male Homosocial Desire* (New York: Columbia University Press, 1985), 83–96, and idem, "The Beast in the Closet," in *Sex, Politics, and Science in the Nineteenth-Century Novel*, ed. Ruth Bernard Yeazell (Baltimore: Johns Hopkins University Press, 1986), 148–55. George Mosse's analysis of the Nazi *Männerbund* and the homophobic violence it engendered provides further historical confirmation of this phenomenon. See in particular the chapter "Fascism and Sexuality," in *Nationalism and Sexuality*, 153–80.

31. F. T. Marinetti, *Al di là del comunismo*, in *Teoria e invenzione*, 475.

32. Ibid., 476.

33. Ibid., 477.

34. F. T. Marinetti, *Come si seducono le donne* (Florence: Edizioni da Centomila Copie, 1916), 33.

35. Ibid., 40.

36. Ibid., 140–41.

37. The Pact of London (April 16, 1915) committed Italy to intervention in the war in return for Istria, the Trentino, the Alto-Adige, and a portion of Dalmatia.

38. F. T. Marinetti, "Discorso futurista agli inglesi," from *Guerra sola igiene del mondo*, in *Teoria e invenzione*, 282–83.

39. For an analysis of D'Annunzio's use of christological language, see Barbara Spackman, "*Il verbo (e)sangue:* Gabriele D'Annunzio and the Ritualization of Violence," *Quaderni d'italianistica* 4, no. 2 (1983): 219–29, and Giorgio Barbéri Squarotti, "D'Annunzio scrittore 'politico,'" in *D'Annunzio politico: Quaderni Dannunziani*, 1–2 (Milan) (1987): 319–48.

40. Gabriele D'Annunzio, "Non abbiamo sofferto abbastanza (11 settembre 1919)," from *Il sudore di sangue*, in *Prose di ricerca . . .* (Milan: Mondadori, 1966), 1:980.

41. See, for example, Emilio Gentile, "La politica di Marinetti," *Storia contemporanea* 7, no. 3 (1976): 415–38.

42. I place "feminist" between quotation marks simply because what fascists meant by feminist has very little in common with what feminists themselves, whether during the fascist period or after, mean by it. On the "masculinization" of women, see Piero Meldini, *Sposa e madre esemplare: Ideologia e politica della donna e della famiglia durante il fascismo* (Rimini-Firenze: Guaraldi, 1975), an invaluable source of rank-and-file writings on the subject of the "fascist woman." A typical example of the rhetoric to which I refer is the following statement from the "Programma Statuto" of the Gruppo Femminile Fascista Romano in 1921, quoted in Meldini, *Sposa*, 132–33 (who in turn cites from G. A. Chiurco, *Storia della rivoluzione fascista 1919–1922*, 5 vols. [Florence: Vallecchi, 1929], 4:26–27): "Even as she prepares herself to give to fascism everything and anything she can — and even more — within the limits of her feminine possibilities, the fascist woman will avoid taking on masculine attitudes and invading the field of male action unless it is required by absolute necessity. She knows that woman can be of greater use to the ideal for which she works if she tries to develop to the fullest her feminine aptitudes, rather than establishing herself in the field of male action where she would always be imperfect and would not inspire the trust necessary to the success of her propaganda." Elisabetta Mondello summarizes this position as "a thesis repeatedly expressed during the fascist period: the emancipated woman is a masculinized virago, evirating, void of all social utility, and so much the more so when she is a suffragette or a feminist, without family and children" (see Elisabetta Mondello, *La nuova italiana: La donna della stampa e nella cultura del Ventennio* [Rome: Riuniti, 1987] 28).

43. This does not mean, of course, that misogyny is absent from his works. See my *Decadent Genealogies: The Rhetoric of Sickness from Baudelaire to D'Annunzio* (Ithaca, N.Y.: Cornell University Press, 1989).

44. It is British and American imperialism that D'Annunzio accuses of "adiposity." Leslie Heywood analyzes a similar connection between the anti-imperialist stance and "anorexic logic" in Conrad (see Heywood's *Dedication to Hunger: The Anorexic Aesthetic in Modern Culture* [Berkeley: University of California Press, 1996]).

45. Gabriele D'Annunzio, "Non abbiamo sofferto abbastanza (11 settembre 1919)," in *Il sudore di sangue*, 982.

46. Fiume is grammatically feminine in most of its occurrences in D'Annunzio's speeches, as one would expect of an Italian city-name; on at least one occasion, however, D'Annunzio plays upon the gender of the common noun "fiume" and masculinizes the city, "il Fiume maschio." See "L'Italia alla colonna e la vittoria col bavaglio," in *Prose di ricerca* (Milan: Mondadori, 1966), 1:904.

47. Ibid., 1:889.

48. See Nancy Huston's essay, "The Matrix of War: Mothers and Heroes," in *The Female Body in Western Culture*, ed. Susan Rubin Suleiman (Cambridge, Mass.: Harvard University Press, 1985), 119–36.

49. D'Annunzio, "Non abbiamo sofferto abbastanza (11 settembre 1919)," 982.

50. See Pier Desiderio Pasolini dall'Onda, *Caterina Sforza*, 3 vols. (Rome: Loescher, 1893). The biography was translated into English by Paul Sylvester in 1898 as *Catherine Sforza*, by Count Pier Desiderio Pasolini (London: Heinemann, 1898) and reprinted in a four-volume edition in 1968 by Edizioni Letterarie Artistiche (Rome).

51. Ernest Breisach, *Caterina Sforza: A Renaissance Virago* (Chicago: University of Chicago Press, 1967), 103. I am here following Breisach's account of the episode.

52. Pasolini dall'Onda devotes a considerable number of pages to attempting to deny the historical accuracy of this, to his mind, indecorous response and concludes by inverting the scene altogether: "The person who appeared and spoke to the crowd was the castellane; Catherine was not on the battlements, but in bed, and when she did appear, wore, not armour, but her shift, which she was probably the last to perceive. At that moment the dauntless Countess was not alarming, but alarmed" (*Caterina Sforza*, 131).

53. John Freccero, "Medusa and the Madonna of Forlì: Political Sexuality in Machiavelli," in *Machiavelli and the Discourse of Literature*, ed. Albert R. Ascoli and Victoria Kahn (Ithaca, N.Y.: Cornell University Press, 1993).

54. See Catherine Gallagher, "Response from Catherine Gallagher," in Hertz, *End of the Line*, 194–96.

55. See Federico Sanguineti, *Gramsci e Machiavelli* (Rome-Bari: Laterza, 1981), 3–22.

56. Maternal love was, for Aristotle, the unique source of courage in women, as it was in bears. Summarizing Aristotle, Suzanne Saïd writes: "Au courage virile s'oppose l'amour maternel, chez les hommes comme chez les animaux" [Maternal love can be set against virile courage, in both men and animals] (Saïd, "Féminin, femme, et femelle dans les grands traités biologiques d'Aristote," in *La femme dans les sociétés antiques: Actes des colloques de Strasbourg [mai 1980 et mars 1981]*), ed. Edmond Lévy [Strasbourg: AECR, 1983], 98).

57. On fascist mothers as "guerriera per interposta persona" [warrior by proxy], see Anna Bravo, "Simboli del materno," in *Donne e uomini nelle guerre mondiali* (Bari: Laterza, 1991), 96–134.

58. Macciocchi, "Les femmes," 1:147.

59. See Christine Buci-Glucksmann, "Culture de la crise et mythes du féminin: Weininger et les figures de l'Autre," in *Femmes et Fascismes*, ed. Rita Thalmann (Condé-sur-Noireau: Editions Tierce, 1986), 16.

60. D'Annunzio belongs to this line both as metonym for his texts and as biographical D'Annunzio. I have elsewhere noted the way in which D'Annunzio's critics read him as a "feminizer." In *La Storia d'Italia dal 1871 al 1915* (Bari: Laterza), Benedetto Croce had

written that D'Annunzio lacked the "virility" of a Giosuè Carducci or Giacomo Leo-pardi, a virility without which greatness is not possible; Carlo Salinari, in *Miti e coscienza del decadentismo italiano* (Milan: Feltrinelli, 1960), remarks that D'Annunzio "svirilizza" or evirates Nietzsche. D'Annunzio's own self-presentation as womanizer also rendered him a feminizer, a sensualist whose "onanist" tendencies the Duce will repudiate. See Victoria De Grazia, *How Fascism Ruled Women: Italy 1922–1945* (Berkeley: University of California Press, 1992), 67; see also Giancarlo Fusco, ed., *Playdux: Storia erotica del fascismo* (Rome: Tattilo Editrice, 1973).

61. D'Annunzio, "Non abbiamo sofferto abbastanza (11 settembre 1919)," 982.

62. For a discussion of the regime's propaganda and of women's manipulations of the "maternal code," see Anna Bravo, "Simboli del materno," in *Donne e uomini nelle guerre mondiali,* ed. Anna Bravo (Bari: Laterza, 1991), 96–134.

63. Benito Mussolini, "42esima Riunione del gran consiglio del Fascismo (22 luglio, 1924)," in *Opera omnia,* ed. Edoardo and Duilio Susmel (Florence: La Fenice, 1956), vol. 21.

64. Gadda, *Eros e Priapo,* 14.

65. Eugen Weber, *Varieties of Fascism* (New York: Van Nostrand Reinhold, 1964), 35.

66. Macciocchi, "Les femmes," 1:157.

67. See ibid., 187–92. For a detailed and nuanced account of women in the workforce during the fascist regime, see De Grazia, *How Fascism Ruled Women,* especially the chapter entitled "Working," 166–200.

68. Macciocchi's essay has received harsh criticism, due in part to rejections of its psychoanalytic orientation and in part to reactions against its polemical stance with regard to the "innocence" of women under fascism. See in particular Enzo Santarelli, "Il fascismo e le ideologie antifemministe," *Problemi del socialismo* 17, no. 4 (1986): 75–107; and Robin Pickering-Iazzi, "Unseduced Mothers: The Resisting Female Subject in Italian Culture of the Twenties and Thirties," *Working Papers from the Center for Twentieth-Century Studies* 1 (fall–winter 1990–91): 1–31.

69. Macciocchi, "Les femmes," 1:128.

70. The notion of "hom(m)o-sexual" economy, and its necessary differentiation from a "homosexual" economy, is discussed in chapter 3.

71. In his essay on Hitler's *Mein Kampf,* Kenneth Burke notes yet another twist on this scenario: "Hitler also strongly insists upon the total identification between leader and people. Thus, in wooing the people, he would in a roundabout way be wooing himself" (see Kenneth Burke, "The Rhetoric of Hitler's 'Battle,'" in *The Philosophy of Literary Form* [1941; reprint, Berkeley: University of California Press, 1973], 195n.).

72. Walter Benjamin, "The Work of Art in the Age of Mechanical Reproduction," in *Illuminations,* ed. Hannah Arendt, trans. Harry Zohn (New York: Schocken, 1969), 218. References to the original German will be to "Das Kunstwerk im Zeitalter seiner tech-nischen Reproduzierbarkeit," in *Illuminationen* (Frankfurt: Suhrkamp, 1955). All subsequent references will appear in the text.

73. For a discussion of the aura specifically in relation to film, see Miriam Hansen, "Benjamin, Cinema and Experience: 'The Blue Flower' in the Land of Technology," *New German Critique* 40 (winter 1987): 179–224.

74. See, for example, Russell Berman's summary of the final move of the essay in "The Wandering Z: Reflections on Kaplan's *Reproductions of Banality,*" in Kaplan, *Repro-ductions,* xix; see also Martin Jay's summary in *The Dialectical Imagination: A History of the Frankfurt School and Institute of Social Research, 1923–1950* (Boston: Little, Brown and Com-pany, 1973), 210–11. For a critique of the notions about Italy that underlie Benjamin's diagnosis of fascism, see Russell Berman, "The Aestheticization of Politics: Walter Benjamin on Fascism and the Avant-Garde," *Stanford Italian Review* 8, nos. 1–2 (1990): 35–52.

75. Zohn's translation is consistent in softening the effect: the "apparatur," which Zohn elsewhere translates as "camera," "equipment," or "apparatus," is here rendered with the most abstract of the terms; the masses, flung dramatically to the ground in the German, are simply forced to their knees in the English.

76. Monique Plaza, cited by Teresa de Lauretis in *Technologies of Gender* (Bloomington: Indiana University Press, 1987), writes: "It is *social sexing* which is latent in rape. If men rape women, it is precisely because they are women in a social sense." And, de Lauretis continues, "When a male is raped, he too is raped 'as a woman'" (37). See Monique Plaza, "Our Costs and Their Benefits," trans. Wendy Harrison, *m/f* 4 (1980): 31.

77. Just as the rape anthropomorphizes fascism. Having raped the masses and the camera, fascism will soon after *speak* in the text: "'Fiat ars — pereat mundus' sagt der Faschismus" ['Let there be art — and let the world perish,' says fascism] (Benjamin, "Das Kunstwerk," 169).

78. See Jay, *Dialectical Imagination*, 175, for a discussion of their style.

2 / Fascist Women and the Rhetoric of Virility

1. Susan Sontag, "Fascinating Fascism," in *Under the Sign of Saturn* (New York: Farrar, Straus, Giroux and 1980), 73–105; on "compulsory heterosexuality," see Adrienne Rich, "Compulsory Heterosexuality and Lesbian Existence," *Signs: Journal of Women in Culture and Society* 5, no. 4 (1980): 631–59.

2. Sontag, "Fascinating Fascism," 104; Sigmund Freud, *Beyond the Pleasure Principle,* in *The Standard Edition of the Complete Psychological Works of Sigmund Freud,* ed. and trans. James Strachey (1955; reprint, London: Hogarth Press, 1986), 18:1–64. See also Kaja Silverman's discussion of *Beyond the Pleasure Principle* in relation to Liliana Cavani's *Night Porter,* in "Masochism and Subjectivity," *Framework* 12 (1980): 2–9.

3. See Judith Butler's theorization of parody as denaturalizing strategy in *Gender Trouble* (New York: Routledge, 1990).

4. The tax on "celibates," or nonreproductive men, was instituted in 1926 and exacted 25 percent of the offending man's wages.

5. See Asvero Gravelli, *Vademecum dello stile fascista, dai fogli di disposizione del Segretario del Partito* (Rome: Nuova Europa, n.d.).

6. Scipio Sighele, *Eva moderna* (Milan: Treves, 1910), 51–52. The notion of a masculine soul in a female body, of course, recalls the medicolegal notion of inversion, according to which male homosexuality is imagined as a woman's soul trapped in a man's body, and female homosexuality is figured as a man's soul trapped in a woman's body.

7. See, for example, Benito Mussolini, "Macchina e donna," in *Opera Omnia di Benito Mussolini,* ed. Edoardo and Duilio Susmel (Florence: La Fenice, 1961), 310–11 (originally published in *Il popolo d'Italia* 206 [August 31, 1934]: 21): "The demographic question intersects with the question of unemployment in the working woman. When work is not a direct impediment to reproduction, it is a distraction, foments an independence and resultant physical and moral habits contrary to childbirth. Man, disoriented and above all "unemployed" in all senses, ends up renouncing the family. Today, the machine and woman are the two major causes of unemployment. In particular, woman often saves a family in trouble or even herself, but her work is, in the general framework, a source of political and moral bitterness. The salvation of a few individuals is paid for with the blood of a multitude. There is no victory without some deaths. The exit of women from the workforce would undoubtedly have an economic repercussion on many families, but a legion of men would raise their heads, now hung in shame, and a hundredfold new families would suddenly enter

into the life of the nation. We must convince ourselves that the same work that causes the loss of reproductive attributes in woman brings to man a robust physical and moral virility. A virility that the machine should help along."

8. See Piero Meldini, *Sposa e madre esemplare: Ideologia e politica della donna e della famiglia durante il fascismo* (Rimini-Florence: Guaraldi, 1975); Maria Antonietta Macciocchi, *La donna "nera": "Consenso" femminile e fascismo* (Milan: Feltrinelli, 1976); Alexander De Grand, "Women under Italian Fascism," *Historical Journal* 19, no. 4 (December 1976): 947–68; Stefania Bartolini, "La donna sotto il fascismo," *Memoria* 10 (1982): 124–32; Maria Fraddosio, "Le donne e il fascismo: Ricerche e problemi di interpretazione," *Storia contemporanea* 1 (1986): 95–135; Enzo Santarelli, "Il fascismo e le ideologie antifemministe," *Problemi del socialismo* 17, no. 4 (1986): 75–107; Elisabetta Mondello, *La nuova italiana: La donna nella stampa e nella cultura del ventennio* (Rome: Riuniti, 1987); Marina Addis Saba, ed., *La corporazione delle donne: Ricerche e studi sui modelli femminili nel ventennio* (Florence: Vallecchi, 1988); Victoria De Grazia, *How Fascism Ruled Women: Italy 1922–1945* (Berkeley: University of California Press, 1992).

9. See Michel Foucault, *The History of Sexuality,* vol. 1, *An Introduction,* trans. Robert Hurley (New York: Vintage, 1980), esp. 100–102.

10. Valentine de Saint Point, "Manifeste de la femme futuriste: Réponse a F. T. Marinetti," in *Futurisme: Manifestes, proclamations, documents,* ed. Giovanni Lista (Lausanne: Éditions L'Age d'Homme, 1973), 329.

11. See Zeev Sternhell, *Neither Left nor Right: Fascist Ideology in France,* trans. David Maisel (Berkeley: University of California Press, 1986).

12. Lucia Re makes this argument in her reading *in bono* of Valentine de Saint Point's position (see Re, "Futurism and Feminism," *Annali d'Italianistica: Women's Voices in Italian Literature* 7 [1989]: 259–61). It is, to be sure, the *lectio difficilior,* for de Saint Point's manifesto also proclaims itself antifeminist and ends with a call to mothers to produce heroes. For readings *in malo,* see Anna Nozzoli, *Tabù e coscienza: La condizione femminile nella letteratura italiana del novecento* (Florence: La Nuova Italia, 1978), 41–64; and Rita Guerricchio, "Il modello di donna futurista," *Donne e politica* 4 (Rome) (August–October 1976): 35–37.

13. De Saint Point, "Manifeste," 330.

14. See Juliana Schiesari's brilliant essay, "In Praise of Virtuous Women? For a Genealogy of Gender Morals in Renaissance Italy," *Annali d'italianistica: Women's Voices in Italian Literature* 7 (1989): 66–87. I take the expression "beyond their sex" from the collection of that title, *Beyond Their Sex: Learned Women of the European Past,* ed. Patricia H. Labalme (New York: New York University Press, 1984).

15. Paola Bono and Sandra Kemp, "Introduction: Coming from the South," in *Italian Feminist Thought,* ed. Paola Bono and Sandra Kemp (Cambridge, Mass.: Basil Blackwell, 1991), 15. See also Carla Lonzi, "Let's Spit on Hegel," 40–59, in the same volume, as well as the Milan Women's Bookstore Collective, *Sexual Difference: A Theory of Social-Symbolic Practice,* trans. Patricia Cicogna and Teresa de Lauretis (Bloomington: Indiana University Press, 1990). On the equality versus difference debate within feminism, see Joan W. Scott, "Deconstructing Equality-versus-Difference: Or, The Uses of Poststructuralist Theory for Feminism," in *Conflicts in Feminism,* ed. Marianne Hirsch and Evelyn Fox Keller (New York: Routledge, 1990), 134–48. For a proposal of "equivalent" rather than "equal" rights, see Drucilla Cornell, "Gender, Sex, and Equivalent Rights," in *Feminists Theorize the Political,* ed. Judith Butler and Joan W. Scott (New York: Routledge, 1992), 280–96.

16. Enif Robert, "Una parola serena," *L'Italia futurista* 2, no. 30 (October 7, 1917): 1; now in Claudia Salaris, *Le futuriste* (Milan: Edizioni delle Donne, 1982), 108.

17. De Saint Point, "Manifeste," 330.

18. See the dossier of discussions that ends with an invocation of Caterina Sforza: Neil Hertz, "Medusa's Head: Male Hysteria under Political Pressure"; Catherine Gallagher, "Response from Catherine Gallagher"; Neil Hertz, "In Reply"; all in Neil Hertz, *The End of the Line: Essays on Psychoanalysis and the Sublime* (New York: Columbia University Press, 1985), 161–96; 206–15; and John Freccero, "Medusa and the Madonna of Forlì: Political Sexuality in Machiavelli," in *Machiavelli and the Discourse of Literature,* ed. Albert R. Ascoli and Victoria Kahn (Ithaca, N.Y.: Cornell University Press, 1993).

19. Guerricchio, "Il modello," 35–37.

20. For a critique of such notions, see Pier Giorgio Zunino, *L'ideologia del fascismo* (Bologna: Il Mulino, 1985).

21. See Alice Y. Kaplan, *Reproductions of Banality: Fascism, Literature, and French Intellectual Life* (Minneapolis: University of Minnesota Press, 1986); and Ernesto Laclau, "Fascism and Ideology," in *Politics and Ideology in Marxist Theory* (New York: Verso, 1977).

22. Marina Addis Saba, "La donna muliebre," in *La corporazione delle donne: Ricerche e studi sui modelli femminili nel ventennio fascista,* ed. Marina Addis Saba (Florence: Vallecchi, 1988), 5. This divided call is itself riven by yet other divisions, among them the contradiction between the representation of woman as rural mother, product of fascism's demographic delirium, and the construction of woman as urban consumer, product of the "Americanization" that accompanies capitalism. See Victoria De Grazia, *How Fascism Ruled Women,* and idem, "La nazionalizzazione delle donne: Modelli di regime e cultura commerciale nell'Italia fascista," *Memoria* 33, no. 3 (1991): 95–111; and Mondello, *La nuova italiana,* 111.

23. See Emma Scaramuzza, "Professioni intellettuali e fascismo: L'ambivalenza dell'Alleanza muliebre culturale italiana," *Italia contemporanea,* fasc. 151–52 (September 1983): 111–33.

24. Ibid., 114n.

25. Teresa Labriola, "Il nostro programma," *La donna italiana* 6, no. 12 (December 1929): 656. On Teresa Labriola, see Luigi dal Pane, "Antonio e Teresa Labriola," *Rivista internazionale di filosofia del diritto* 22, ser. 2 (1942): 49–79; Enzo Santarelli, "Protagoniste femminili del primo novecento: Schede biobibliografiche," in *Problemi del socialismo* 4 (1976): 248–49; Addis Saba, "La donna muliebre," 1–71; Sara Follacchio, "Conversando di femminismo: 'La donna italiana,'" in *La corporazione delle donne,* 171–225; De Grazia, *How Fascism Ruled Women;* Mondello, *La nuova italiana.*

26. See Mondello, *La nuova italiana,* 180–81.

27. Quoted in Denise Detragiache, "Il fascismo femminile da San Sepolcro all'affare Matteotti (1919–1925)," *Storia contemporanea* 14, no. 2 (April 1983): 227.

28. The leftist strain is so faint that some hear it not at all. Certain that the egalitarian, emancipationist route is inseparable from feminism, Franca Pieroni Bortolotti in particular is unwilling to grant any authenticity to Labriola's "feminism." Already in the prefascist era, writes Pieroni Bortolotti, "Labriola called for the advancement of European women in order to counterbalance the rise of 'negroes.'" The term "emancipation" linked the abolitionist and feminist causes, something that Bortolotti claims Labriola knew quite well. Labriola's severing of those causes and her attack on emancipationist feminism (of the left) in an attempt to distinguish from it a "pure feminism" (of the right) are, Bortolotti argues, evidence of "indifference to truth, ideological ignominy, and a talent for imbroglio." Bortolotti blames on Labriola the subsequent resistance of the Italian proletariat to feminism: "From that moment, within Italian democracy and its corresponding workers' movement, the term 'feminism' will be unconsciously associated with antidemocratic and antisocialist positions, and as such it will be unconsciously rejected." See Franca Pieroni Bortolotti, *Socialismo e questione femminile in Italia, 1892–1922* (Milan: Mazzotta, 1974), 12, and passim; idem, *Femminismo e partiti politici in Italia 1919–1926* (Rome: Riuniti, 1978), 244, and

passim; and idem, *Alle origini del movimento femminile in Italia, 1848–1892* (Turin: Einaudi, 1963).

29. On Latin feminism, see De Grazia, *How Fascism Ruled Women*.

30. See George Mosse's important study, *Nationalism and Sexuality: Respectability and Abnormal Sexuality in Modern Europe* (New York: Howard Fertig, 1985).

31. See Adriana Cavarero, "Per una teoria della differenza sessuale," in *Diotima: Il pensiero della differenza sessuale* (Milan: Tartaruga, 1987), 43–75.

32. Teresa Labriola, *I problemi sociali della donna* (Bologna: Zanichelli, 1918), 60–61.

33. This splitting causes confusion even within a single work, where virility and masculinity at one moment appear to be synonyms, and at another virility is degendered. Thus in *I problemi sociali della donna*, Labriola writes: "In a society that has so clearly shown itself to be animated by virile spirit, guided by virile will and capable of expansion solely through the traditional means of male society, that is, war, the development of feminine activities necessarily follows the line of development of masculine organization. Feminine activity is locked within dams." When, however, Labriola turns to the development of women's activities in the new nation, "virility" returns as a positive rather than negative term, whose connotation is clearly that of ungendered dedication to the nation.

34. Teresa Labriola, "L'assistenza quale dovere nazionale," *La donna italiana* 10, no. 2 (February 1933): 67; idem, "Nell'orbita del femminismo: Valori reali e correnti fittizie nell'ora presente," *La donna italiana* 7, no. 10 (October 1930): 547.

35. Teresa Labriola, "Il femminismo italiano nella rinascita dello spirito," *La donna italiana* 1 (1924): 13.

36. Labriola, "Nell'orbita del femminismo," 544.

37. Teresa Labriola, "Spunto polemico," *La donna italiana* 11, no. 5 (May 1934): 258. Julius Evola's elaborate theories can be boiled down to two statements: "In special regard to the sexes, whoever is born a man must complete himself as a man, and whoever is born a woman must complete herself as a woman in everything and for everything, overcoming any mixture or promiscuity." "Mixed beings," as Evola puts it, smack of "the abnormal inclinations of the 'third sex,'" beings who "in their souls are neither man nor woman, or rather the woman is a man and the man, a woman" (Julius Evola, *Rivolta contro il mondo moderno* [1934; reprint, Rome: Edizioni mediterranee, 1969], 202, 209).

38. Teresa Labriola, "Nell'orbita del fascismo (Elogio della donna nuova)," *La donna italiana* 4, no. 9 (September 1927): 562.

39. Teresa Labriola, "Nell'orbita del fascismo (Elogio della donna nuova)," in *La donna italiana* 4, no. 10 (October 1927): 645.

40. Teresa Labriola, "La donna nella cultura e nelle professioni (Conservazione e dispersione delle energie)," *La donna italiana* 9, no. 10 (October 1932): 537.

41. See Teresa Labriola, "Parlando con le lettrici," *La donna italiana* 8, no. 2 (February 1931): 69–73. Her point is not that women should be expelled from professions: "The profession is the condition for the harmonious development of feminine qualities; it is above all beneficial from an intellectual, ethical, and economic point of view. And besides, it corresponds to the concrete way of life of modern society" (72–73).

42. See Joan Rivière, "Womanliness as Masquerade," in *Formations of Fantasy*, ed. Victor Burgin, James Donald, and Cora Kaplan (New York: Routledge, 1986), 35–44 (originally published in *The International Journal of Psychoanalysis* 10 [1929]).

43. Labriola, "La donna nella cultura," 537.

44. Ibid., 538. Alexander De Grand attributes to Labriola the position that "the desire to send young women to the universities was mere middle-class snobbishness," and he cites in support the 1933 article "Per la riforma della cultura," *La donna italiana* 10, nos. 7–8 (July–August 1933): 385–87 (De Grand, "Women under Italian Fascism," 958). While it

is true that she associates the bourgeoisie with a "paper chase" mentality interested only in degrees and diplomas for pragmatic reasons, she does not address the question of the university in that article, which is devoted to the problems of childhood and adolescence, nor does she draw the conclusion that De Grand attributes to her. In a follow-up essay, "Sempre in tema di cultura" (September 1933), Labriola writes that culture is of no use to woman understood as "a completely physiological being" (a conception she rejects); that woman understood as "a spiritual, sacerdotal being" also has no need of culture, since she comes "originally" to that vocation; but that culture is indispensable for woman as "educator of the nation, for the nation, understood as a living reality that transcends the species," which is to say, as nationalized mother. See "Sempre in tema di cultura," *La donna italiana* 10, no. 9 (September 1933): 466–67.

45. Labriola, "Parlando con le lettrici," 71.

46. See, for example, "Doveri di madri," in *La donna italiana* 12, no. 1 (January 1935): 10–12.

47. Labriola, "La donna nella cultura," 537.

48. On the ideal of (homosocial) manliness and its abjection of certain sexualities and sensualities (particularly male homosexuality), see Mosse, *Nationalism and Sexuality.*

49. Labriola, "Nell'Orbita del fascismo (Elogio della donna nuova)," 648.

50. Schiesari, "In Praise of Virtuous Women," 15.

51. Labriola, *I problemi sociali della donna,* 49.

52. Ibid., 67.

53. Ibid., 106.

54. In a 1930 essay, Labriola writes that "under the pretext of protection, there has been and in part still is today in world history a sort of enslavement of women," but in a 1935 article, she argues that "woman must be protected above all" because of her "natural physical inferiority." See Labriola, "Nell'orbita del femminismo," 545; and idem, "Doveri di madri," 11–12.

55. See Teresa Labriola, "Problemi morali del femminismo," in *La donna italiana* 7, no. 6 (June 1930): 334; on Roman law, see Yan Thomas, "The Division of the Sexes in Roman Law," in *A History of Women in the West,* vol. 1, ed. Pauline Schmitt Pantel, trans. Arthur Goldhammer (Cambridge, Mass.: Harvard University Press, 1992), 83–137.

56. Though Labriola never quite arrives at this conclusion explicitly, she tiptoes around it, introducing the *materfamilias* in a 1935 article, "Suffragismo francese e sodalismo italiano," *La donna italiana* 12, no. 4 (April 1935): 194; and reluctantly admitting that physical maternity had a role to play in a 1936 article, "Madri e istitutrici," *La donna italiana* 13, nos. 6–8 (June–August 1936): 246: "OK, physical maternity is the basis, or better, it is the condition for the exercise of complete maternity. But it is not enough. We must affirm the value of spiritual maternity. If we don't affirm it, we are in Bolshevism."

57. Labriola was reacting to the recognition of "natural maternity" by the National Agency for Maternity and Infancy, which provided services for unwed mothers and illegitimate children. Its roots, according to De Grazia, were indeed in "prewar social reformism rather than fascist pronatalism" (see De Grazia, *How Fascism Ruled Women,* 60–68). On fascist maternity policies, see also Annarita Buttafuoco, "Motherhood as a Political Strategy: The Role of the Italian Women's Movement in the Creation of the Cassa Nazionale di Maternità," in *Maternity and Gender Policies: Women and the Rise of the European Welfare States, 1880s–1950s,* ed. Gisela Bock and Pat Thane (New York: Routledge, 1991), 178–95; and Chiara Saraceno, "Redefining Maternity and Paternity: Gender, Pronatalism and Social Policies in Fascist Italy," also in *Maternity and Gender Policies,* 196–212.

58. Labriola, "Il pericolo latente," in *La donna italiana* 15, no. 1 (January 1938): 2.

59. Ibid. On women and sports during the fascist regime, see Rosella Isidori Frasca, "L'educazione fisica e sportiva, e la 'preparazione materna,'" in *La corporazione delle donne,* 273–304, and Isidori Frasca, . . . *e il duce le volle sportive* (Bologna: Pàtron, 1983).

3 / Mafarka and Son

1. Zeev Sternhell, "Fascist Ideology," in *Fascism: A Reader's Guide,* ed. Walter Laqueur (Berkeley: University of California Press, 1976), 334.

2. See Zeev Sternhell, *The Birth of Fascist Ideology,* with Mario Snzajder and Maia Asheri, trans. David Maisel (Princeton, N.J.: Princeton University Press, 1994), 8.

3. The volume *Futurismo, cultura e politica,* ed. Renzo De Felice (Turin: Fondazione Giovanni Agnelli, 1988) contains yet other examples of ways in which texts are bypassed in arriving at the conclusion that they are fascist. Umberto Carpi's argument that Marinetti's constant need to justify his adhesion to the regime is in fact the paradoxical demonstration and confirmation of the weight of the leftist leanings of futurism slips and slides between "Marinetti" and "il futurismo marinettiano," between biography and text (see Umberto Carpi, "Futurismo e sinistra politica," 67–78); Emilio Gentile finds a "permanent affinity" between futurism and fascism in their "attitudes toward life" and, like Sternhell, lists elements abstracted from the texts: irrationalism, antihistoricism, anthropological pessimism, tragic and active enthusiasm, a sense of movement, and the myth of the future (Emilio Gentile, "Il futurismo e la politica: Dal nazionalismo modernista al fascismo [1909–1920]," 105–60); leaving the texts entirely behind, Enrico Crispolti addresses not ideological affinities but rather the degree of legitimation of futurism within fascist cultural policies (see Enrico Crispolti, "La politica culturale del fascismo, le avanguardie e il problema del fascismo," 247–82).

4. I therefore disagree with Robert Dombroski when, in *L'esistenza ubbidiente: Letterati italiani sotto il fascismo* (Naples: Guida, 1984), he argues that "if it were true that there were no relations of interdependence between the literary product and the true life of the writer (a hypothesis contrary to all the norms of historical and critical reconstruction), it would be useless to proceed not only in our study but in any project that aims for either a historical or a psychological understanding of art" (9). His own methodology, however, turns out not to be in need of biography and to be a good deal closer to my own interest in examining what he calls "the specific contents of the imaginary" in order to find, again in his words, "a plane on which [literature and politics] may coincide and exhibit a single ideological substance" (11).

5. Sternhell, "Fascist Ideology," 318.

6. Ibid., 320. Pier Giorgio Zunino argues precisely the opposite: "It might seem paradoxical at first, but in order to grasp the meaning of the life of fascism, one must first of all reconsider the way in which it dies. What is not true for men is true instead for regimes and institutions: their last moments constitute a faithful and revealing reflection of essential aspects of their entire existence" (Pier Giorgio Zunino, *L'ideologia del fascismo* [Bologna: Il Mulino, 1985], 25).

7. Zeev Sternhell, *Neither Right nor Left: Fascist Ideology in France,* trans. David Maisel (Berkeley: University of California Press, 1986), 3. Sternhell's valorization of the "source" goes hand in hand with his privileging of France as birthplace of fascist ideology. See also his *Birth of Fascist Ideology.* Zunino, on the other hand, makes use of the river metaphor to emphasize the heterogeneity of the sea that is fascist ideology: "Paradoxically, one could say that fascism's refusal of an organic complex of ideas was the fruit of an overabundance

of ideal (ideological) inspirations. Into fascism flowed ideological rivers and streams that descended from far-off springs" (*L'ideologia del fascismo,* 153–54).

8. Ernesto Laclau, "Fascism and Ideology," in *Politics and Ideology in Marxist Theory* (New York: Verso, 1977), 99.

9. See Louis Althusser, "Ideology and Ideological State Apparatuses: Notes toward an Investigation," in *Lenin and Philosophy,* trans. Ben Brewster (New York: Monthly Review Press, 1971), 127–86.

10. See Laclau, "Fascism and Ideology," and Alice Y. Kaplan, *Reproductions of Banality: Fascism, Literature, and French Intellectual Life* (Minneapolis: University of Minnesota Press, 1986).

11. See, for example, Mario de Micheli: "In some respects this novel by Marinetti can be considered a caricature of Flaubert's *Salammbô.* Flaubert's taste for atrocity here becomes grotesque ostentation, eroticism becomes a licentious running on at the mouth, and Africa is a stereotypical bazaar" (Mario de Micheli, *La matrice ideologico-letteraria dell'eversione fascista* [Milan: Feltrinelli, 1976], 30). Rinaldo Rinaldi notes that Emilio Salgari's Orientalist adventure novels are also among the sources of *Mafarka* (see Rinaldo Rinaldi, "Le plagiat de l'avant-garde: *Mafarka le futuriste* de Marinetti," in *Vitalité et contradictions de l'avant-garde: Italie — France 1909–1924,* ed. Sandro Briosi and Henk Hillenaar [Paris: Librairie José Corti, 1988], 117–24).

12. F. T. Marinetti, *Mafarka le futuriste* (Paris: Christian Bourgois, 1984), 16; henceforth, citations of this work will be given in the text. The novel was originally written in French in 1909 (*Mafarka le futuriste: Roman africain* [Paris: E. Sansot, 1909]) and translated into Italian by Marinetti's secretary, Decio Cinti, as F. T. Marinetti, *Mafarka il futurista,* trans. Decio Cinti (Milan: Edizioni futuriste di "Poesia," 1910).

13. For a discussion of this notion as it appears in Flaubert, see Edward Said, *Orientalism* (New York: Random House, 1979), 113–15.

14. See Liz Constable, "Sentencing the Other: The Rhetoric of Colonial Rape in *Mafarka,*" unpublished paper.

15. For an extended analysis of this and related notions, see Johannes Fabian, *Time and the Other: How Anthropology Makes Its Object* (New York: Columbia University Press, 1983).

16. See Donna Haraway, "A Manifesto for Cyborgs," in *Feminism and Postmodernism,* ed. Linda J. Nicholson (New York: Routledge, 1990), 190–233.

17. Jean-Joseph Goux, *Symbolic Economies: After Marx and Freud,* trans. Jennifer Curtiss Gage (Ithaca, N.Y.: Cornell University Press, 1990), 213.

18. Ibid., 199. The idealist nature of this project goes unremarked in attempts to describe futurism's theory and practice as "materialist," just as the extent to which "technology" is *reproductive* technology has been elided in discussions, whether glorifying or not, of futurism's relation to "the machine." For analyses of all technologies as reproductive, see Zoë Sofia, "Exterminating Fetuses: Abortion, Disarmament, and the Sexo-Semiotics of Extraterrestrialism," *Diacritics* (summer 1984): 47–59, and Donna Haraway, "Manifesto for Cyborgs." For a theoretically informed discussion of Marinetti and technology, see Andrew Hewitt, *Fascist Modernism* (Stanford, Calif.: Stanford University Press, 1992).

19. Goux, *Symbolic Economies,* 224.

20. As Alice Kaplan writes, "The earth is played by woman — so is war, the machine, the sea, and, in fact, nearly every possible thing except woman herself, who, having given over her essence to everything around her, is completely void of intrinsic meaning" (*Reproductions of Banality,* 86). On *Mafarka* and the feminine, see Cinzia Blum's chapter in *The Other Modernism: Marinetti and the Futurist Fiction of Power* (Berkeley: University of California Press, forthcoming). See also Carol Diethe, "Sex and the Superman: An Analysis of the Pornographic Content of Marinetti's *Mafarka le futuriste,*" in *Perspectives on Pornography: Sex-*

uality in Film and Literature, ed. Gary Day and Clive Bloom (New York: Macmillan, 1988), 159–74.

21. See Said, *Orientalism,* 182. Mafarka in fact gives in to temptation only once, after the construction of his son is well underway.

22. My understanding of Marinetti's use of "pederasty" in the manifestos is that he is not being philologically precise, not using "pederasty" to refer to man-boy relations, but rather as a generic slur on all male same-sex relations.

23. Kaplan, *Reproductions,* 83.

24. F. T. Marinetti, "Contro il lusso femminile," from *Futurismo e fascismo,* in *Teoria e invenzione futurista,* 547.

25. Luce Irigaray, "Commodities among Themselves," in *This Sex Which Is Not One,* trans. Catherine Porter (Ithaca, N.Y.: Cornell University Press, 1985), 193 (originally published as "Des marchandises entre elles," *La quinzaine litteraire* 215 [August 1975]). Irigaray's formulation has been much misunderstood and accused of the very homophobia that her theory explains. Included among the accusers is Eve Sedgwick, in spite of what seems to be a congruence between their theories. In *The Epistemology of the Closet* (Berkeley: University of California Press, 1990), Sedgwick writes that Irigaray's writing about the hom(m)o-sexual "is the locus classicus" of a trajectory "according to which authoritarian regimes of homophobic masculinist culture may be damned on the grounds of being *even more homosexual* than gay male culture" (154). For other examples of this reading of Irigaray, see Jonathan Dollimore, *Sexual Dissidence: Augustine to Wilde, Freud to Foucault* (Oxford: Oxford University Press, 1991), 249–50, and Joseph Bristow, "Homophobia/Misogyny: Sexual Fears, Sexual Definitions," in *Coming on Strong: Gay Politics and Culture,* ed. Simon Shepherd and Mick Wallis (London: Unwin Hyman, 1989), 64. Dollimore cites Bristow approvingly: "Such an argument gives the impression that gay men are the culprits of the sexual inequalities — between homosexual and heterosexual, man and woman — we have to struggle against. The glaring contradiction — that homosexual desire creates the oppression of homosexuality — appears over and again in sociology, literary theory and varieties of feminist criticism." If we rewrite the central phrase according to what it seems to me Irigaray is saying, we get a slightly different formulation: hom(m)o-sexual, which is to say, homosocial, desire, already mediated through women, creates the oppression of homosexuality.

26. Rinaldo Rinaldi argues that the 1908 Messina earthquake was the inspiration for this ending and that Marinetti delayed publication of both the "Founding Manifesto" and *Mafarka* in order to exploit the "coincidence" of this "réclame in natura" (see Rinaldi, "Le plagiat de l'avant-garde," 117–24).

27. Richard Burton, "Terminal Essay," in *A Plain and Literal Translation of the Arabian Nights' Entertainments, Now Entituled The Book of the Thousand Nights and a Night with Introduction Explanatory Notes on the Manners and Customs of Moslem Men and a Terminal Essay upon the History of The Nights* (London: Burton Club, 1886), 10:206–7.

28. Karen Pinkus links this rope-penis to the anthropological figure of the trickster in folktales. See her analysis of *Mafarka* in *Bodily Regimes* (Minneapolis: University of Minnesota Press, 1995). The source of the enormous *zeb* itself may well be the 1908 J. C. Mardrus translation of the *Milles et une nuits* and specifically the description of the demon Kaschkasch who, in addition to six horns, each four cubits long, three forked tails of the same length, eyes planted lengthwise in the middle of this face, and hands larger than cauldrons, is the bearer of a "zebb deux fois plus gros que celui de l'éléphant" [*zeb* twice as big as that of an elephant]. See *Le livre des mille nuits et une nuit,* trans. J. C. Mardrus (Paris: Fasquelle, 1908), 3:17. The description appears in the tale told the 182nd night, under the general rubric of the "Histoire de la princess Boudour." A thematic connection to *Mafarka* is present as well: the

tale concerns the young prince Kamaralzamân, whose aversion to women is so great that he threatens suicide in response to his father's insistence that he marry. Burton's translation refers to the demon as Kashkash and to the tale as "The Tale of Kamar al-Zaman"; no reference is made to the *zeb.* I am indebted to Liz Constable for this tidbit.

29. Alice Kaplan, in fact, takes the meaning of the tale to be the phallic power of storytelling.

30. Goux, *Symbolic Economies,* 207.

31. Irigaray, "Commodities," 193.

32. See Karl Marx, *Grundrisse: Foundations of the Critique of Political Economy,* trans. Martin Nicolaus (New York: Vintage, 1973), 234.

33. Constable, "Sentencing the Other." I would like here to acknowledge the importance that Constable's work on "colonial crises" has had for my thinking about *Mafarka.*

34. While both Giovanna Tomasello, in *La letteratura coloniale italiana dalle avanguardie al fascismo* (Palermo: Sellerio, 1984), and Mario de Micheli, in *La matrice ideologico-letteraria dell'eversione fascista,* understand Mafarka to be a "re negro," it is clear to me both from the color-coding of Mafarka as "fauve," "bronze," and "le teint des belles terres cuites" and from the insistence with which his enemies are referred to as coffee-colored "nègres," that we are to understand that Mafarka is a North African Arab, but not a black African.

35. See Jean Laplanche and J.-B. Pontalis, "Fantasy and the Origins of Sexuality," *International Journal of Psychoanalysis* 49 (1968): 1–18.

36. The economic function of the paste thus differentiates it from the "bloody miasma" analyzed by Klaus Theweleit. Theweleit discusses the obsession with the reduction of the human body to paste, and argues that the soldier male differentiates himself only by mashing others, particularly women, to pulp (see Klaus Theweleit, *Male Fantasies* [Minneapolis: University of Minnesota Press, 1987], esp. 2:272–89).

37. J. K. Huysmans, *A rebours* (Paris: Gallimard, 1977), 214–15.

38. J. K. Huysmans, *Against Nature,* trans. Robert Baldick (New York: Penguin, 1979).

39. See Barbara Spackman, *Decadent Genealogies: The Rhetoric of Sickness from Baudelaire to D'Annunzio* (Ithaca, N.Y.: Cornell University Press, 1989).

40. See César du Marsais's *Traité des tropes* (Paris: Le Nouveau Commerce, 1979) as well as Pierre Fontanier: "By this word [hypallage] one understands the transfer made to one of the elements of a sentence of something that really seems to be appropriate to another element to which it has some relation. But if this transfer is legitimate and conforms to the spirit of the language, then it belongs to the category of another figure, such as *metaphor,* and one should not consider it a separate figure; if it is not legitimate, then one should consider it a vice of style and not a figure" (Pierre Fontanier, *Les Figures du discours* [Paris: Flammarion, 1977], 266).

41. See Gérard Genette, "Métonymie chez Proust," in *Figures III* (Paris: Seuil, 1972), 41–63.

42. Fredric Jameson, *Fables of Aggression: Wyndham Lewis, the Modernist as Fascist* (Berkeley: University of California Press, 1979), 29.

43. Pasquale Turiello, *La virilità nazionale e le colonie italiane: Memoria letta alla R. Accademia di Scienze Morali e Politiche della Società Reale di Napoli* (Naples: Tipografia della Regia Università, 1898), 3.

44. Ibid., 47.

45. Ibid., 59.

46. See Giuseppe Carlo Marino, *L'autarchia della cultura: Intellettuali e fascismo negli anni trenta* (Rome: Editori Riuniti, 1983), 181.

47. Some of the paradoxes and uneven exchanges that result from this logic are apparent in a 1940 economic treatise, Raffaele Basile-Giannini's *Autarchia dell'Africa italiana*. Published in "Anno XIX," according to the calendar of the regime, it lays out plans for the autarky of Italian Africa as well as for the autarky of the "Madre-patria," or Mother-fatherland (another male mother?). The African landscape it describes is an unpeopled one where colonial products — coffee from Ethiopia, bananas from Somalia, grain from Libya, livestock (what the text refers to as the "African zootechnical patrimony") — stand ready for importation to the "Madre-patria." Or rather, they stand ready to be "contributed" to the autarky of the empire: after initially describing the exchanges between colony and nation as imports and exports, the text switches to "apporto" and "contributo" and speaks of "la possibilità di eliminazione delle importazioni metropolitane attraverso l'apporto dell'Africa Italiana" [the possibility of the elimination of metropolitan imports through the contribution of Italian Africa]. Like the "male ovary," the Italian colony is part of a one-way deal; part of the empire as it contributes, it is however to be independent of the nation. Imperial and nationalist rhetorics crisscross, absorbing and re-expelling the colony as necessary.

48. The campaign against the *Lei,* the second-person singular formal pronoun that is homonymous with the third-person singular feminine pronoun, was begun in 1938. Xenophobia, the campaigns for *romanità* and for linguistic autarky as well as the rhetoric of virility colluded in attempting to expel the *Lei:* its roots were in Spanish rather than Latin, and thus the pronoun was denounced as a residue of foreign invasions; the use of the feminine form for the formal "you" led to caustic attacks on its evirated, bourgeois, slavish connotations. The *Lei* was to be replaced by the more virile, more Latin, more Roman *voi.*

4 / D'Annunzio and the Antidemocratic Fantasy

1. One critic, Glauco Viazzi, has suggested that *Mafarka* is a response to D'Annunzio's botched attempt at creating what Charles Klopp has referred to as his "Superbambino." See Glauco Viazzi, "Di alcune funzioni segniche e corrispondenze nelle *Vergini delle rocce,*" in *Gabriele D'Annunzio, la scrittura e l'immagine,* vol. 12, no. 23 of *ES* (January–August 1980), 33n, and Charles Klopp, *Gabriele D'Annunzio* (Boston: Twayne, 1988), 53.

2. Paolo Alatri, "Ideologia e politica in D'Annunzio," *D'Annunzio a Yale, Quaderni dannunziani* 3–4 (1988): 33.

3. Fredric Jameson, *Fables of Aggression: Wyndham Lewis, the Modernist as Fascist* (Berkeley: University of California Press, 1979), 15.

4. Alice Y. Kaplan, *Reproductions of Banality: Fascism, Literature, and French Intellectual Life* (Minneapolis: University of Minnesota Press, 1986), 33.

5. Jameson, *Fables of Aggression,* 15.

6. Ernesto Laclau, "Fascism and Ideology," in *Politics and Ideology in Marxist Theory* (New York: Verso, 1977), 111.

7. On "artecrazia," see Claudia Salaris, *Artecrazia: L'avanguardia futurista negli anni del fascismo* (Florence: La nuova italia, 1992).

8. Cf. Jameson (*Fables of Aggression*), who argues that the populist component in Wyndham Lewis is expressed through his stylistic practice.

9. Gabriele D'Annunzio, *Le vergini delle rocce, Prose di Romanzi,* ed. Annamaria Andreoli and Niva Lorenzini (Milan: Mondadori, 1989), 1:29. Hereafter cited in the text.

10. Gabriele D'Annunzio, *The Maidens of the Rocks,* trans. Annetta Halliday-Antona and Giuseppe Antona (New York: George H. Richmond and Son, 1898), 43. Hereafter cited in the text; I have modified the translations as necessary.

11. The Marinettian version of such ridicule takes "equality" to be equivalent to "monotony" and mediocrity. In "Ad ogni uomo, ogni giorno un mestiere diverso! Inegualismo e artecrazia" [To every man, every day, a different trade! Inegalitarianism and artocracy!] (from *Futurismo e fascismo,* in *Teoria e invenzione futurista,* ed. Luciano de Maria [1968; reprint, Milan: Mondadori, 1983], 551–52), Marinetti glosses his refrain "Abbasso l'eguaglianza! Abbasso la giustizia! Abbasso la fraternità!" [Down with equality! Down with justice! Down with fraternity!] with the exclamation "Abbasso l'eguaglianza! Infatti, non sono l'eguale di nessuno. Tipo unico. Modello inimitabile" [Down with equality! In fact, I'm not the same as anyone! One of a kind. Inimitable model]. "L'inegualismo" is defined as variety, difference, distinction, and diversity: "Gloria alle Differenze!...Morte alla monotonia! Varietà, varietà, varietà! [Glory be to Differences!...Death to monotony! Variety, variety, variety!]. Mussolini (with the help of Giovanni Gentile) also mistakes equality for mediocrity. In the entry "fascismo" written for the *Enciclopedia Treccani* and reprinted in volume 34 of the *Opera Omnia,* Mussolini writes: "Il fascismo...afferma la diseguaglianza irrimediabile e feconda e benefica degli uomini che non si possono livellare attraverso un fatto meccanico e estrinseco com'è il suffraggio universale" [Fascism...affirms the irremediable, fecund, and beneficent inequality of men, who can't be brought to the same level by means of such a mechanical and extrinsic thing as universal suffrage] (Mussolini, "Dottrina del fascismo," in *Opera Omnia,* ed. Edoardo e Duilio Susmel [Florence: La Fenice, 1956], 34, 126).

12. On kinds of antiparliamentarism current in Italy at the time, see Carlo Salinari, *Miti e conscienza del decadentismo italiano* (Milan: Feltrinelli, 1960), 62–64, and A. James Gregor, *The Ideology of Fascism: The Rationale of Totalitarianism* (New York: Free Press, 1969), 36–54.

13. Karl Marx, *Capital: A Critique of Political Economy,* ed. Frederick Engels, trans. Samuel Moore and Edward Aveling (New York: International Publishers, 1974), 1:59.

14. Ibid., 59.

15. Ibid., 60.

16. Jean de Néthy's essay "Nietzsche-Zarathustra" appeared in *La revue blanche* (April 1892): 206–12. See Guy Tosi, "D'Annunzio découvre Nietzsche, 1892–1894," *Italianistica* 2–3 (September–December 1973): 481–513. D'Annunzio's essay "La bestia elettiva" appeared in *Il mattino* 25–26 (September 1892) and is reprinted in *Quaderni dannunziani* 3–4 (1988): 48–59, with an introduction by Jeffrey T. Schnapp.

17. See Schnapp's introduction to "La bestia elettiva," in *Quaderni dannunziani,* 48–50.

18. Such is Peter Carravetta's strategy in his discussion of *Maia* in "Dopo Zarathustra: Temi e figure tra Nietzsche e D'Annunzio," *Quaderni dannunziani* 3–4 (1988): 223–49.

19. In *Gabriele D'Annunzio e le estetiche della fine del secolo* (L'aquila: Japadre, 1976), 18–22, Maria Teresa Marabini Moevs notes that Carlyle's "On Heroes, Hero Worship and the Heroic in History" is a possible source of this passage.

20. Lucia Re, "Gabriele D'Annunzio's Novel *Le vergini delle rocce:* 'Una cosa naturale vista in un grande specchio,'" *Stanford Italian Review* 3, no. 2 (1983): 260.

21. Ibid., 260.

22. Friedrich Nietzsche, *The Genealogy of Morals,* trans. and ed. Walter Kaufmann (New York: Random House, 1969), 20.

23. Marx, *Capital,* 57n.

24. Slavoj Žižek, *The Sublime Object of Ideology* (New York: Verso, 1989), 25.

25. Ibid., 26.

26. Marx, *Capital,* 57.

27. See Ernst H. Kantorowicz, *The King's Two Bodies: A Study in Mediaeval Political Theology* (Princeton, N.J.: Princeton University Press, 1957).

28. Žižek, *Sublime Object,* 33.

29. Another proponent of a split reading, Lucia Re, has yet a different name for the blockage: an aporia in which Claudio's narrative stands in relation to the narrative of the virgins as the Lacanian imaginary stands in relation to the symbolic. This relation would be, she argues, a dialectic without synthesis, in which the "second functions as a critical gloss on the first, and there is no synthesis" (Re, "Gabriele D'Annunzio's Novel," 258). The "symbolic" undermines the project of the "imaginary" by threatening to reintroduce the "law." The function of Re's intervention is a salutary one in relation to the split readings of a Salinari; her strategy is to devote her attention to the narrative of the virgins as a corrective to what she calls "scape-goatings" of D'Annunzio by critics reacting to a "secret sense of [political] shame in themselves" (251). The result, however, is that Claudio's narrative, as a "day-fantasy" that articulates "socially unacceptable" contents, is exempted from political critique and read as a wish-fulfilling fantasy of "fullness of being."

30. Salinari, *Miti e conscienza,* 40; my translation.

31. Benito Mussolini, "Agli operai del Monte Amiata," August 31, 1924, in *Scritti e discorsi di Benito Mussolini* (Milan: Hoepli, 1934–39), 4:257; cited in Paola Desideri, "Appunti per una analisi della oratoria mussoliniana: Processi discorsivi e strategie persuasive," in *Quaderni dell'Istituto di Linguistica dell'Università di Urbino* 1 (1983): 108.

32. Hermann Ellwanger, *Sulla lingua di Mussolini* (Milan: Mondadori, 1941), 33.

33. Žižek, *Sublime Object,* 146. Care must be taken in applying Žižek's analyses of the totalitarian leader to questions of Italian fascism because Žižek is more often than not referring to communist regimes rather than fascist ones. Similarly, his insights into fascism frequently refer to Nazism rather than Italian fascism. With this caution in mind, however, it is also the case that some of his analyses hit the fascist nail on the head.

34. Žižek, *Sublime Object,* 146.

35. See, for example, Denis Mack Smith's biography of Mussolini, *Mussolini* (New York: Knopf, 1982).

36. The "split" reading is masterfully continued by Salinari, who dips in and out of the *Le vergini,* the "political manifesto of the superman," then in and out of *Trionfo della morte,* read as the "sexual manifesto of the superman," in and out of *Il fuoco,* read as the "artistic manifesto of the superman," with stops along the way in articles on the organization of the Italian navy, passages from *Odi navali,* and so on. Jared Becker adopts a similar "splitting" strategy in his essay entitled "Homoeroticism and Nationalism in D'Annunzio," *Stanford Italian Review* 11:1–2 (1992): 139–53. The result in both cases is a more homogeneous political discourse than the internally split one I am suggesting. My strategy insists upon a notion of the text and of fascist discourse as heterogeneous materials that get bound together, buttoned down (or "quilted," as Žižek, after Lacan, would say). The ideological value of those materials is not fixed in advance but determined only through their binding.

37. Freud, "Fetishism," in *The Standard Edition of the Complete Psychological Works of Sigmund Freud,* trans. James Strachey (1961; reprint, London: Hogarth Press, 1978), 21:153.

38. See Jacques Derrida, *Glas* (Paris: Galilée, 1974); Sarah Kofman, "Ça cloche," in *Lectures de Derrida* (Paris: Galilée, 1984); Octave Mannoni, "Je sais bien, mais quand même...," in *Clefs pour l'Imaginaire ou l'Autre Scène* (Paris: Seuil, 1969).

39. On fetishism and suspense, see Gilles Deleuze, *Coldness and Cruelty,* in the volume, entitled *Masochism* (New York: Zone, 1989), that also contains Leopold von Sacher-Masoch's *Venus in Furs.*

40. Freud symptomatically "forgets" this temporality in the fetishism essay and collapses the two moments into one. He thus turns his own theory (and the infantile theory of the child) into a "sight," whereas in the essay entitled "Anatomical Differences" a threat of castration intervenes between the first sight and its understanding through deferred action.

41. On the Freudian connections between mother, casket, and castration, see Stephan Broser's essay, "Kästchen, Kasten, Kastration," trans. Barbara Spilmann, in *Cahiers: Confrontation* 8 (1982): 87–114. The incestuous suggestion in the passage is taken up in the story of the fountain.

42. See John Freccero's classic essay "Medusa: The Letter and the Spirit," in *Dante: The Poetics of Conversion* (Cambridge, Mass.: Harvard University Press, 1986).

43. Sigmund Freud, "The Theme of the Three Caskets," in *The Standard Edition of the Complete Psychological Works of Sigmund Freud,* trans. James Strachey (1958; reprint, London: Hogarth Press, 1986), 12:293.

44. See the entry for "Gorgones," in *Lemprière's Classical Dictionary* (1788; reprint, London: Routledge and Kegan Paul, 1984), 256–57.

45. Shakespeare, *The Merchant of Venice* 3.2.

46. Freud, "Theme of the Three Caskets," 294n.

47. See Paolo Valesio, "'That Glib and Oylie Art': Cordelia and the Rhetoric of Anti-rhetoric," *VS* 16, no. 5 (1977): 91–115.

48. Shakespeare, *King Lear,* 1.1.

49. I learned of these two citations from Nancy Vicker's brilliant essay, "'The Blazon of Sweet Beauty's Best': Shakespeare's *Lucrece,*" in *Shakespeare and the Question of Theory,* ed. Patricia Parker and Geoffrey Hartman (New York: Methuen, 1985), 95–115.

50. Plato, *The Symposium* 198c.

51. Cited in Vickers, "Blazon," 110.

52. On Freud's reduction of multiplicities, see Gilles Deleuze and Félix Guattari, "1914: One or Several Wolves," in *A Thousand Plateaus,* trans. Brian Massumi (Minneapolis: University of Minnesota Press, 1987), 26–38.

53. See, again, Neil Hertz, "Medusa's Head: Male Hysteria under Political Pressure," in *The End of the Line: Essays on Psychoanalysis and the Sublime* (New York: Columbia University Press, 1985).

54. Vickers, "Blazon," 112.

55. Freud, "Theme of Three Caskets," 299.

56. Carlo Salinari calls it "the political manifesto of the superman" in *Miti e coscienza,* 82. Michael Ledeen entitles his book on D'Annunzio at Fiume *The First Duce: D'Annunzio at Fiume* (Baltimore: Johns Hopkins University Press, 1977).

57. For much criticism of the novel, it matters not at all, and the fact that no child is conceived, let alone born, is oddly elided. Jeffrey T. Schnapp, for example, establishes continuity between *Le vergini* and D'Annunzio's takeover of Fiume by noting that the "solution (of *Le vergini*) is equally Fiuman: the institution of a new realm of force by means of the birth of a miraculous progeny in whom the ancient seed of Rome will flower again" (see Schnapp, "Le parole del silenzio," *Quaderni dannunziani* 3–4 [1988]: 39).

58. Paolo Valesio, *Gabriele D'Annunzio: The Dark Flame* (New Haven, Conn.: Yale University Press, 1991), 37–38. Espousing the D'Annunzian ideological fantasy, Valesio locates the difference between fascism and D'Annunzio in the relation of the leader to the masses; for Valesio, fascism cuts the "delicate mediation of a crepuscular elite" that is found in D'Annunzio's version of the "Overman." Fascism, for Valesio, turns the Overman into an "overseer."

59. This is the problem we encountered in the discussion of Marinetti's fantasy of sexual autarky and its relation to the fascist regime's fantasy of economic autarky. The relation between the two is neither causal nor prophetic but is established through the critic's reading and interpretation.

60. Cited in Frank Kermode, *The Genesis of Secrecy: On the Interpretation of Narrative* (Cambridge, Mass.: Harvard University Press, 1979), 18.

61. See Erich Auerbach's essay "Figura" on the question of the Old Testament as "phenomenal prophecy" (Auerbach, "Figura," trans. Ralph Manheim, in *Scenes from the Drama of European Literature* [Minneapolis: University of Minnesota Press, 1984], 11–76).

62. On the temporality of filiation, see Carla Freccero, *Father Figures: Genealogy and Narrative Structure in Rabelais* (Ithaca, N.Y.: Cornell University Press, 1991).

63. This same structure is operative in the way in which D'Annunzio constructs himself as precursor by reading retroactively his own (borrowed) name. D'Annunzio plays on the name "D'Annunzio" as being that of the Precursor, the Announcer, yet in order to become such a precursor he had to replace the name "Rapagnetta" with that of D'Annunzio. "Self-naming" is the giving of the patronymic. This "self-naming" is, therefore, a renaming of *the father* such that in the act of naming himself D'Annunzio he christens his father "D'Annunzio" as well; the son fathers the father, precurses the past.

64. Žižek, *Sublime Object,* 126.

65. Alexander De Grand, *The Italian Nationalist Association and the Rise of Fascism in Italy* (Lincoln: University of Nebraska Press, 1978), 1.

66. Pier Giorgio Zunino, *L'ideologia del fascismo* (Bologna: Il Mulino, 1985), 123. Zunino notes that this sense of the past differentiates Italian fascism from that of Maurras in France (69).

67. Emilio Gentile, *Le origini dell'ideologia fascista (1918–1925)* (Bari: Laterza, 1975), 392.

68. Benito Mussolini, "Mussolini rivela il suo segreto," in *Opera Omnia,* 22:286 (originally published in *Il Popolo d'Italia,* December 14, 1926).

5 / Fascism as Discursive Regime

1. Benito Mussolini, "L'azione e la dottrina fascista dinnanzi alle necessità storiche della nazione (Discorso pronunciato a Udine, nel teatro Sociale, la mattina del 20 settembre 1922)," in *Opera Omnia,* ed. Edoardo e Duilio Susmel (Florence: La Fenice, 1956), 18:411; references to Mussolini's *Opera omnia* will hereafter appear as *OO*.

2. Benito Mussolini, "The Italy We Want Within, and Her Foreign Relations," in *Mussolini as Revealed in His Political Speeches (November 1914–August 1923),* ed. and trans. Barone Bernardo Quaranta di San Severino (New York: Howard Fertig, 1976), 143. I have modified the translation, which, in an attempt to make fascism more palatable to its audience, neglects to include "democratic" among the modifiers of oratory and omits a section critical of the British.

3. Umberto Eco, "Il linguaggio politico," in *I linguaggi settoriali in Italia,* ed. Gian Luigi Beccaria (Milan: Bompiani, 1973), 91–106. Eco argues that rhetoric as bombast is the natural degeneration of rhetoric as an honest and productive exercise and identifies Mussolini in particular with such a degeneration: "It's easy to understand how the astute use of premises and commonplaces validated by a long tradition makes it possible to elicit favorable emotional reactions, almost by reflex-action. This constitutes a clear example of degenerated rhetoric. All of Mussolini's speeches belong to this kind of political argumentation" (95). Mario Isnenghi, on the other hand, characterizes as passé the association of a negatively assessed "rhetoric" and totalitarian regimes and argues for the importance of studying it as cultural institution. See Isnenghi, "Il fascismo come 'regno della parola?'" in *Intellettuali militanti e intellettuali funzionari* (Turin: Einaudi, 1979), 29–32.

4. See, for example, Luigi Rosiello's introduction to Erasmo Leso et al., eds., *La lingua italiana e il fascismo* (Bologna: Consorzio Provinciale Pubblica Lettura, 1977), 7.

5. The best survey of such interpretations of fascism remains Renzo De Felice, *Interpretations of Fascism,* trans. Brenda Huff Everett (Cambridge, Mass.: Harvard University Press, 1977). The fascism-irrationalism line is opposed by another line of interpretation, according to which fascism was produced from within the Western conception of reason. See, for example, Theodor Adorno and Max Horkheimer, *The Dialectic of Enlightenment,* trans. John Cumming (New York: Seabury Press, 1972), and Philippe Lacoue-Labarthe, *Heidegger, Art and Politics,* trans. Chris Turner (Cambridge, Mass.: Basil Blackwell, 1990).

6. See Julia Kristeva, *Polylogue* (Paris: Seuil, 1977), 7.

7. "Technology" as an explanatory category in studies of Italian fascism is largely a transference from studies of the case of Germany, where it more closely corresponds to the state of industrialization. In Italy, where fascism took power in 1922 but gathered support even earlier, recourse to reproductive technologies (film, radio, and so on) as an explanation of the success of fascism is less firmly grounded historically. (See, for example, the comparative statistics on radio subscriptions and on the existence of movie theaters, in Italy and in Germany, in Victoria De Grazia, *How Fascism Ruled Women: Italy 1922–1945* [Berkeley: University of California Press, 1992], 131. In *Mussolini immaginario* [Rome-Bari: Laterza, 1991], Luisa Passerini argues that, until 1940, the written word was the most important medium for the creation and diffusion of the image of the Duce.) Indeed, Fredric Jameson comments that "technology" may be neither the problem nor the answer but a figure for the problem: a lack of understanding of the whole. Jameson argues that the fetishization of the communication and information technologies may in fact be an allegory "of something else, of the whole unimaginable decentered global network itself." In the local case of studies of Italian fascism, "technology" may have the function of allegorizing our lack of understanding of the "whole" of fascism (see Fredric Jameson, *The Geopolitical Aesthetic: Cinema and Space in the World System* [Bloomington: Indiana University Press, 1992], 11–13).

8. A useful overview of such studies can be found in Gian Carlo Jocteau, "La lingua e la storia del fascismo: Un difficile terreno di ricerca," in an issue of *Movimento operaio e socialista* 7, no. 1. n.s. (1984): 7–14, entitled *Parlare fascista: Lingua del fascismo, politica linguistica del fascismo.* Erasmo Leso's work has been fundamental to analyses of Mussolini's rhetoric, beginning with the 1973 essay "Aspetti della lingua del fascismo: Prime linee di una ricerca," in *Storia linguistica dell'Italia nel Novecento,* ed. Maurizio Gnerre, Mario Medici, and Raffaele Simone (Rome: Bulzoni, 1973), 139–58, followed by "Osservazioni sulla lingua di Mussolini," in *La lingua italiana e il fascismo,* Erasmo Leso et al. (Bologna: Consorzio Provinciale Pubblica Lettura, 1977). Michele Cortelazzo's work also focuses on Mussolini's rhetoric: see "Lingua e retorica di Mussolini oratore socialista," *Lingua nostra* 36, no. 3 (September 1975): 73–77; "La formazione della retorica mussoliniana tra il 1901 e il 1914," in *Retorica e politica,* ed. D. Goldin (Padua: Liviana, 1977), 177–91; "Mussolini socialista e gli antecedenti della retorica fascista," in Leso et al., eds., *La lingua italiana e il fascismo;* and "Il lessico del razzismo fascista (1938)," in *Parlare fascista,* 57–66. Of related interest are Paolo Agosto, "Mussolini: Strumentalizzazione e desemantizzazione di lessemi marxisti," in *Parlare fascista,* 15–23; Paola Desideri's essays on Mussolini's rhetoric, "Appunti per una analisi della oratoria mussoliniana: Processi discorsivi e strategie persuasive," in *Quaderni dell'Istituto di Linguistica dell'Università di Urbino* 1 (1983): 101–20, and "Il linguaggio politico mussoliniano: Procedure pragmatiche e configurazioni discorsive," in *Parlare fascista,* 39–48; and Augusto Simonini, *Il linguaggio di Mussolini* (Milan: Bompiani, 1978). Studies that focus more generally on the fascist period, but take Mussolini's rhetoric into consideration, include Giovanni Lazzari, *Le parole del fascismo* (Rome: Argileto, 1975), and Daniele Rambaudi, *Politica e argomentazione: Strategia e tecniche del consenso nelle società di massa* (Milan: Marzorati, 1979). Studies that focus on the linguistic politics of the regime include Fabio Foresti, "Proposte interpretative e di

ricerca su lingua e fascismo: La 'politica linguistica,'" in Leso et al., eds., *La lingua italiana e il fascismo,* and "Il problema linguistico nella politica indigena del colonialismo fascista," in *Parlare fascista,* 133–55; Giovanni Lazzari, "Linguaggio, ideologia, politica culturale del fascismo," in *Parlare fascista,* 49–56; Gabriella Klein, "L''Italianità della lingua' e l'Accademia d'Italia: Sulla politica linguistica fascista," in *Quaderni storici* 47 (1981): 639–74, and *La politica linguistica del fascismo* (Bologna: Il Mulino, 1986). See also Mario Isenghi's "Per una mappa linguistica di un 'regime di parole': A proposito del convegno 'Parlare fascista' in 'Italia Anni Cinquanta,'" *Movimento operaio e socialista* 7, no. 2, n.s. (1984): 263–75, and the chapter "Viene da lontano la lingua nera" in *Intellettuali militanti e intellettuali funzionari* (Turin: Einaudi, 1979), in which Isenghi is sharply critical of the couplings fascism-irrationality and antifascism-rationality particularly as they appear in Lazzari's work. Of additional interest are the apologists contemporary to the regime: Eugenio Adami, *La lingua di Mussolini* (Modena: Società Tipografica Modenese, 1939); Giuseppe Ardau, *L'eloquenza mussoliniana* (Milan: Mondadori, 1929); and Hermann Ellwanger, *Studien zur Sprache Benito Mussolins* (Florence: Sansoni, 1939), translated into Italian as *Sulla lingua di Mussolini* (Milan: Mondadori, 1941).

    9. The expression is Franco Venturi's; see "Il regime fascista," in *Trent'anni di storia italiana (1915–1945)* (Turin: Einaudi, 1961), 186–87.

    10. This is perhaps the place to acknowledge the essays of the historian Walter L. Adamson, whose work I came upon as I finished this chapter. Adamson has proposed a thesis similar to the one that has guided my work, namely, that a study of fascist rhetoric is necessary in order to gain an idea of the functioning of fascist ideology. In "Modernism and Fascism: The Politics of Culture in Italy, 1903–1922" (*American Historical Review* 95, no. 2 [April 1990]: 359–90), Adamson writes: "Fascism was, especially in Mussolini's hands, a kind of 'anti-ideology ideology,' which celebrated its own incoherence as a virtue, as indicative of its commitment to the priority of spontaneous action and its contempt for intellectualism. Mussolini fully understood that appealing to 'faith' rather than rational (interest-based or utilitarian) argument could be a source of strength for fascism as a political culture. The important issue, therefore, is not the content of fascist ideology but the cultural sources of fascist rhetoric" (363). In another essay ("The Language of Opposition in Early Twentieth-Century Italy: Rhetorical Continuities between Prewar Florentine Avant-gardism and Mussolini's Fascism," *Journal of Modern History* 64 [March 1992]: 22–51), Adamson pursues his research on "culturally available language" and performs a valuable Burkean rhetorical analysis of the rhetorics of prewar cultural and political movements, as these relate to Mussolini's language in the years between 1915 and 1922. Specifically, Adamson gives a breakdown of "nationalist rhetoric," "syndacalist rhetoric," "Florentine avant-gardist rhetoric," "futurist rhetoric," and "Mussolinian rhetoric" as these mix and match similar elements.

    11. Leso, "Osservazioni," 33.

    12. Ibid., 45–46.

    13. Ibid., 51. Lazzari echoes Leso's conclusions when he refers to the "*magnetism* found on the lexical level, that, through the musical effect of the words, mystifies the slight or nonexistent semantic value of speech" (see Lazzari, "Linguaggio," 52).

    14. Rosiello, introduction to *La lingua italiana,* 7. Rosiello's summary of Leso's work is typical of the tendency I am criticizing. He writes: "The irrationalist ideology present both in the socialist Mussolini and in the fascist Mussolini determined without substantial discontinuities the linguistic practices of political discourse, whether propagandistic or oratorical, on which the language of fascism and the fascists is modeled: a language that negates the rational properties of signifieds and that tends to cause emotional behaviors and to create an immediate consensus not based on the participation of the rational faculties, rather than to sketch an analysis of reality" (9).

15. Fredric Jameson, *Late Marxism: Adorno, or, the Persistence of the Dialectic* (New York: Verso, 1990), 236–37.

16. See Jean Luc Nancy, "Our History," *Diacritics* 20, no. 3 (fall 1990): 97–115, and De Felice, *Interpretations of Fascism*, as well as Alice Y. Kaplan, *Reproductions of Banality: Fascism, Literature, and French Intellectual Life* (Minneapolis: University of Minnesota Press, 1986).

17. See Jean Pierre Faye, *Langages totalitaires* (Paris: Hermann, 1973).

18. See Norberto Bobbio, "La cultura e il fascismo," in *Fascismo e società italiana*, ed. Guido Quazza (Turin: Einaudi, 1973), 240.

19. "Semplice, evidente, maschio" (see *Il selvaggio* 10, no. 1 [February 15, 1933], 8); "Chiarezza concisa e rilievo monumentale" (see Ellwanger, *Sulla lingua di Mussolini*, 72).

20. Chaim Perelman and L. Olbrechts-Tyteca, *The New Rhetoric: A Treatise on Argumentation*, trans. John Wilkinson and Purcell Weaver (Notre Dame, Ind.: University of Notre Dame Press, 1969), 157.

21. Ibid., 158.

22. Erich Auerbach, *Mimesis*, trans. Willard R. Trask (Princeton, N.J.: Princeton University Press, 1953), 107, 111.

23. Ibid., 110.

24. Ibid., 113.

25. On the "totalitarian" interpretation, see De Felice, *Interpretations of Fascism*, 60–67; Hannah Arendt, *The Origins of Totalitarianism* (New York: World, 1961); Carl J. Friedrich and Zbigniew K. Brzezinski, *Totalitarian Dictatorship and Autocracy* (Cambridge, Mass.: Harvard University Press, 1965).

26. Benito Mussolini, "L'azione e la dottrina fascista," 414.

27. See Theodor Adorno, "Parataxis," in *Notes to Literature*, ed. Rolf Tiedemann, trans. Shierry Weber Nicholson (New York: Columbia University Press, 1992), 1:109–49.

28. And without re-essentializing the "nature" of the people, as does Augusto Simonini in *Linguaggio:* "The people love simple and natural things, and binary and ternary rhythms are the simplest and most natural. Simple and natural means commensurate with the structure of man, with his physiology, so that everything appears to be as easy and spontaneous as breathing" (64). Sharp criticism of Simonini's methods and conclusions can be found in Giulio C. Lepschy, "The Language of Mussolini," *The Journal of Italian History* 1, no. 3 (winter 1978): 531–34. For a discussion of fetishizations of the "people" in studies on fascism, see chapter 4, above.

29. See Cortelazzo, "La formazione," 186.

30. See Luisa Passerini, *Torino operaia e fascismo: Una storia orale* (Bari: Laterza, 1984), 136.

31. Jacques Derrida, "Economies de la crise," *La quinzaine littéraire* 399 (August 1983): 4–5.

32. Piero Bargellini, *Ritratto virile* (Brescia: Morcelliana, 1939), 241.

33. Ellwanger, *Sulla lingua di Mussolini*, 120.

34. Leso, "Osservazioni," 39.

35. Benito Mussolini, "Il discorso dell'ascensione," OO 22:382.

36. Michele Cortelazzo, "Mussolini socialista," 68.

37. Benito Mussolini, *Citazioni: Il manuale delle guardie nere* (Rome: XX Secolo Editore, 1969), 18.

38. Pier Giorgio Zunino, *L'ideologia del fascismo* (Bologna: Il Mulino, 1985), 154.

39. Leso, "Osservazioni," 38.

40. Kenneth Burke, "The Rhetoric of Hitler's 'Battle,'" in *The Philosophy of Literary Form* (1941; reprint, Berkeley: University of California Press, 1973), 216.

41. In "Prolégomènes à une théorie du discours fasciste," *Analytica* 33 (1983): 41–54, Mladen Dolar argues that one of the principal characteristics of fascist discourse (though he addresses only Nazism) is the foreclosure of the economic register.

42. See Michael Ledeen, *The First Duce: D'Annunzio at Fiume* (Baltimore: Johns Hopkins University Press, 1977).

43. "We may make use here of the great historical example provided by the persecutions which Christians were obliged to suffer during the first centuries. Modern authors have been so struck by the language of the Fathers of the Church and by the details given on the acts of the Martyrs, that they have generally imagined the Christians as outlaws whose blood was continually being spilt.... What was of much greater importance than the frequency of the torments were the remarkable occurrences which took place during the scenes of martyrdom. The Christian ideology was based on these rare but very heroic events" (Georges Sorel, *Reflections on Violence,* trans. T. E. Hulme and J. Roth [Glencoe, Ill.: Free Press, 1950], 204–7).

44. Emilio Gentile, "Fascism as Political Religion," *Journal of Contemporary History* 25, nos. 2–3 (May–June 1990): 229–51.

45. Croce's countermanifesto was published in *Il mondo,* May 1, 1925, under the title: "Una risposta di scrittori, professori e pubblicisti italiani, al manifesto degli intellettuali fascisti." It is reprinted in Emilio R. Papa, *Fascismo e cultura* (Venice-Padua: Marsilio, 1975), 211–17. Papa also reprints Gentile's "Manifesto degli intellettuali del fascismo," 186–94.

46. Croce, "Una risposta," 213.

47. Jacques Derrida, seminar on "testimony" at University of California—Irvine, April–May 1993.

48. On the 1932 exhibition, see Jeffrey T. Schnapp, "Epic Demonstrations: Fascist Modernity and the 1932 Exhibition of the Fascist Revolution," in *Fascism, Aesthetics, and Culture,* ed. Richard J. Golsan (Hanover, N.H.: University Presses of New England, 1992), 1–37.

49. On D'Annunzio at Fiume, see Renzo De Felice, *D'Annunzio politico 1918–1938* (Bari: Laterza, 1978); the issue of *Quaderni dannunziani* devoted to "D'Annunzio politico," n.s. 1–2 (1987); George Mosse, "The Poet and the Exercise of Political Power," *Yearbook of Comparative Literature* 22 (1973); and Spackman, "*Il verbo (e)sangue:* Gabriele D'Annunzio and the Ritualization of Violence," *Quaderni d'italianistica* 4, no. 2 (1983): 218–29.

50. Leso, "Osservazioni," 24; Simonini, *Linguaggio,* 24.

51. See Natalia Aspesi, *Il lusso e l'autarchia: Storia dell'eleganza italiana 1930–1944* (Milan: Rizzoli, 1982), 71.

52. On the history of the terms *fascio* and *fascismo,* see Erasmo Leso, "Storia di parole politiche: Fascista (fascio, fascismo)," in *Lingua nostra* 32, no. 2 (1971): 54–60, as well as the entry "Fascio" in the Treccani Encyclopedia.

53. See Ernesto Laclau, "Fascism and Ideology," in *Politics and Ideology in Marxist Theory* (New York: Verso, 1977), 120.

54. See Zunino's discussion of the relation between democracy and dictatorship, *L'ideologia del fascismo,* 181; and Mussolini's 1932 "Dottrina del fascismo," in OO 34:127, in which he writes: "Il fascismo potè da chi scrive essere definito una 'democrazia organizzata, centralizzata, autoritaria" [Fascism can be defined by yours truly as an organized, centralized, authoritarian democracy].

55. Franco Venturi, "Il regime fascista," in *Trent'anni di storia italiana (1915–1945)* (Turin: Einaudi, 1961), 186–87.

56. Mario Isnenghi discusses Venturi's definition and juxtaposes it to Tullio De Mauro's observation that "words are themselves facts" in *Intellettuali militanti e intellettuali funzionari: Appunti sulla cultura fascista* (Turin: Einaudi, 1979), 29–32. On "discursive totalities," see

Ernesto Laclau and Chantal Mouffe, "Post-Marxism without Apologies," in *New Reflections on the Revolution of Our Time* (New York: Verso, 1990), 97–132.

57. Ellwanger, *Sulla lingua di Mussolini*, 24.

58. See Denis Mack Smith, *Mussolini* (New York: Knopf, 1982), 87.

59. For historical details and further bibliography, see Renzo De Felice, *Mussolini il fascista*, vol. 1, *La conquista del potere 1921–1925* (Turin: Einaudi, 1966).

60. Benito Mussolini, "Discorso del 3 gennaio," *OO* 21:238; hereafter references to this work will be given in the text.

61. "Cheka" refers to the Soviet security service organized by Lenin in 1918 and is short for "Extraordinary commission."

62. My analysis of the orders of cognition and fiction, and of the performative, is indebted to Paul de Man, "Excuses," in *Allegories of Reading: Figural Language in Rousseau, Nietzsche, Rilke, and Proust* (New Haven, Conn.: Yale University Press, 1979), 278–301.

63. See Zunino's discussion of this notion in *L'ideologia del fascismo*, 11–29.

64. This is, for example, the meaning given to virility in Giovanni Papini's *Maschilità* (Florence: Quaderni della Voce, 1915).

65. De Felice, *Mussolini il fascista*, 622.

66. Sigmund Freud, *Jokes and Their Relation to the Unconscious*, in *The Standard Edition of the Complete Psychological Works of Sigmund Freud*, vol. 7 (London: Hogarth Press, 1953–1974).

67. De Man, "Excuses," 299.

68. See Teresa de Lauretis, "The Violence of Rhetoric: Considerations on Representation and Gender," in *Technologies of Gender* (Bloomington: Indiana University Press, 1987), 31–50.

69. See Catherine MacKinnon, *Sexual Harassment of Working Women: A Case of Sex Discrimination* (New Haven, Conn.: Yale University Press, 1979), 219.

70. Benito Mussolini, "Il discorso dell'ascensione," *OO* 22:367; hereafter references will appear in the text.

71. The criterion of intelligence is in this speech, as in the "Discorso del 3 gennaio," inseparable from violence; as we will later read, "It is stupid to have an opposition in a totalitarian regime."

72. Zunino's *L'ideologia del fascismo* (esp. 245–309) is an exception to this rule. On Italian fertility, see Massimo Livi Bacci, *A History of Italian Fertility during the Last Two Centuries* (Princeton, N.J.: Princeton University Press, 1977); on the falling birthrate during the regime as "demographic resistance" on the part of women, see Luisa Passerini, *Torino operaia*.

73. See the notes to chapter 3 for works on studies of women and fascism.

74. See Mussolini, "La razza bianca muore?" in *OO* 26:312–15. Citing a publication of the National Alliance for the Increase of the French Population, Mussolini writes that "I dieci milioni di francesi non nati fra il 1870 e il 1914 hanno creato quel fatale disquilibrio fra le due masse di popolazione al di qua e al di là del Reno, squilibrio demografico e quindi militare, a sanare il quale sono stati necessarî il concorso e il sangue di quasi tutti i popoli della terra" (313) [The ten million French not born between 1870 and 1914 created that fatal imbalance between the two masses of population on either side of the Rhine, a demographic and therefore military imbalance that it took the blood and participation of almost all the peoples of the earth to right]. He had already touched on the topic in his conversations with Emil Ludwig: "If in 1914 France had had fifty-five million inhabitants rather than thirty-five, Germany would not have made war" (Emil Ludwig, *Colloqui con Mussolini: Riproduzione delle bozze della prima edizione con le correzioni autografe del duce* [1932; reprint, Milan: Mondadori, 1950], 165).

75. See Slavoj Žižek, *The Sublime Object of Ideology* (New York: Verso, 1989), 126. On the "impossibility of society," see Ernesto Laclau and Chantal Mouffe, *Hegemony and Socialist Strategy* (New York: Verso, 1985).

76. One of the commonplaces of the *ventennio*, this association returns again and again in Mussolini's speeches and writings in the 1930s. He puts it particularly succinctly in a 1933 article: "La città tentacolare è al crepuscolo: non vi nasce più nessuno e la morte vi impera" [The tentacular city is on the wane; no one is born there, and death reigns] ("Cifre," in *OO* 26:124–25; from *Il Popolo d'Italia*, no. 301, December 20, 1933).

77. Benito Mussolini, "Il discorso dell'ascensione," in *Scritti e discorsi di Benito Mussolini* (Milan: Hoepli, 1934), 6:76.

78. Žižek (*Sublime Object*, 87–110, 145–48) discusses the relation of the party to the people in communist regimes; the fascist analogue is rather the relation of the state to the people. Žižek borrows the notion of rigid designation from Saul Kripke's *Naming and Necessity* (Cambridge, Mass.: Harvard University Press, 1980). For a discussion of Žižek's use of Kripke, see Judith Butler, "Arguing with the Real," in *Bodies That Matter* (New York: Routledge, 1993), 187–222.

79. Cited in Laclau and Mouffe, *Hegemony and Socialist Strategy*, 187; see Claude Lefort, *L'invention démocratique* (Paris: Fayard, 1981), 100.

80. Other measures may be listed, including the prohibition of homosexual acts among men in the 1931 penal code; the institution of fatherhood as a prerequisite to certain careers — mayor, professor, university dean; the obstruction of information about contraception. See De Grazia, *How Fascism Ruled Women*, 42–45.

81. This fantasy is similar to the one analyzed by Beverly Allen in her study of genocidal rape in Bosnia Herzegovina, insofar as that fantasy imagines that the offspring of genocidal rapes will genetically embody an ethnicity. See Allen's *Rape Warfare* (Minneapolis: University of Minnesota Press, 1996).

82. Before the Pact of Steel, Mussolini repeatedly ridiculed the notion of "racial purity." In his conversations with Emil Ludwig, he was asked by Ludwig whether he believed that there were "pure races" in Europe. Mussolini responded: "Naturally there no longer exists a pure race, not even the Jewish one. But it's precisely from happy mixtures that the strength and beauty of a nation arise. Race is a feeling, not a reality; 95 percent is feeling. I will not believe that it can be proved biologically that a race is more or less pure. Those who declare the Germanic race noble are coincidentally all not Germanic: Gobineau is French, Chamberlain British, Woltmann Israeli, Lapouge another Frenchman. Chamberlain went so far as to call Rome the capital of chaos. Such a thing will never happen in Italy....National pride has no need of racist delirium" (Emil Ludwig, *Colloqui con Mussolini: Riproduzione delle bozze della prima edizione con le correzioni autografe del duce* [1932; reprint, Milan: Mondadori, 1950], 71–72). This is not to say, however, that racism did not exist in Italy, before, after, or during fascism; for a brilliant study of racism in fascist advertising, see Karen Pinkus, *Bodily Regimes* (Minneapolis: University of Minnesota Press, 1995). The same can be said of anti-Semitism; see, among others, Renzo De Felice, *Storia degli ebrei italiani sotto il fascismo* (Turin: Einaudi, 1961). For a study of anti-Semitism in nineteenth-century Italian literary and medico-legal texts, see Nancy Harrowitz, *Antisemitism, Misogyny, and the Logic of Cultural Difference: Cesare Lombroso and Matilde Serao* (Lincoln: University of Nebraska Press, 1994).

Index

Barbara Spackman received a B.A. in comparative literature from the University of Wisconsin, Madison, and a Ph.D. in Italian literature from Yale University. She has taught at Yale, Northwestern, the University of California, Irvine, and currently teaches at New York University where she is associate professor of Italian. She is the author of *Decadent Genealogies: The Rhetoric of Sickness from Baudelaire to D'Annuzio.*